THE ELEMENTS OF

THE GRAIL
TRADITION

John Matthews

ELEMENT BOOKS

© John Matthews 1990
First published in Great Britain in 1990 by
Element Books Limited
Longmead, Shaftesbury, Dorset

Cover design by Max Fairbrother
Cover illustration by Pam Jenkins
Designed by Jenny Liddle
Typeset by Selectmove Ltd, London
Printed and bound in Great Britain by
Billings, Hylton Road, Worcester

British Library Cataloguing in Publication Data
Matthews, John 1948–
The elements of the Arthurian tradition
1. Legends. Characters: Arthur, King
I. Title
398'.352

ISBN 1-85230-074-4

CONTENTS

To
the memory of David Jones (1895 – 1974)
artist and writer
who saw the totality of the Grail.

THE MYSTERIES OF THE GRAIL

The dead King lies in the perilous bed
Uncorrupt, his soul caught in a wrack of air,
His hands folded in a long dream of day.

The Grail Knight, distant, wrought of clay
Dreams of a King whose wounds will never heal
Unless the Cup is brought to birth.

In the silence of the dark earth
The waters stir to life
The King's hands wake and move.

The hands of the Knight eschew strife;
He holds the sword from the red stone
And wields the bonds of love.

The neophytes who watched the sky above
The Castle of the Grail, awake
To see the Mystery complete.

John Matthews

Acknowledgements

To Caitlin Matthews for making the intricacies of Peredur sensible to me, for allowing me to ransack the researches for her forthcoming study, *Sophia: Goddess of Wisdom* (Unwin Hyman, 1990) for parts of Chapters 2 and 3. And as always for all her support and love during the writing of this and other books. You're wonderful!

To Gareth Knight for allowing me to use my version of the meditation in Chapter 5, originally devised for a weekend course at Hawkwood College in 1986.

Parts of Chapters 2 and 3 originally formed part of an unpublished manuscript worked on by the present author with Caitlin Matthews in 1982. Grateful acknowledgement is given to her for permitting this material to be used.

Thanks to all those who willingly talked of their own Grail experiences and permitted the inclusion of them within these pages.

INTRODUCTION:
WHAT IS THE
GRAIL TRADITION?

LOOKING AT THE MYTH

The Grail Tradition is the embodiment of a dream, an idea of such universal application that it appears in a hundred different places as the teaching of sects, societies and individuals. Yet, although its history, both inner and outer, can for the most part be traced, it remains elusive, a spark of light glimpsed at the end of a tunnel, or a reflection half-seen in a swiftly-passed mirror.

Nor must we forget that the stories which make up the Grail Tradition contain the basic teachings of a Mystery School, its tests, its trials, and its initiations, all hidden within the rich symbolic core of the Grail texts. These are themselves part of a larger Tradition, that of the Arthurian Legends[62], which also constitute the framework of a secret body of teaching.

The legends of chivalry are veiled accounts of man's eternal search for truth. These beautiful stories are not, however, merely folklore. They are parts of an orderly tradition, unfolding through the centuries and bearing witness to a well-organised plan and program. Like the myths of classical antiquity, the hero tales are sacred rituals belonging to secret Fraternities perpetuating the esoteric doctrines of antiquity[35].

These words, written by the founder of the Philosophical Research Society, Manly P. Hall, sum up as well as one could wish the reality

1

of the Grail Tradition. But there are problems, both of definition and methodology, which must be met with before one can really begin to understand them. Another great modern seeker, Rudolf Steiner, spoke of the difficulty involved in getting the mystery at the heart of the Grail into proper focus. He added that,

> In occult research ... it has always seemed to me necessary, when a serious problem is involved, to take account not only of what is given directly from occult sources, but also of what external research has brought to light. And in following up a problem it seems to me specially good to make a really conscientious study of what external scholarship has to say, so that one keeps ones feet on the earth and does not get lost in cloud-cuckoo-land[81].

All too many Grail seekers have wandered into just such a place, frequently to remain there. It is very easy to follow a seemingly exciting clue into deep waters where the currents run strongly, and to suddenly find oneself out of one's depth. This is in part due to the extraordinary diversity of the Grail Tradition, which this book can do little more than touch upon. But it is also due to a certain 'light-headedness' which tends to come upon the would be seeker. The Grail can bring about extraordinary effects within the individual psyche, as we can see from the personal accounts to be found in Chapter 6.

But it has been open season on the Grail for a long time now – people have been putting forward theories ever since the twelfth century when French poet Chrétien de Troyes left his *Story of the Grail*[13] unfinished and started a trail of wonder which is still being followed. Some of the theories are sensible, some are not. In recent years for example the Grail has been compared to, or identified with, a number of actual cups, bowls, stones, or jewels. It has been described as a container for the Shroud of Turin[17]; as the mysterious Altar of St Patrick[30]; as a Bloodline[38]; and as a sacred relic[1]. People seem desperate to pin it down, to say what it is and where it is. Yet somehow, despite all this, the theorists have managed by and large to keep one fact clearly in mind. The Grail itself, whatever its origins, is somehow special, connected in some way to the idea of spiritual awakening.

The great mythographer Joseph Campbell has a passage in one of his books, which says it all very well:

> It is one of the prime mistakes of many interpreters of mythological symbols to read them as references, not to

2

mysteries of the human spirit, but as earthly or unearthly scenes, and to actual or imaginal historical events: the promised land as Canaan, for example: heaven as a quarter of the sky; the Israelites passage of the Red Sea as an event such as a newspaper reporter might have witnessed. Whereas it is one of the glories of [the Grail Tradition] that in its handling of religious themes, it retranslates them from the language of imagined facts into a mythological idiom; so that they may be experienced, not as time-conditioned, but as timeless; telling not of miracles long past, but of miracles potential within ourselves, here, now, and forever[10].

The Grail may be all of the things mentioned above – or it may be none of them. It may be something else entirely, something which has no form, or more than one form – it may not even exist at all in this dimension. The important thing is that it provides an object for personal search, for growth and human development, for healing.

In fact, it is more often not the object itself that we are concerned with but the **actions** of the Grail that we seek – the way it causes changes to happen – in the heart, in the mind, in the soul. It is these actions, and the way they came to be recorded, that we shall be exploring throughout this book – and perhaps also learning to work with, if we follow the exercises which are to be found at the end of each chapter.

But to begin with we need signposts. There is no point in simply stepping off into inner space with no idea of what we are looking for. So let us begin with a breakdown of the essential story. This is taken from a number of texts and will not therefore be found within any one account, but it combines most of the elements and gives a broad idea of what we shall be looking at in more detail later on.

THE ESSENTIAL STORY

Some traditions hold that the Grail originated as a jewel – an emerald – from the crown of the Light Bringer, Lucifer, the Angel of the Morning, which fell to earth during the war between the Angels. Others believe that Seth, the child of Adam and Eve, returned to the Garden of Eden in search of a cure for his father's illness, and was given not a remedy for Adam's sickness, but one for the sickness of all men, as well as a promise that God had not forgotten us – the Grail. Whatever theory we choose, the Grail makes its first physical appearance in recorded history at the time of the Crucifixion.

The story begins with Joseph of Arimathea, a wealthy Jew to whose care Christ's body is given for burial and who, according to some accounts, also obtained the Cup used by Christ at the Last Supper. While the body is being washed and prepared for the tomb, some blood flows from the wounds which Joseph catches in the vessel. After the Resurrection, Joseph is accused of stealing the body, and is thrown into prison and deprived of food. Here Christ appears to him in a blaze of light and entrusts the Cup to his care. He then instructs Joseph in the mystery of the Mass and the Incarnation, before vanishing. Joseph is miraculously kept alive by a dove which descends to his cell every day and deposits a wafer in the cup. He is released in AD 70, and joined by his sister and her husband Bron, goes into exile overseas with a small group of followers. A table called the First Table of the Grail is constructed, to represent the Table of the Last Supper. Twelve may sit there, and a thirteenth seat remains empty either in token of Christ's place, or that of Judas. When one of the Company attempts to sit in it he is swallowed up and the seat is thereafter called the Perilous Seat.

Joseph next sails to Britain, where he sets up the first church here in Glastonbury, dedicating it to the Mother of Christ. Here the Grail is housed, and serves as a chalice in the celebration of Mass in which the whole company participate, and which becomes known as the Mass of the Grail.

In other versions Joseph goes no further than Europe and the guardianship of the Grail passes to Bron, who becomes known as the Rich Fisherman after he miraculously feeds the company from the Cup with a single fish. The company settles at a place called Avaron (again perhaps, Avalon) to await the coming of the third Grail Keeper, Alain.

A temple is built at Muntsalvache, the Mountain of Salvation, and an Order of Grail knights comes into being to serve and guard the vessel. They sit at a Second Table, and partake of a sacred feast provided by the Grail. A form of Grail Mass once again takes place, in which the Grail keeper, now called a King, serves as priest. Shortly after, he receives a mysterious wound, variously in the thighs or more specifically the generative organs, caused by a fiery spear. Thereafter the guardian is known as the Maimed or Wounded King and the countryside around the Grail Castle becomes barren and is called the Waste Land – a state explicitly connected with the Grail Lord's wound. The spear with which he is struck becomes identified with the Lance of Longinus, the Roman centurion who in Biblical tradition pierced the side of Christ on the Cross. From this time on there are four objects in the castle – the Cup itself, the Spear, a Sword which is said to break in the hands of its wielder at a crucial moment, and either a shallow dish or a Stone. These are the Hallows, the four sacred treasures which must be sought, and wielded, in a mysterious way, by those who seek the Grail. Each of them, in a certain sense, is the Grail, which is thereafter said to have five mysterious forms – of which we shall hear more later.

By this time, but only now, we have reached the Age of Arthur, and the scene is set for the beginning of the great Quest. The Round Table is established by Merlin as the Third Table of the Grail (though the vessel is absent). A fellowship of Knights, called the Knights of the Round Table, meet there and are bound by a code of chivalry. At Pentecost the Grail makes an appearance, floating on a beam of light through the hall of Camelot, and each and every person there receives the food he likes best (we may see this if we like as Spiritual food) – whereupon the knights all pledge themselves to seek the holy object.

There follows an extraordinary series of initiatory adventures, featuring in the main five knights: Gawain, Lancelot, Perceval, Galahad and Bors. Of these, and of the many knights who set out from Camelot, only three are destined to achieve the Quest. Lancelot, the best knight in the world fails because of his love for Arthur's queen. Gawain, a splendid figure who may once have been the original Grail knight, is shown in the medieval texts as being too worldly, though he comes close to the heart of the mystery.

For the rest: Galahad, who by a marvellous law of change and substitution is the son of Lancelot and the Grail Princess, is destined from the beginning to sit in the Perilous Seat and to achieve the Quest. Perceval, like Gawain originally a successful candidate, is partially ousted by Galahad, so that while he is permitted to see the Grail – and to use the Spear to heal the Wounded King – at the end of the Quest he returns to the Grail Castle where he apparently becomes the new guardian. Because once the Grail has been achieved in that time, and since it is fully achieved by one person only – Galahad – rather than the whole world for whom it is meant, the Grail is withdrawn – but not entirely, not forever. Perceval takes up residence again in the empty castle to await the return of the Grail, which will thereafter be once again available for all true seekers. (And this is still the pattern today – even if someone were to achieve the Grail right now, it would still become available in the next moment – and so it will continue to be until the end of all things or the final achievement of the great Quest.)

Bors, the last of the three knights to come in sight of the Mystery, to experience the Grail directly, is the humble, dogged, 'ordinary' man, who strives with all his being to reach towards the infinite, and who succeeds, voyaging with Galahad and Perceval to the Holy City of Sarras, far across the Western sea. Of the three, he alone returns to Camelot to tell of what has happened. For despite Galahad's personal success – he looks into the Grail and expires in a transcendent moment of Glory – the Quest has been a failure. Merlin, serving the great powers of Creation, had wished to build a perfect kingdom – Logres within Britain – into which the Grail would come and which would then be transformed into the Holy City on Earth, the Earthly Paradise – from which the whole world would be renewed. As it is, the best that can be achieved is the healing of the Waste Land – a kind of inverse Paradise in ruins – and the Maimed King.

Arthur's realm, the earthly world, suffers from the actions of the Grail rather than benefiting from them. Many of the Round Table knights are killed on their search, or anyway die in the attempt, and Lancelot, his great heart almost broken by his rejection at the very door to the chapel of the Grail, returns to his old love and ushers in the downfall of the Table and of Arthur's and Merlin's dream.

THE TRUE MYTH

Such is the story in its essentials. We are dealing here with high things, with a Mystery that is almost too much for us. But we can learn, and grow, from studying it, by sharing the adventure of the Quest with those far-off people of the Arthurian world, who in truth are not so far off at all. Whatever else it may be, the Arthurian Tradition is first and foremost pure myth. And like all myths it is filled with archetypes. The smallest episode within the huge, rambling edifice may contain enough material to furnish a dozen meditations. And it must be said that this is still the best way of getting 'inside' the stories. Of course we must begin by reading the texts: most are currently available in English, and though there are many of them, each one contains something of value, But once we have become familiar with the world of the great Arthurian forest – that seemingly trackless wilderness through which the Quest knights wander, encountering fresh adventures at every crossroad, bridge or clearing – once we have entered and begun to explore that world for ourselves, then we really begin to understand what the Grail is and why it is worth looking for.

POSTSCRIPT

While I was completing the final stages of this book, I encountered a wonderful example of the living quality of the tradition. The latest, spectacular motion picture of *Indiana Jones and the Last Crusade*[50] opened in London to packed houses. It concerns, basically a modern Grail quest, and adds a new chapter to the myth. Indiana Jones goes in pursuit of his father, who is the greatest living expert on the Grail and who has been taken prisoner by the Nazis. After many adventures the cup is discovered in 'a certain valley in Hatay'. It is a plain wooden cup, which nonetheless heals the mortally wounded scholar, and brings death to the evil seeker after eternal life. Then, it is lost again, in the depths of the earth.

Familiar themes abound. The Grail is guarded by an ancient crusader, one of three brothers whose lives were extended beyond mortal span by the power of the Cup. Images of the Wounded King, the three knights of the Grail, and the power of the vessel to bring either life or death are clearly present in the film. The tradition is thus shown to be as vibrant and living as ever, and for the first time since Chrétien de Troyes is received by a large and rapturous audience!

John Matthews
London, 8 July 1989

7

PART ONE:
HISTORY

1 · THE
CAULDRON OF REBIRTH:
THE CELTIC GRAIL

We must look a long way back in time for the origins of what is today understood to be the Grail Tradition. Not for us the panoply of King Arthur and his Round Table Fellowship; we see no shining Cup or radiant maiden, bearing the holy relic through a hall of Medieval splendour. Instead we find an ancient cauldron, intricately carved, its rim set with pearls 'warmed', according to one text, 'by the breath of nine attendant muses'[49]. And this cauldron has the power to grant life, to give forth rich foods, and to bestow upon its owner rare favours. It is possessed by gods and goddesses, it is stolen and stolen again. Hidden and revealed, it lies at the centre of the ancient British (which is to say Celtic) mysteries. And it is sought after as a talisman of power, just as the Grail was to be in the time of Arthur.

Many of the attributes and qualities of the Cauldron are to be found, still present and active, within the later traditions of the Medieval romancers who compiled the vast body of material which became known as *The Matter of Britain*, the stories of Arthur and his knights, and of their great quest for the miraculous Cup.

It is thus to the mysterious realm of the Celtic imagination that we must look for much that is otherwise obscure in the later texts, and in particular to the earliest owners of the wondrous vessel – the

11

The Grail Procession by Howard Pyle

gods and goddesses, and the heroes who even then had begun the search[54].

THE CAULDRON OF CERIDWEN

Of all the God or Goddess-owned cauldrons mentioned within Celtic tradition, one of the earliest and most important is that of the Sow Goddess Ceridwen, one of the most important Celtic deities.

The story goes that Ceridwen had a son named Avagddu, which means 'darkness', who was of such terrible hideousness that no one could bear to look upon him. So the Goddess decided to brew an elixir of pure wisdom and knowledge which would equip her offspring to fare better in the world. She set out to gather the ingredients which would go into the brew, and she set her servants, an old blind man named Morda and a boy named Gwion, to boil her great Cauldron.

The ingredients were gathered and the Cauldron heated. Then Ceridwen went out again, leaving Gwion to stir the mixture. While she was away however, three drops flew out of the Cauldron and scalded Gwion's finger. Automatically, he thrust the finger into his mouth and thereby gained all knowledge, for the three drops were the distillation of Ceridwen's brew.

At once Gwion was aware that the Goddess knew what had occurred, and that she was coming after him in anger. With his newly found powers, he changed his shape to that of a hare and fled. Ceridwen changed her shape to that of a greyhound and gave chase. Through several more metamorphoses of animal, bird and fish Gwion fled and the Goddess pursued, until finally in desperation he became a grain of wheat in a heap of chaff. But Ceridwen took the form of a red-crested hen and swallowed the grain. And thereafter she bore a son in her womb and gave birth to him nine months later.

Ceridwen would have killed the child but she saw that he was beautiful beyond measure, and so she put him into a leather bag and cast him into the sea, where he floated for nine nights and nine days until the bag caught in the weir of the Chieftain Gwyddno Garanhir. There it was found by Gwyddno's son Elphin, an unlucky youth, who had lost all his goods and had been awarded the fateful May-Eve catch of salmon which always came to his father's nets on that day. This time however there was no salmon, only a leather bag which squirmed and wailed. And when Elphin took it forth, bemoaning his evil luck, and opened it, he found the child within, and one of his men remarked at once on the beauty of the infant, and especially his broad white brow. 'Taliesin be he called' said Elphin, for the word meant 'radiant brow', and thus he was called ever after. And though he was still but a new born child he made a song for Elphin which was to be the first of many[30]:

Fair Elphin, dry thy cheeks!
Being too sad will not avail,
Although thou thinkest thou hast no gain
Too much grief will bring thee no good;
Although I am but little, I am highly gifted.

Weak and small as I am,
On the foaming beach of the ocean,
In the day of trouble I shall be
Of more service to thee than three hundred salmon . . .
There lies a virtue in my tongue
While I continue thy protector
Thou hast not much to fear.

Thus was Taliesin, Primary Chief Bard to the Island of Britain, born of the Goddess from the child Gwion. He became the greatest bard of the age, and went on to prove himself a powerful magician and prophet in the tradition of Merlin, whose successor he became when the great enchanter withdrew into the Otherworld. But all his power came from

13

the Cauldron of Ceridwen, and the three drops of inspiration which he had accidentally imbibed.

This is an ancient tale, and an even older theme. We may believe without fear of contradiction that it hides an ancient initiatory experience, in which the candidate was given a drink containing elements to send him into a visionary trance in which he saw past and future events and was put in touch with the *awen*, or inspiration, becoming at once a poet and a prophet. The nature of the transformations, into bird, beast and fish, indicate the shamanic nature of the experience, since all shamans were taught to discover and identify with various totem animals, who became their guides and helpers in the inner realms, whence they travelled to learn the secrets of creation. Taliesin's story is one of the clearest we possess of this initiatory sequence, and the present author has written elsewhere at length on its profound meaning[60].

Elsewhere the theme appears in the story of the famous Irish hero Fionn MacCumhail, who in his youth was set to catch the Salmon of Knowledge for his master Fintan, and when he has done so, is given the task of cooking it. Then, as he lifts it from the fire to give to Fintan, he burns his thumb on the hot flesh and thrusts it into his mouth just as Gwion does in the story outlined above. Fionn too learns thus the power of animal and bird speech, and can read the future by putting his thumb into his mouth and biting upon it.

The salmon was long recognised by the Celts as a bearer of wisdom; surely such a long-lived creature, who knew how to find its way back to its spawning grounds, could only be a symbol of the gods. Therefore to eat of its flesh was to partake of the nature of the Divine, just as Taliesin does by being reborn of the Goddess.

The idea of placing the thumb or fingers into the mouth seems to be reflected in one of the few references to Celtic methods of divination of which we have knowledge. This is known as *dichetel do chennaib* which may be translated as 'divination by finger ends' and possibly refers to the ancient, magical language of Ogham, which consisted of numbers of horizontal strokes crossing a vertical line in various combinations. 'Finger Ogham' could be made by using one finger to form the 'stave' and the others the crossing strokes. This was almost certainly used as a method of conveying messages between one initiate and another[59].

Thus in the very first example of the appearance of the Cauldron we see that it gives wisdom, knowledge, inspiration, and the ability to shape change – all necessary aptitudes for crossing the divide into the Otherworld.

THE CAULDRON OF BRAN

The second example of the Celtic fascination with Cauldrons – and one which brings us firmly into the realm of the Grail – is that of the God Bran, whose title, 'the Blessed', indicates in what degree of reverence he was held. The story comes, as does that of Taliesin, from the collection of Celtic wonder-tales gathered together under the title *Mabinogion*[30], which means literally 'tales of youth' or as we might say, 'tales of young heroes'. It contains most of the earliest reference to Arthur and the Grail, as well as an astonishing collection of magical stories unequalled anywhere.

In the story of *Branwen Daughter of Llyr* we find the following account.

Bran the Blessed was King of Britain, and he arranged for his sister Branwen to marry Matholwch, the King of Ireland. At the wedding feast one of his brothers, Evnissien, took slight at the Irish king and mutilated his horses. Strife seemed imminent, but Bran offered Matholwch the Cauldron of Rebirth, into which dead warriors were placed and came forth alive again. Matholwch already knew of the Cauldron which came originally from Ireland and was owned by a giant and his wife, Llassar Llaes Gyfnewid and Cymidei Cymeinfoll, who gave birth to a fully armed warrior every six weeks. They had been driven out of Ireland and had taken refuge with Bran.

Branwen now went to Ireland, where she bore Matholwch a son, but was so unpopular with the people that she was forbidden his bed and put to work in the kitchens. There she trained a starling to carry a message to her brother, who once he heard of her ill treatment came with all his warriors across the sea. Matholwch retreats and sues for peace, which is granted on condition that he abdicates in favour of Gwern, his son by Branwen.

At the feast which ensues, Evnissien again brings disaster by thrusting the child into the fire. Fighting breaks out and the Irish are winning because they put their fallen warriors into the Cauldron. Evnissien then crawls inside and stretching out, breaks both the vessel and his own heart. Bran is wounded in the foot by a poisoned spear and instructs his surviving followers, who number only seven, to cut off his head and bear it with them.

They journey to an island named Gwales, where they are entertained by the head of Bran and the singing of the Birds of Rhiannon for eight-five years, during which time they know no fears or hardship and forget all that they have suffered. Then one of their number opens a forbidden door, and at once the enchantment ceases and they remember everything. Bran's head tells them to carry it to London and bury it beneath the White Mount with its face towards France. The seven then return to Bran's country and find it under the power of a magician named Caswallawn. The remainder of the story is told in the next tale in the *Mabinogion*, but does not concern us here.

Here the Cauldron is shown to have definite Otherworldly status. The gigantic man and woman, Llassar Laes Gyfnewid and Cymideu Cymeinfoll can persuasively be identified with Tegid Foel and Ceridwen with whom she is partnered in later traditions. Both are said to come from a lake with an island in the centre and both possess a wonder-working cauldron. We may perhaps go no further with this identification than to say that both couples seem to represent an earlier, more primeval tradition of the Otherworld, connected in some way to the race of aboriginal giants hinted at elsewhere in Celtic mythology. But it is worth remembering that the woman of the pair in *Branwen* is said to give birth to fully armed warriors – which seems itself like another echo of the Cauldron story, where it is seen as giving life to (previously dead) warriors.

We are told that Matholwch soon discovered the mistake he had made by allowing the couple to remain in his court: they had multiplied so rapidly and committed such outrages that in less than four months we find the Irish King trying to be rid of them. They do this by building a huge iron house which is then heated, with the giants inside it, in an attempt to destroy the unwanted guests. This theme seems to originate in an Irish tale called *Borama* where the king is actually called Brandub, which is the probable reason why the story became attached to the story of Bran the Blessed. Once again there is the suggestion of a giant cauldron, in which the giant and his wife were placed in the hope that they would be destroyed. This is reminiscent of certain Alchemical practices which we shall examine in more detail in Chapter 3. Here the alchemical King and Queen are placed in a huge bath which is then heated. They emerge renewed and transformed. The idea is ultimately the same – those placed into the Cauldron of Rebirth, come forth renewed.

In *Branwen*, of course, the giants escape and go to Britain, where they become peaceable citizens. Here, unlike the treatment they received in Ireland, they are made welcome and Bran 'quarters them throughout every part of the kingdom' – a reference no doubt to the breeding properties of the giantess, who appears to provide excellent soldiers for the British army!

And so we move towards the next appearance of the Cauldron. Bran learns of his sister's ill treatment and arrives in Ireland with an army. Negotiations take place and at Branwen's suggestion the Irish king has a hall built for Bran – again perhaps a reference to a giant cauldron? But what occurs then is tragic: Branwen's child is thrown into the fire and consumed, Bran receives a wound in the thigh and in the ensueing battle the Cauldron is brought into play by the Irish to revive their dead. Until, that is, Evnissien, finally regretting his earlier actions, himself gets into the vessel and breaks it – and his heart – in the process.

THE PIERCED THIGH

Meanwhile, Bran has seized Branwen and cries aloud the words which are usually translated as 'Dogs of Gwern, beware of Morddwyd Tyllion'. This is a very important sentence, because although it sounds virtually meaningless in this context, it becomes clearer if one translates Morddwyd Tyllion as 'Pierced Thigh'. This, as we shall see, is a suitable title for Bran. 'Dogs of Gwern' has been taken to refer to the Irish followers of the boy Gwern, who is, however briefly, their king. But if we again translate the word 'gwern' literally, as 'alder swamp', the whole sentence then reads 'Dogs of the alder swamp' (that is, the Irish) beware the Pierced Thigh (that is, Bran).

The importance of this epithet, as applied to Bran, becomes apparent if we look ahead to the medieval Grail stories, where we find the figure known as the Wounded King, who suffers an unhealing wound in the thigh (generally recognised as a reference to the genitals) which is the ultimate cause of the wasting of his lands – a condition which can only be remedied by the coming of the destined Grail champion, who will bring about the healing of both the king and the land. If we also notice that one of the foremost kings of the Grail lineage is named Bron, we may begin to see the extensive links which exist between this titanic figure of Celtic myth and the kingdom of the Grail.

It is at this point in the story of *Branwen* that we come to one of the most important, as well as the strangest, episodes in the entire collection of tales which go to make up the *Mabinogion*. Mortally wounded, Bran orders his surviving followers (who significantly number seven) to cut off his head and take it to Bryn Gwyn, the White Mount, in London, and bury it looking towards France. So long as it remains there, no enemy will be able to invade the island of Britain from that direction.

However, the seven do not take a direct route to London. They make two stops along the way – firstly at Harlech, where Branwen dies, and then at the mysterious island of Gwales, where eighty years passed in feasting and song. During this time Bran's head continues to speak with and entertain the company as though he was still alive, for which reason the period is known as 'The Entertainment of the Noble Head' and the seven men as 'The Company of the Noble Head.'

Both Helaine Newstead[72] and R.S. Loomis[49], both noted authorities, affirm that this episode arises from a misunderstanding of the word pen, which can mean both 'head' and 'chief', – the implication being that Bran was present in his entirety during the period of feasting and song and on the journey to London. Certainly Taliesin, who was one of the seven, refers in a poem to singing before the sons of Llyr – Bran and Manawyddan – at Aber Henvellen (the place towards which it was forbidden to look), suggesting that both were in fact alive.

If we accept this interpretation the island of Gwales becomes an aspect of the Celtic Otherworldly paradise, where heroes spent a timeless period in feasting and song, and which is incidentally a clear precursor of the paradisal realms sought by the Grail questers. It is also wholly consistent with descriptions of the island of Caer Sidi, the Feary Fortress described by Taliesin in another poem as:

Perfect is my seat in Caer Siddi.
Nor plague nor age harms him who dwells therein.
Manawyddan and Pryderi knew it.
Three tuneful instruments around the fire play before it
And around its corners are ocean's currents.
And the wonder-working spring is above it
Sweeter than white wine is the drink in it . . .[60]

THE VOYAGE TO HELL

Bran thus becomes a type of the Otherworldly host who feasts heroes in his magic hall, feeding them from an inexhaustible Cauldron which 'will not boil the food of a coward'. We can see another example of this kind of vessel, and incidentally complete the connections of Bran and the various cauldrons with the Grail quest by looking at another poem, Preiddeu Annwn, attributed to Taliesin (whom we should remember was present at the Entertainment of the Noble Head, and is himself one of the Cauldron-Born, an initiate of the sacred vessel).

The poem begins thus:

Perfect was the prison of Gweir in Caer Siddi
According to the testament of Pwyll and Pryderi;
No one before him was sent into it.
A heavy blue chain held the youth,
And before the spoiling of Annwn gloomily he sang;
Till released he continues his song.
Three times the fullness of Pridwen we went in –
Except seven, none returned from Caer Siddi.

In Caer Pedryvan, four times revolving,
We came upon the Cauldron of Annwn
With a ridge around its edge of pearls.
By the breath of nine muses was it warmed,
Nor will it boil the food of a coward.
Before Hell's portals lights were burning,
And when we went with Arthur, of splendid endeavour,
Except seven, none returned from Caer Veddwid. . . .

(from a reconstruction by the author,[68])

We are hearing of a raid on the Otherworld, lead by Arthur, to steal the magical cauldron of Pen Annwn. Once again the word *pen*, head is important. In this case it refers to the Otherworldly King Arawn, who is here a possessor of a cauldron of incalculable power. Clearly, also, as in the Grail quest, the task is not an easy one. Only seven men – the same number, we note, as returned with Bran from Ireland – come back with Arthur. One of them, again, is Taliesin, who tells the tale. And we may note that the description of the caers (castles) through which the heroes must pass in order to reach Arawn's hall, are remarkably reminiscent of the island of Caer Siddi in Taliesin's other song, and like the island of Gwales in *Branwen*. Indeed, the voyage of Bran to Ireland seemed to have been modelled on the *Spoils of Annwn*, and may at one time have contained only this story, before the account of Branwen's adventures were grafted onto it.

THE KEEPERS OF THE HALLOWS

There is strong evidence, besides, for an identification of Bran with Arthur – not necessarily as identical figures, but as two distinct characters who assume identical roles – as guardians of the Land. We have already seen how Bran fulfils this role in requiring that his head be buried beneath the White Mount in London. Later we are told, Arthur had the head disinterred, declaring that none but he should defend the Island of Britain. Bran's name, which means 'raven' is also linked to Arthur, who in folk-tradition is said to have taken the form of a chough, a type of raven, after his death. To this day ravens frequent the Tower of London, which stand on the White Mount, and it is widely believed that if they ever depart the country will fall – which is why even today the precaution is taken of clipping their wings to make them unable to fly!

All of this raises another question. If Bran is not dead on the island of Gwales, and if, as in the suggested earlier pattern of the story, he carried off the Cauldron (rather than Arthur, who tended to assume the attributes of Bran) then this would make him one of the guardians of the 'Hallows', or 'treasures' of Britain, thus placing him in direct line to the Sacred Kings who were the keepers of the Grail – one of which, as we saw, was called Bron or Brons. This would be quite in line with Bran's title *Bendigeid*, 'Blessed', which for someone who was a type of the Wounded Grail Lord would be perfectly appropriate.

Add to this the fact that Bran is elsewhere associated with a magical drinking horn or platter, and we have what were possibly the Treasures of Annwn, brought back by Arthur/Bran to become the foundation of the later Grail stories where the Hallows were the Cup, the Spear, the Stone and the Dish.

The attribution of the word pen to Bran would have put the story-teller in mind of other, older stories concerning beheadings and oracular heads, of which there were a number in Celtic mythology (hardly surprising in a race which treated the severed head as a cult object). As it is the fact that the Company were in the presence of Bran's head need not imply that it was no longer attached to his body! An otherworldly feast presided over by Bran could well be the root of a story which was later added to the tradition of the sacred head of a chieftain buried under the White Mount to guard either the land or an object of special significance.

THE HEAD IN THE DISH

There is another story concerning a severed head which brings us firmly into the realm of the Grail myths. This is the story of *Peredur*. It is also to be found in the *Mabinogion*, and though controversy still rages over its actual date and provenance it can safely be assumed to contain material from a far earlier time than the later medieval romance of the Grail written by Chrétien de Troyes[53].

Brought up in woodland seclusion by his mother, Peredur grows up in ignorance of arms. On seeing some of Arthur's knights, he mistakes them for angels. He is soon enlightened and vows to follow them to Arthur's court where he too will become a warrior. His mother gives him misleading advice which causes him to be thought boorish. At court, he defends Gwenhwyfar's honour and rescues her gold cup. After a sojourn with his first uncle where he tests his strength with a sword which breaks and is miraculously reunited again, he meets his second uncle, the Wounded King. Following his mother's original advice, he forbears to ask what is happening when the Grail procession enters the hall. He sees a spear which drips blood and a head floating in a dish of blood but remains silent: an act for which he is later rebuked by the Black Maiden, since, had he asked about it, the land might have been healed along with the Wounded King, but Peredur has, by his thoughtlessness, delayed the day of restoration. In a series of adventures Peredur is enamoured of a beautiful woman, learns arms from the Nine Witches of Gloucester, slays a serpent and gains the ring it guards, overcomes a giant, kills another serpent and wins the gold-granting stone it guards, and finally comes upon the Woman of the Mound, who gifts him with a ring of invisibility which aids him to overcome a third monster.

Peredur is transfixed with love for her but finds himself entering the Otherworld. During his sojourn, he presents himself to the Empress of Constantinople (conceived of as a Faery Queen) and overcomes all the knights in the tournament which she has called. Peredur kills three cup-bearers and sends their cups to his hostess during the tourney – a miller's wife. He then marries the Empress who is none other than the Woman of the Mound who originally helped him. After fourteen years in the Otherworld, Peredur returns to Arthur's court where a Black Maiden comes to rebuke him for delaying the healing of the land. The Grail quest proper begins. During this quest, Peredur comes upon a castle where there is a chessboard which plays by itself. The side Peredur supports loses and he casts the board into a lake. He is forced to retrieve it, since it belongs to the Empress. He has to overcome the monstrous black man, Ysbidinongyl. He then kills a unicorn whose horn is causing the waters to dry up. Finally, he comes to the Castle of Wonders – the Grail Castle – where it is revealed that many characters within the story were Peredur's cousin in disguise. The head in the dish belonged to another of his cousins. Peredur and Gwalchmai, with the help of Arthur, finally defeat the Witches of Gloucester who have caused the enchantments.

Here the object which in Chrétien's version of the story becomes the Grail, is a dish, and instead of containing holy blood, or spiritual food, it contains a severed human head – that of Peredur's cousin whom he seeks to revenge. Although at one level this turns the story into a quest for vengeance, we must not forget the Celtic obsession with the human head, which as we saw in the story of Bran became an object for reverence which magically provided food and entertainment for the whole company – just as, later on, the Grail was to do for the company of the Round Table.

Other talismanic objects abound in this story: the ring guarded by the serpent of the mound; the ring given to Peredur by the Woman of the Mound; the ring he takes from the Maiden of the Tent; the cup stolen from Guinevere and later restored to her; the magical chessboard won from Ysbidinongel; the unicorn's head won by Peredur for the Empress; and of course the Spear Which Drips Blood and the head in the dish, which is seen but not won by the hero.

This list can be matched with the list of the Thirteen Treasures of the Island of Britain[58], which tradition ascribes to the guardianship of Merlin, on an island not unlike that in both the *Spoils* and *Branwen*. For a full and detailed discussion of the intricate relationship of these items to the Grail mystery the reader is referred to *Arthur and the Sovereignty of Britain* by Caitlin Matthews, especially Chapters 7 and 9.

For the moment we need to look more closely at the idea of the otherworldly island on which the Hallows are kept, and which provides us with further analogies with the story of the Grail.

THE FORBIDDEN DOOR

We are told in *Branwen* that on the island of Gwales the Birds of Rhiannon sang to the company, and that as long as no one opened the forbidden door that looked towards Aber Henvellen, then all would be well. The Birds of Rhiannon belong to the Goddess of that name. They are of the kind that sing so sweetly that those who hear them no longer notice the passage of time or feel any sorrow or fear. That these are otherworldly sirens is clear, as is the fact that it is *they* rather than the presence of Bran's head which keeps the company in a state of suspended life. There is a very close analogy of this episode in the later medieval text of *Perlesvaus*, in which the heroes visit the Island of Ageless Elders.

> They looked beneath a tall tree with branches spreading wide, and saw the clearest and most beautiful fountain that any man could describe. . . . Beneath the fountain two men were sitting,

with air and beards whiter than new-fallen snow, yet their faces seemed young indeed[6].

They go into a wonderful hall and there see:

> The richest tables of gold and ivory [they] had ever seen. One of the masters sounded a gong three times, and into the hall came thirty-three men, all in one company; they were dressed all in white, and each bore a red cross on his chest; and they all seemed to be thirty-two years old. (ibid)

When this company sit at table a golden crown on a chain descends from above, and a pit is opened in the middle of the hall: '. . . the moment the pit was uncovered, the greatest and most lamentable cries ever heard rose up from below; and when the worthy men in the hall heard them they . . . began to weep.' (ibid) What happens to put an end to the idyllic life? In *Perlesvaus* the wondrous hall is built above a pit of lamenting souls. In *Peredur* one of the company, Heilyn son of Gwyn the Old, decides that he cannot rest until he knows what lies behind the Forbidden Door. The result we already know: the Company remember their former lives and the sorrows they had experienced, and immediately set out for London to inter the head of Bran.

All of this seems like a clear parallel to the Christian Fall. The knowledge which comes from opening the forbidden door, like that which comes from eating of the fruit of the tree of Good and Evil, is the same, sorrow and dismissal from Paradise. Yet this is part of the lot of humanity, that they should not remain in paradise so long as that means remaining in ignorance (even though protected) of the true state of Creation.

In this Celtic version, instead of the angelic guardians of Eden, there are the Birds of Rhiannon, spinning a dream around the heroes so that they forget themselves. But there is a built-in fail-safe, which is *already known to Bran* before even the seven set out for Gwales with the miraculous head. In the text Bran *tells* them they will remain for an exact number of years (eighty-seven) and this is shown to be the case. Bran must also know the nature of the magical birds. Was it they who were imprisoned behind the forbidden door, so that when it was opened they flew away? Perhaps they should also be seen as Branwen's birds, comparable with the tame starling who carries a message to her brother?

Far more is intended to be understood by the opening of the door than we are told in *Branwen*. It is a doorway between worlds which is

23

opened, one which allows for passage both ways, between this world and the other, of those who dwell in either place. In setting Bran's head to watch over the land of Britain from the White Mount, there is also a sense in which the inner archetype of Bran is placed in a position of guarding the otherworld as well – the exchange taking place by way of the door – which we must remember we are not told is *closed* again after the departure of the seven, only that it was opened.

THE ISLAND OF WONDERS

Another, later, text, makes the symbolism even clearer. *Sone de Nausay*[49] is a medieval story, but as is often the case it contains material from significantly earlier sources. Here we find related the adventures of the brave knight Sone, who takes service with the king of Norway. Most of the story is not relevant to our present exploration, but one episode is of vital importance for the clues it offers both to the identity of the island of Gwales and its place in the Grail mysteries.

In order to receive the grace necessary to overcome a gigantic warrior, Sone and Alain travel to a mysterious island named Galosche, where they find a beautiful castle with four towers at each of the four corners and in the centre a great hall. This castle is curiously inhabited by monks, who however, possess two wondrous relics: the uncorrupted body of Joseph of Arimathea and the Grail itself. . . . These are shown to Sone and the story of the vessel retold. Long after, Sone returns to the island to be married and is permitted to carry the Grail in procession, with the Spear, a piece of the True Cross, and a candle which had been carried by the Angel of the Annunciation!

The description given here of the Island of Galosche (Wales? Gwales?) is typical of the Grail castle and the turning island and the four-cornered city in *Preiddeu Annwn*. But there is so much here that bears a resemblance to episodes in *Perlesvaus* that one might be forgiven for believing they shared a common source. Both texts describe a collection of paintings depicting the Annunciation and the Harrowing of Hell. In both, a coffin containing the body of a great man, in this case Joseph of Arimathea. And both texts contain a description of a land under the curse of barrenness, though here it is Logres rather than the Island of Need which is in question.

The Substitution of Joseph for Bran in *Sone* is possibly due to a misunderstanding on the part of some unknown copyist of the word *cors*, which while it can mean body, also means horn. We remember that Bran was the possessor of a remarkable horn; when this was read as body it would have been natural for the medieval writer, who knew the Grail story, to replace the pagan god with the figure of Joseph, whom he probably mistook for the wounded King, retaining the image of Bran's wound at the same time.

The seven followers of Bran have become twelve in both *Sone de Nausay* and *Perlesvaus*, where there are twelve monks and twelve ageless elders respectively. But we can still see the influence of the earlier story in the ageless men in the latter text, as we can also see echoes of the sorrowing Company of the Noble Head in *Branwen*, in the weeping and wailing monks in *Sone*, and the sorrowful sounds emanating from the pit on the island of Ageless Elders.

In the *Historia Meriadoci*[18], a thirteenth century romance written in Latin, we find the island of Gundebaldus, which is square, lies at the centre of a bog and is only connected to dry land by a narrow causeway (elsewhere this becomes the famous Sword Bridge leading to the Castle of the Grail). There are four castles on this island, as there are in the *Preiddeu Annwn*, and in the centre is a beautiful hall with gardens. The hero, Meriadoc, meets the wizard Gundebaldus on the causeway and fights him, successfully knocking him into the bog. The name Gundebaldus has been identified as a variant of Gwynas or Gwynn, another name for the King of Annwn. The name of the fictitious king of Norway in *Sone* is given as Alain, a name also attached to one of the later Grail kings, and which may well be a corruption of Arawn, the owner of the Cauldron in *Preiddeu Annwn* . . . !

In the Celtic wonder-tale *The Voyage of Maelduin*[58], there is another island, divided in four by walls of precious substance: gold, silver, copper, and crystal, and each quarter allocated to kings, queens, youths, and maidens respectively. These refer to the four elements and the four directions on the shamanic Wheel of the Year, and on each of the four quarters of the island can be placed one of the four ancient Hallows of the Grail which first appear in their Celtic forms as: The Stone of Fal from Falias; The Spear of Lugh from Gorias; The Sword of Nuadu for Findias; and The Cauldron of the Dagda from Murias.

THE PLACE OF THE FOUR HALLOWS

From all the above we arrive at a picture. It is of an island four square, perhaps made of glass or crystal according to other Celtic sources, divided in four or with four towers or castles at each corner. At the centre is a mysterious enclave surrounded by a wall or fence that is difficult to penetrate. Here the Grail is sometimes to be found, and all who sit down at its table are fed with the food they most desire. In some mysterious way this is the heart centre of both land and people, even though it is often situated on an island off the coast of the mainland.

Here all things are balanced and there is no hardship or anger, fear or hatred or dread. In fact the paradisial realm of the Grail. It is possible to make a glyph of this:

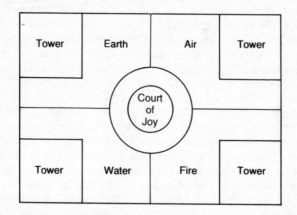

Figure 1: The Blessed Realm/The Realm of the Grail.

Here the four directions/elements meet in harmony. Add to this the shape of the Grail cup in its more abstract design, and we arrive at a mandala of the Grail, where all things meet and are balanced, where the aspirations of humanity meet the desire of God to be reunited with His creation.

Caswallawn, the new ruler, is presented as an infamous magician, who slew six of the seven guardians while wearing a cloak of invisibility. Caradac, Bran's son, broke his heart at the sight of his friends falling to an invisible opponent. There is a strong echo here of the later episodes, which will be dealt with fully in Chapter 4, where the knight Balin, staying at the castle of the Grail king, sees a knight struck down by the king's invisible brother. Though Balin does not die of grief, his reaction, the slaying of the invisible attacker, does bring death and destruction in its wake, and his own death follows shortly.

The Company is, in a very real sense, without its 'head'; Bran is buried in the land as its new palladium. He thus joins a select group of figures whose importance must be recognised for the part it, too, plays in the formative history of the Grail.

It has already been suggested that Bran shares enough common factors with the Grail king to substantiate his identity as a prototype of the Maimed King. His guardianship of the Cauldron, and ultimately of Britain, further identify him as a type of *genius loci*, such as Arthur later became, sleeping beneath the land until he is needed to reaffirm his lordship. Another such figure, from Classical mythology, who shares these attributes, as well as Bran's gigantic stature, is Cronos, the father-god of the Greeks. If we turn to Classical literature and to a text by Plutarch, which has often been quoted to show how Britain was seen as an otherworldly realm by the rest of the ancient world, we get a vivid picture of the buried God. The quotation comes from a work entitled *The Silence of Oracles*[75] which tells how a Greek named Demetrius visited Britain to investigate the island's religious traditions.

This image is reflected almost universally, whether it be in one of the marvellous mandalas of the mystic Hildegard of Bingen, or a Hopi Indian sand painting, where the power of the four directions is recognised. Here we see the reconciliation of head and heart, the balancing of male and female, the above and below, the placing of the four Hallows on the Table of Creation, and the Elements in the Divine Cauldron of Time and Space.

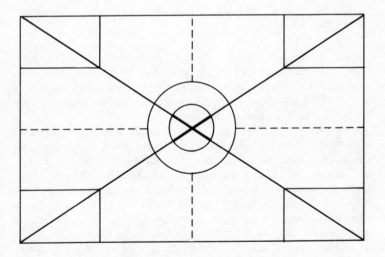

Figure 2: The Mandala of the Grail.

THE SLEEPING TITAN

When the Company of the Noble Head return to Britain, they find that time has moved on. The seven men left behind to guard the kingdom have all been overthrown and killed, including Bran's son. Caswallawn, son of Beli, now rules over the land. There is again a sense that just as there is an inner and outer Bran, so the seven men left behind are somehow surrogates for the seven who were present at the Entertainment of the Noble Head. There is, too, an echo of the episode we looked at from *Perlesvaus* where Arthur, absent from the land, is thought to be dead and other events take their course as though he were indeed no longer ruling.

'There is' he says, 'an island there where Cronos is a prisoner guarded by Briarius in his sleep – sleep was the fetter devised for Cronos, and many daimons lie around him as servants and followers.' This is further amplified in *The Face of the Moon*[75], also by Plutarch, where it is said that:

> The natives [of Britain] have a story that in one of these [islands] Cronos has been confined by Zeus, but that he, having a son as a gaoler, is left sovereign lord of those islands ... Cronos himself sleeps within a deep cave resting on rock which looks like gold ... birds fly in at the topmost part of the rock, and bare him ambrosia, and the whole island is pervaded by the fragrance shed from the rock. (ibid.)

Not only is this astonishingly reminiscent of descriptions of the aged Grail king kept alive by a host brought to him by a dove from heaven, but it also establishes clearly the nature of the sleeper and reminds us as well of the island on which Bran resides, with the company of the Noble Head and the Birds of Rhiannon.

In Greek myth Cronos is the last of the Titans, who having castrated his father Uranus, becomes lord of the world. He later consumed all the children of his wife Rhea except for Zeus who finally overthrew him and chained him in the Islands of the Blessed. He is thereafter seen as ruling over a lost Golden Age much as Bran (also 'the Blessed') during the feasting of the Noble Head. Both are shown as sleeping beneath the land, guardians of the door between the upper realm and the otherworld. Arthur joins them as the latest in a line of guardians – the Pendragons, the Chieftains of Annwn – who await the call to come forth from their magical sleep and defend their country.

All of this throws a new light on the idea of the Grail kings and their origins. They are a part of the legacy of Celtic tradition which helped shape the future development of the Grail myths, and which are felt throughout most of the medieval retellings which followed. For something like five hundred years these and other stories continued to circulate, first in Britain and later in Europe. Eventually, they returned, christianised and shaped anew, but with the same underlying elements still perceivable beneath the layers of new material which had been grafted upon them. We shall see something of what occurred in the next chapter.

EXERCISE 1: THE COMPANY OF THE NOBLE HEAD

Close your eyes and sinking deeply into meditation, prepare to embark on a journey. Visualise before you this scene: a low-lying level plain, with long grass waving in the gentle breeze of midsummer. Above you the sun is high in a clear blue sky. Ahead see a low mound, scarcely a hill, almost certainly man-made. In the centre of the side facing is a door made of two mighty upright stones capped with a huge lintel. As you approach great wooden doors fold inward on noiseless hinges. Within, all seems dark, but as you go forward you see a dim light which grows brighter the further you go, until you find yourself at last standing in what seems to be a long hall, high-ceilinged, supported upon huge timbers carved with intricate spiralling designs. As you look about you see that the walls themselves seem to be of wood, and that everywhere they are carved in reliefs depicting scenes of people hunting, of warriors battling and drinking, of men and women making love. . .

In the centre of this great hall burns a great fire, casting a warm red glow over everything, flickering across the walls, so that the carved figures seem to move. . . . Around the fire pit are benches and tables, arranged in a rough circle, and, as you watch, the hall, which had seemed empty, begins to fill up with people. Proud, fine-boned men with strong, fierce faces, many sporting long moustaches: slender fair women, some with hair unbound, others with plaits reaching below the knee. All alike are dressed in bright colours: brilliant reds and blues, deep greens and startling yellows.

You notice three in particular who stand out from the rest, who sit upon ornate chairs where the rest throng noisily onto the benches. These are two men and a woman; the men both handsome and dark-haired, the woman, who might be their sister, white-skinned as the moon, with dark, red hair and keen, far-seeing eyes. She it is who now looks towards you, and beckons you forward. You are invited to join the company, to sit on one of the benches and room is made for you.

Once you are seated, liquor is brought round, a foaming brew served in rough leather tankards. It tastes somewhat like cider, but with a deep sparkling freshness which leaves you feeling more alive after you have drunk it.

Now you see a figure step forth into the firelight: a tall slender man dressed in simple green. He carries a small harp and round about his brows is a fillet of silver which glows like starlight. As he begins to play you are entranced, for the music seems like the most sweet and lovely sound you have ever heard. You may feel tears starting to your eyes as you listen, but you are aware also that the eyes of the harpist are upon you, and that his cool gaze looks deeply into you, reading all that is there to see . . .

As you listen to the music of the harpist, you lose all sense of time. You have perhaps sat there for only a few moments, or maybe far, far longer, when at last you become aware that the music has ceased, a new element has been added to scene. Across the room from the three carved chairs you see a huge, wise and gentle head. It is as though it is floating there, yet there is nothing fearful or repellent about this; the face is so filled with joy and merriment; the eyes brimming over with life, the lips smiling . . .

After a moment of complete silence, when even the bright throng of men and women have fallen completely still, you hear again the sound of the harp, and now a voice is raised in song, high and sweet and more pure than anything you have ever heard. At first you cannot quite hear the words, but slowly you realise that the song is coming from the mouth of the Noble Head, though it seems to be made up not of one voice, but of many. Gradually you begin to pick out the words and to realise that what is being sung is meant directly for you and you alone. Although all who are present listen with such attention that maybe all hear something which is of particular significance to them.

Listen carefully and try to remember what you hear. . .

At length, the Great Song is ended. If you have listened with heart as well as ears, you will have learned much that will be of help to you in the months and years ahead. For you are now one of the Company of the Noble Head and once you have heard the Song that is sung you can never wholly forget it. As you look the great face slowly fades from sight and you find yourself once again in the great wooded hall beneath the green mound. It is time to depart and sadly you take leave of the bright gathering. As you rise from your place and return the way you came, you notice that on three sides of the hall are great wooden doors securely barred and bolted. The wood from which they are made seems more ancient than that of the rest of the hall, blackened and weathered by countless fires burning in the great hall. You may wonder about the doors later on and one day you may return to see them opened . . .

Now as you return the way you came, the light begins to fade and you see before you the archway of the door by which you entered. Outside is bright sunlight, but when you step through the doors you find that it is the cold light of midwinter. You have been within the mound for a full half year.

Slowly now let the scene begin to fade from you and become aware again of your surroundings. In your own time re-establish contact with the world around you. But always remember what you learned in the Hall of Blessed Bran.

2 · CHRIST'S CUP:
THE CHRISTIAN DIMENSION

A NEW DIMENSION

By the late twelfth century the stage was already set for a new epiphany of the Grail. The Middle Ages had achieved their first flowering: a springing forth of new ideas and beliefs in minds freed at last from the sheer effort of survival. Art, architecture and literature were in their vernal aspect; Chartres cathedral was still under construction, and complex webs of theology and mysticism were being unwound in both monastery and university. The relationship of mankind with creation, and with God, were amongst the all important questions of the age.

Despite, or perhaps because of the fact that literacy was a skill reserved almost exclusively for clerics, memory was correspondingly stronger than today. The ear, not the eye, was the gateway to the imagination; when it came to storytelling, there were always willing listeners to wonder-tales in which a semi divine hero slew beasts and overcame implacable enemies in order to rescue and eventually marry, archetypal maidens.

There was also a stronger sense of conceptual or symbolic understanding. Labourers were known by their implements of toil, religious by their habit, nobility by their rich apparel, knights by their mounts and weapons. Although the liturgy of the Mass was in

Latin, except perhaps for the sermon, which may have been in the vernacular, this did not seem to matter; the actions of the priest at the altar were necessarily mysterious, emblematic of the way in which he mediated between heaven and earth on behalf of the congregation.

Factors such as these helped prepare the way for the return of the Grail, as did the political state of Europe at this time. Prior to the spread of Christianity the whole of the Western world had been torn apart by war and insurrection; orphaned from its Classical roots by Barbarians who eventually made the West their own homeland, Europe remained a tangle of petty kingdoms, each one battling for supremacy.

Each kingdom, however small, had its own capital. The archetype for these capitals was, religiously, Jerusalem, the city of the Divine King; mythically, it was Camelot, the stronghold of the Earthly King, Arthur of Britain. And indeed, the role of kingship within European society was a significant one: kingship sprang from a divine source as it had from the Goddess of Sovereignty in Celtic times, and kings were annointed with oil just as priests were – emphasising the priest-like nature of the office.

This descent of kings from a divine source was of the greatest importance to medieval man. We must remember that Europe was a wilderness of forest and trackless waste, partitioned by rivers and lakes and still very much under the influence of tutelary gods and goddesses. Each tree, hill and well had its guardian spirit; standing stones, circles and sacred groves retained a sense of the numinous. Although only folk memory of these things survived, the king had to be a consort of the gods as well as the people if he was to wield any power.

It is this which makes the idea of the Wounded King, which we saw springing from Celtic myth, such a powerful theme within the Grail cycle. The wounding of the king caused the wounding of the land because of the deep and indissoluble links between them. Its presence within the Arthurian stories demonstrates how thin was the veneer of Christianity upon the original beliefs of the West. The power of Rome had not yet assumed the extremes which resulted in reformation and counter-reformation, but few had the strength to step outside its laws.

The further the influence of the Church spread through Europe, the more exoteric became its expression. Yet even within such strictures, the real message of Christ managed to survive; a body of mystical and esoteric teaching was upheld by isolated people: mystics, solitary madmen, who were either ignored, lauded as exemplary members of

33

the Church, or if their doctrines attracted undue attention, summarily dismissed as heretics.

It is perhaps significant that there are no 'Grail Saints', no officially approved expositors of what might be termed the Grail 'school' of mysticism, any more than there is either specific recognition or denial of the Grail itself. There is merely a deafening silence which, in an age of relic-hunting, is itself as telling.

THE NEW CORPUS

Almost the entire corpus of Grail literature was written between 1170 and 1225, appearing suddenly and ending almost as abruptly. We can only guess at the extent of oral tradition behind their composition. Certainly the Arthurian canon was already established well before the twelfth century, deriving its roots from the Celtic sources discussed in Chapter 1. Story-tellers such as the trouvères, wandering singers and poets who were able to cross all boundaries, both physical and religious, fused the pagan and the Christian ethos with Chivalric achievement and folk culture, forming an archetypal world which lived in the imaginations of all kinds of people.

Two authors who may be seen as helping to establish the canon of the Grail were Chrétien de Troyes and Robert de Borron. Chrétien was already famed throughout Europe for his Arthurian poems, in which he had introduced such originally Celtic figures as Lancelot, Gawain and Geraint to a Norman French, courtly society who were hungry for more. The Matter of Britain, as it was known, became all the rage, with countless new stories appearing all the time. Chrétien's last work, left unfinished at his death, was *The Conte Del Graal* or Story of the Grail[13], in which he told of the adventures of a young, innocent youth named Perceval, who happened to catch sight of two knights – whom he took for angels – in the forest where he had been brought up in ignorance of all manly pursuits. From this moment he desired only to follow them and to discover where and how they lived. He met many adventures on the way, but the strangest of all was that of the Grail.

Finding himself at the Castle of his uncle the Fisher King, Perceval witnesses a mysterious procession in which a vessel called the Graal is born through the hall and is used in some way to sustain a wounded man. Perceval, either from politeness or ignorance, fails to ask the meaning of these things, and finds himself outcast to wander in the wilderness of the Waste Land as a result. A hideous damsel chides him for his failure and tells him that had he asked the required question the land and the king would have been restored. Thereafter the foolish youth has to suffer in the wilderness for some time before he finds his way back to the castle; but the outcome is never revealed since the poem breaks off before the mystery of the Grail is explained.

The enigma of this story touched the imagination of the Western world, expressing feelings that were already latent within the consciousness of Medieval man. A Swiss knight named Robert de Borron, who may have already been working on a Grail text of his own prior to Chrétien, took the story back through time to the days when Christ walked the earth, telling how Joseph of Arimathea, who gave up his own tomb to contain the body of the Crucified Messiah, had given into his keeping, by no lesser person than Jesus himself, the Cup of the Last Supper[64].

Other writers, notably Wolfram von Eschenbach, whose *Parzival*[92] brought in much of the Orientalism to be discussed in the next chapter, and the anonymous authors of *The Elucidation*[22], the *Didot Perceval*[78] and the vast compilation known as the *Vulgate Cycle*[56] added to and strengthened both the Arthurian background and the mystical dimension.

The dangers of such rival interest was not lost upon the Church which, perhaps in the interest of survival, did its best to exclude troubadours and other story-tellers from communion on the grounds that they were agents of the devil. Eventually, the Church itself took over the office of story-teller; texts such as *Perlesvaus* and the *Vulgate Cycle* were both written down by Cistercian monks who incorporated the uncanonical writings of earlier writers to produce a version which, though it suffers at times from a heavy moral underscoring, yet expresses one of the finest and most complete visions of the Grail to date.

It was these writers who first introduced the figure of Galahad, the stainless, sinless knight destined from birth to succeed in the Quest for the Grail. Yet, he was the son of Lancelot, the strongest physically of all the Arthurian knights, and yet possessed of a fatal flaw – his love for Arthur's Queen. The anonymous author of the *Vulgate Quest*, perhaps seeking a way to Christianise the overt Paganism of the earlier Grail texts, brought about the birth of Galahad by having Lancelot tricked into believing he was lying with Guinevere, when in fact the lady in his bed was the Grail Princess.

One writer has described this as 'one of the greatest moments of imagination ever permitted to man', adding that:

The absurd nonsense that has been talked about [Galahad] being
'unhuman and unnatural' misses altogether the matter of the
mystically enchanted fatherhood ... where the Princess of the
Grail abandoned her virginity and Lancelot was defrauded of his
fidelity, so that the two great Ways [of Camelot and Carbonek]
might exchange themselves for the begetting of Galahad[90].

The author (or compiler) of *Perlesvaus* added a further strand of
veracity to the claims made for the myth, telling us that:

The Latin text from which this story was set down in
the vernacular was taken from the Isle of Avalon, from
a holy religious house which stands at the head of the
Lands Adventurous; there lie King Arthur and his Queen,
by the testimony of the worthy religious men who dwell
there, and who have the whole story, true from beginning
to end[6].

The 'holy religious house' mentioned here is meant to be Glastonbury, where the supposed bones of Arthur and Guinevere were
discovered in 1184. Also there are the 'worthy religious men', the
Benedictines of Glastonbury Abbey – though whether they indeed
had 'the whole story' is a matter for speculation.

What is interesting is that both the Isle of Avalon, a recognised
name for the Celtic otherworld, and the holy religious house, stood 'at
the edge of the Lands Adventurous'. It seems that even the monkish
chroniclers recognised that the Archetypal world of the Grail and the
Arthurian heroes stood at one remove from everyday life, accessible
not only in legend but also physically.

The spate of texts continued unabated. Chrétien's *Story of the Grail*
now boasted four continuations, by different hands, which extended
and detailed the original by thousands of lines. Robert de Borron
had completed his trilogy: a *Merlin*, a *Joseph d'Arimathie* and a
Perceval[64]. Versions of these stories began to appear throughout
Europe, drawn now into the whirlpool of Arthurian literature.
Descriptions of the Grail and of the mysterious procession, some
based on Chrétien's original version, others displaying a degree of
originality, appeared in Germany, Italy, and Spain[26]. The mighty
Vulgate Cycle was begun, perhaps to give a more authoritative
Christian stamp to the material.

THE OLDEST CHURCH

Yet another strand in the strange and wondrous history of the Grail was its part in the division between Rome and the so called Celtic branch of Christianity. Robert de Borron had connected the Grail with Joseph of Arimathea, and had brought his Saintly hero to Britain along with the Grail. Here he had founded the first church in these islands, substantially *before* the Church of Rome and with the apparent warrantry of both Christ and his mother. In more than one Church Council thereafter British Bishops claimed the right to prior speech before those of other countries, solely on account of this early ascription of Christianity to Britain.

The Wattle Church

Celtic Christendom was discouraged and secretly considered heretical by Roman missionaries, who found it well established when they arrived in the first century. Even after the Synod of Whitby in AD663, which established such matters as the tonsure of monks and the date of Easter, all was not as it might have been between the different professions. Monks and clerics of the Celtic rite were rarely considered for high office within the Church.

But it was within the boundaries of Celtic Christendom that the stories of the Grail arose. We have to look at the wonder voyages of monks like St Brendan, written in Latin in the ninth century, to see the tendency among such Celtic monkish scribes. The *Navigato Sancti Brendani*[58] is rife with elements which might just as well have come from an Arthurian or Grail adventure: the bold adventurer who goes in search of God's mysteries, treasure, beautiful maidens, monsters, islands shimmering in the seas of the West – the Lands Adventurous indeed.

Such writings as these were the product of a solitary, hermetic existence, suited to the isolated island bothy rather than the community life as witnessed in Benedictine or Cistercian houses. It is perhaps significant that Palagius, a fifth century theologian and exegete, whose doctrine was that man could take the initial step towards salvation by his own efforts, and apart from Divine Grace, should also have originated in Britain. There has always been something sanguine in the British make-up which has not reacted well with the Augustinian doctrine of Original Sin, and we may see in the Grail Tradition this same yearning towards independent salvation – for the meaning of the Grail seems to have little to do with the established means to such an end.

Is it possible that the Grail legends share in the accusation of heresy levelled against Pelagius? It has been noted before that: '. . . its [the Grail's] effects upon those who see it are made to correspond closely with the effects of Holy Communion upon communicants'[16]. Which may explain why the Grail seekers found it necessary to go on quest for something which was ostensibly to be had daily on every altar in every church in the Christian world. But there is something deeper than this yet. The seeker was looking for a level of mystical experience demonstrably not present in the fundamental teachings of the Church.

THE INNER LIFE

The basis of the Christian mystery teaching is that it consists of a series of initiations into the life of Christ himself, a sharing of his experience within the compass of our own. We have only to look at the course of Perceval's life within the earlier Grail texts, especially that of Chrétien, to see the parallels which exist there.

Perceval, like all Christians according to accepted dogma, is in a state of sin – his innocence, his ignorance, does not preclude his share in the collective sin of mankind. The Fall, according to Origen[16] occurred because the Beginning [of Creation] was unstable, and unstable because it was innocent. The Beginning is dependent upon redemption through the action of the Apocatastasis (the Restoration of All Things). Just as Christ had to live through the sacred drama of Incarnation, Nativity; Initiation in the desert (an image of the Waste Land), Active Ministry, and Crucifixion, so the Grail hero has to

38

acquire experience on his quest to abrogate the seeds of his own innocence. Christ thus becomes the divine archetype of the Grail initiate – he is seeded in the Grail womb of the Virgin, he vivifies and translates water in the vessel of Cana; he descends into the waters of the Jordan, taking on him the sins of those whom John the Evangelist has previously baptised; he offers his flesh and blood in the Passover meal to his disciples in order that they might literally 'pass over' into the Promised Land of the redeemed (the Otherworld of spiritual mysticism); he begs that the chalice of suffering be taken from him – but nevertheless drinks it to the dregs; he is buried in a hollow tomb after his essential moisture (blood and sweat) have been collected by Joseph of Arimathea; he is resurrected, going first to harrow Hell in an action which is paralleled by the freeing of the waters in the Grail story.

Perceval, on the other hand, is as innocent as Adam before the temptation. It is not until he has failed to ask the all important question about the Grail procession that he becomes alive to the possibility of suffering and its both evil and redemptive consequences. He is informed, quite bluntly, of the death of his mother – he is himself the instrument of her death. We see in him the Fool perpetually innocent and blameworthy; he is smeared with the same blood as Adam and shares his sin. Like a bystander at the Crucifixion he beholds the Grail and the suffering of the Wounded King yet fails to ask why these things should be so. It is possible that:

> The final answers might have been: 'The Lance bleeds to reveal the hope of salvation', and 'In the contents of the Grail which come to you from God the Father and are served to all Christian folk, lies the source of *caritas*, redemption of sin and the getting of salvation'[84].

Yet, though he is 'witless of the Trinity' in Chrétien, Perceval eventually does succeed in his quest precisely because of his innocence/ignorance. He goes through all the levels of initiation in unknowing imitation of Christ; lead through necessary suffering in order to reach the Paradisial object of his search – the Grail itself.

> For there is a foolishness of the Grail as there is a foolishness of the Cross (I Cor, I, 8–23) and the predestined are 'peculiar' in more than once sense; they are not only different, but God's or the Grail's, own possession[11].

This element of predestination runs through all of the Christian Grail texts. It is evident that Perceval, and after him Galahad, partake more

39

closely than the common run of humanity in the mysteries. Perceval's unusual ignorance of even the basic tenets of faith set him apart from the experience of the Medieval Christian in search of salvation. Yet for all that he comes nearer than the great 'worldly' knights, Lancelot and Gawain who, though schooled in the ways of Christianity, turn away and reject the inner life for its outer rewards.

THE TWO WAYS

[handwritten annotation: Is a real pain!]

That wise and astute commentator Joseph Campbell recognised in the dichotomy which runs throughout the whole of the Grail corpus a reflection of a similar disharmony within Christendom itself. Taking the text of Wolfram von Eschenbach's *Parzival* as exemplar he notes:

> This calamity [the wounding of the Grail King Anfortas], in Wolfram's meaning, was symbolic of the dissociation within Christendom of spirit from nature: the denial of nature as corrupt, the imposition of what was supposed to be an authority supernaturally endowed, and the actual demolishment of both nature and truth in consequence. The healing of the Maimed King, therefore, could be accomplished only by an uncorrupted youth naturally endowed, who would merit the supreme crown through his own authentic life work and experience, motivated by a spirit of unflinching noble love, enduring nobility, and spontaneous compassion [10].

This seeming dichotomy was present even at the most profound level, in the nature of the Eucharistic sacrament which played so profound a part in the mystical imagery of the Grail. Christ was God: yet he was also man. His nature was heavenly: yet he was also of the earth. The bread and wine, before consecration, were merely bread and wine: afterwards they became the actual body and blood of Christ, although they remained – in appearance – bread and wine.

Just as the early Church laboured to define the nature of Christ, so the Medieval Church sought to define the nature of these things. The precise definition of transubstantiation, as the miraculous change was termed, was not outlined until the Lateran Council of 1215 – at exactly the time when the Grail texts were appearing. Pope Innocent III merely confirmed what everyone knew; there was reason to be semantically precise, because heresy had begun to threaten the fabric of Christianity at this time. Indeed, heresies which denied the mystery of transubstantiation, preferring more rational explanations of the

Eucharistic sacrifice, existed side by side with an almost talismanic belief in the Real Presence of Christ in the species of Blood and Wine.

The daily miracle of the Mass occurred on the altar in every church and chapel, so that the mystery became familiar without losing any sense of its numinosity. Lay-folk in the West were not protected from the divine mysteries by an iconastasis screen, as was the custom in the East, but were actually encouraged to see them taking place – to the extent that the priest elevated the consecrated gifts while the deacon rang the sacring bell to draw their attention to it. In *Perlesvaus* it is at this moment that Arthur witnesses the Grail's most profound mystery – though in a totally different manner to the normal Mass: '. . . looking towards the altar after the preface, it seemed to him that the hermit was holding in his arms a man, bleeding from his side, bleeding from his hands and feet and crowned with thorns'[6].

In both the Vulgate *Quest del Saint Graal* and later in Malory's *Book of the San Greal*, we come across similar events, in which the Grail heroes, or Arthur, witness an actual appearance of Christ. These texts go out of their way to exhibit a similarity between the actions of the Grail and those of the Eucharist.

That this was in itself unusual is evidenced by the fact that at this point in time (eleventh century), the laity did not frequent the sacrament of Communion in order to receive it. It was not until 1215 that the faithful were obliged to make confession and receive the sacrament at least once a year. Nor did they, even then, receive it in both kinds (bread and wine); this was generally forbidden the laity as the danger of spilling the Precious Blood was considered too great. Kings heard Mass before battle, before breakfast, before going hunting – but they seldom received the host; only the priest made his Communion.

THE RESERVED BODY

This makes the actions of the Grail all the more unusual, and leads us to consider another interesting practice. The consecrated bread was, from earliest times, reserved in a box called an *aumbry*. This happened not only within churches but in private houses as well, where the faithful would administer the sacrament to each other in default of priest or deacon, or during times of persecution. The reservation of the sacrament is an intrinsic part of the Grail legends and is mentioned specifically in a translation into Medieval English of Robert de Borron's *Joseph*. In the episode in question Sarracynte, the wife of Evelach of Sarras, one of the earliest Grail Kings, relates how her mother kept the

host in a box, being a Christian secretly for fear of her pagan husband.
Each day she washes her hands and,

> The box anon she opened there;
> Out of the box there issued anon
> Our Holy Saviour in flesh and bone
> In form of bread . . .
> . . . with many tears and sore sighing
> There received she that holy thing. . .[1]

Shortly after this she dies, charging her daughter to keep the box hidden
safely. (Another example of the way in which women seem to have been
the bearers of the Grail mystery while the men were its guardians.)

With regard to the Grail legends it is interesting to note that some
churches are known to have possessed pyxes (receptacles for the
reserved host) in the shape of doves. These were kept over the altar.
In Wolfram's *Parzival*, on Good Friday,

> . . . one can infallibly see a Dove wing its way down from heaven.
> It brings a small white Wafer to the Stone and leaves it there . . .
> from which the Stone receives all that is good on earth of food and
> drink, or paradisial excellence[92].

The stone mentioned here is the Grail, and we shall have more to say
of its significance in the next chapter. Doves seem to have a special
significance within Grail symbology. Again in *Parzival*, we see the
dove as a symbol of hope – the Grail knights see the turtle doves
embroidered on the robes of the hag Kundrie, who is the emissary of
the Grail. They proclaim with evident joy:' Our trouble is over. What
we have been longing for ever since we were answered by sorrow is
approaching us under the sign of the Gral'[92].

REWARDS OF THE JUST

The Grail castle, whilst not in the generally accepted sense a church,
is clearly the focus for sacramental devotion. Its occupants are the
guardians not only of a great treasure, but of a life-giving secret.
The qualities of what is contained in the Grail inspire awesome
joy or reverent dread, and their effects vary from nourishment to
the prolongation of life or the gift of death.

The earliest texts still speak of the Grail in almost Celtic terms as a
cauldron of plenty which nourishes the hungry with their favourite

food, while the sick are healed by a stroke of the sacred Lance. It is not until the later versions of the story that we begin to hear tell of kings suffering mysterious wounds, who are sustained only by a wafer.

In *Parzival* the death of the wounded Anfortas is a release, for while he beholds the Grail he cannot die. Yet again, in Malory, the death of Galahad is the apotheosis of his achievement on earth. At the end of his journey he attends a Mass of Our Lady which is served by Joseph of Arimathea himself in the likeness of a Bishop.

> And when he . . . had done, anon he called Galahad, and said to him, 'Come forth the servant of Jesu Christ, and thou shalt see that thou hast much desired to see'. And then he [Galahad] began to tremble right hard when the deadly flesh began to behold the spiritual things. (52, Bk.XVII. Ch.22.)

Galahad receives the sacrament from his hands and says: 'Now Blessed Lord, would I no longer live'. . . . 'Now wottest thou what I am?' said the good man . . . 'I am Joseph of Arimathea, the which Our Lord hath sent here to thee to bear thee fellowship.' (ibid.) Galahad kneels in prayer and then expires, his soul born to heaven in a manner visible to both Bors and Perceval who remain on earth. Here is one of the central Grail mysteries: it gives life and death, joy and suffering, because it is a vessel, an empty vessel capable of being filled by anything. These great mysteries are indeed akin to that of the Blessed Sacrament; they express, in archetypal terms, the means of salvation and the way to Paradise[61]. But they are mysteries of which it is not meet to speak or to exhibit to the credulous, and thus they are hidden, secrets indeed. It is not without reason that they are guarded by the Grail keepers who, from Joseph of Arimathea to Perceval and beyond, have kept watch over them and passed them down to each succeeding generation.

THE MYSTERIES OF THE GRAIL

These, then, were the sacramental mysteries around which the life of Medieval Christendom revolved. Christ was present among men, not just in the reserved host on the altar, but also in each person who partook of the sacraments. This realisation is an important one. People did not frequent the sacrament in order to be 'good' in some perfunctory manner, but in order to be at one with Christ – in communion. This was, and is, the ultimate aim of every Christian – to be in oneness with God in the person of Christ, whether on earth or in heaven. But the obstacles to this union must be overcome. Man suffers the effects of Original Sin, a loss of sanctifying grace, brought about through Adam's fall. Thus the Grail knights had to struggle against overwhelming odds, always supported and aided by their faith and by the presence of the Holy Hermits who peopled the forest of adventure through which they rode in quest of the miraculous vessel.

The Redemption, whereby man is saved from sin and death, was seen in various ways. In the West, emphasis was given to the expiation of sins through the sacrificial death of Christ; while in the East, the Greek fathers were more concerned with the restoration of man to Divine life – an idea referred to by the term *theosis* or God-becoming. It is a delicate idea to comprehend, and one which the Western Church has understated again and again. Not so the Eastern Church, in which it remains an article of faith.

THE JOURNEY OF SETH

Such intricate webs of symbolism are the underpinning power of the Christian Grail legends. In the great compilation of Biblical legends known as *The Golden Legend*[1], Adam sends his son Seth to seek for the Oil of Mercy with which his father can be cured of age and death. Seth returns with seeds from the Tree of Life which he buries with his father; the Tree sprouts, eventually growing into that from which the Cross on which Christ is crucified comes to be made. The sin of the first Adam is thus redeemed by the second, and symbolically the Tree forms a bridge across which the whole of humanity can pass from death to life.

According to another tradition Seth returns with the Grail, a promise to mankind of the Saviour who will come. While in the *Queste del Saint Graal*, Perceval, Galahad and Bors make their way to the Holy City of Sarras, on a boat made from wood taken from the same Tree. When Galahad lies upon the great bed within the ship he emulates Christ. The ship itself is the Grail knights' way to theosis, the path to God.

AN ALTERNATIVE WAY?

Throughout the Grail corpus there is a thread of independence and individuality which was sufficient to brand it with the taint of heresy. In its literary form it may even have presented a dangerous alternative to the available avenues of Christian fulfilment. Later it was to become associated with the military Order of the Knights Templar and with the heretical Cathars. Both movements were to be stamped out in bloody purges.

44

The fact that the Grail is housed in the castle of Corbenic, which can be translated as meaning 'blessed or transfigured body' is not without significance. Did the Grail offer an alternative way to salvation? Is this the reason why, to answer an earlier question, the knights embarked on a quest for something which could ostensibly be gained by worshipping daily at the sacrament of the altar?

Perhaps the answer is that the Grail legends symbolised man's personal search for perfection; not a narrowing of sights and a cramping of style, but a generous impulse which could not be contained within the straight ways of orthodox belief. The Church had already begun to develop into an administrative organisation concerned with political, as much as religious, motivation. It had established an exoteric mode of expression.

But, when a received tradition begins to petrify in this way, losing its original cutting edge of truth in a tangle of dogmas, it becomes time for an esoteric tradition to arise by which the great truths may not perish but be revivified and transmitted to further generations. When the established hierarchy fails in its duty, it is as though the angelic powers inspirit humankind to produce those who will continue them. These are the people who stand in direct communication with the will of God: the mystics, who interpret the inner workings of creation; the story-tellers, who realise the truths in popular manner; and the heretics, who delve into forgotten or half-forgotten lore, who formulate alternatives to established ways of belief.

Each of these categories can be seen to have influenced the growth of the Grail legends in one way or another. They can be viewed as simple Christian allegory, as straight forward story, or as rank heresy, according to the prevailing tone of the time. Yet there were those who found no dichotomy in such matters, and it was they who kept the idea of the Grail alive throughout the Middle Ages.

There were those who made their own investigations, reaching conclusions which they could speak of only in code. The source was perhaps as unexpected as anyone could have imagined. For a new and profound influence was about to be brought to bear on the formulation of the Grail legends – that of the Orient, in the shape of Islamic teachings brought back from the Crusades.

EXERCISE 2: JOURNEY TO THE GRAIL LANDS

The country of the Grail is really that of the soul but that is itself a place not often frequented nowadays. Not entirely a Wasteland perhaps, but a place where the weeds are grown tall and the paths tangled. If we are to approach the place of the Grail ourselves we may choose to follow in the steps of the Quest Knights, who set forth to journey from Camelot to Sarras; or we may choose to follow our own path. Either way we need signposts.

There are, if one likes, two important points on the path – the A. and the Z of our journey. Point A is our place in the real world, point Z is Sarras, the Holy City of the Grail where all who join the Quest one day hope to arrive. Between these two points stretches a vast divide – a land peopled with beings both wondrous and strange, many of whom are able to help you on your quest. Indeed we should never think as wasted the time we spend in inner colloquy with the folk of the Grail – they can save us many an hour spent in journeying down paths that lead nowhere. This can be done through meditation on one of the many characters to be met with in the texts.

But what are the best methods of gaining access to the Grail country? Perceval sets out, as do many of the Arthurian knights, knowing nothing of the Quest, nor even why the Grail should be sought at all. So, more often than not, we also tend to set out unprepared. How many reading these pages have already set out, fired with enthusiasm, but without *really* comprehending what is entailed?

So we need to begin by considering what our reasons are, what need we are answering as we set out on this long journey. It is like any magical work, which needs to be contemplated and interrogated before it is begun to make sure that there is no intent to seek power or riches or to cause harm to others. Once these things are sorted out, we are in a much better frame of mind and preparedness than before.

The next stage comes with the realisation that we have to make our own maps – there are none printed for us, no 'X marks the spot' where the Grail is to be found. We might select certain episodes from the texts to offset this, meditating upon them until they are firmly established in our own inner world. It is no good simply saying: 'Right, I'm going to meditate on the Grail now.' You might get some interesting and valuable insights, but you are unlikely to get very far on the journey. And the journey is every bit as important as the final goal.

So, take an episode like Gawain's visit to the Chessboard Castle, where the hero arrives at this mysterious dwelling and finds it apparently deserted. On entering he finds a chessboard set up for a game, and when he moves one of the pieces finds himself matched with an invisible opponent. When he is soundly beaten he tries to throw both board and pieces out of the window, but a woman rises from beneath the waters of the moat and challenges him with the failure of his quest and sets him a further series of tests designed to help him on his way.

There are a number of points here on which we could dwell at some length. Who, for instance, is the mysterious dweller in the moat, who seems to know all about Gawain and his quest? And what is the purpose of the magic chessboard? By the time you have answered these questions – and others which will occur to you – you will also have come to know a good deal more about the Grail Castle and its inhabitants, as well as their function within the Grail country. This gives a signpost to which you may return on your next journey into the world you have come to explore.

Another method of working would be to visit one of the Castles mentioned in the texts which have no specific symbolic attributes (Joyous Gard or Tintagel for instance) and to build the image of this over several days of meditation (it can be based on memories or pictures of any castle – this will not detract from the inner reality of the image). When you have successfully completed this part of the exercise you should climb to the top of the castle and look out at the surrounding countryside. You may be surprised how much there is to see, things of which you were hitherto unaware of.

In this way you can build up a quite detailed scenario of the country, and you will soon begin to notice another surprising thing – the land will not always bend to your will; your imagination will not always shape things as you might wish. In fact it will begin to impose itself on your own visualisations, to become 'real' in ways you might never have guessed could happen. From here on you can make further explorations, charting a course through new territories, finding new places or people not necessarily mentioned in existing texts.

Finally, when you feel you are ready, set out consciously to reach Sarras. How will you journey? By ship? By horse? On foot? What sort of country will you pass through? What, or who, will be there when you arrive? The journey may take time but if you persevere you will almost certainly reach there in the end.

3 · THE STONE OF WISDOM:
ORIENTALISM AND THE GRAIL

THE NEW TIDE

The unique quality of European Christianity did not long remain unmixed. Just as it had come to establish itself and was even beginning to seem tame, the rallying call went out through the Western world: '*Aidez le Saint Sepulchre*' (Save the Holy Sepulchre). The city of Jerusalem, long seen as an image of heaven on earth, demanded rescue from the Infidel. It was the beginning of a great and powerful movement, which swept up just about every able-bodied man in Europe and flung them headlong into a venture which was to take them into strange lands. Out of this was to come a new strand in the story of the Grail, which went with the Crusaders in their dreams and their literature, and returned, once again transformed.

So far we have dealt with the Christian and Celtic faces of the Grail Tradition. Now, like true Crusaders, we must venture into the realm of Islam. The third of the so-called religions of the Book – the others are Christianity and Judaism – Islam spread quickly throughout the Middle East, eventually encompassing Egypt, Morocco, Spain, Persia and India. It brought with it a new culture as well as a new religion. In medicine, arithmetic, astronomy, geography and philosophy, it led the world: Islamic scholars had access to major Greek writings long before the West – in fact, it taught the West. We shall examine the element of Alchemy, which has a strong bearing on the Grail texts, later; this too had many proponents among the Moslem world, as we shall see.

NOW RECK I NOT THOUGH I DIE·FOR NOW I HOLD ME ONE OF THE BLESSED MAIDENS OF THE WORLD·THAT HATH MADE THE WORTHIEST KNIGHT OF THE WORLD

The Ship of Solomon by Ann Alexander

Jerusalem had been in Islamic hands for a long time before the beginning of the Crusades. Pilgrimage to the Holy Land was possible, if hazardous, under the Abbasid caliphate; but towards the end of the eleventh century the balance of power changed; under the new Fatimid dynasty, permission to enter Palestine seemed doubtful. It was no accident that Pope Urban II should put up the cry for Crusade in 1095. His motivations may have been politically oriented – he desired above all to see the incipient split between Eastern and Western Christendom, Constantinople and Rome, healed, but he also expressed goodwill and a genuine concern that the Eastern Church should suffer while the Western stood by and did nothing to help its brothers in Christ. He therefore proclaimed at the Council of Clermont that to those who would fight to protect Eastern Christendom from pagan incursions, and go onward to liberate the holy places, he would grant general absolution and remission of sins. To those who forsook their promise, he vowed excommunication.

Urban's clarion call opened the way for Christians to perform their duty in clear and unambiguous terms; he managed, unknowingly, to call into being the best fighting force Europe was to see until the Second World War, and at the same time helped to solve the problem of unfocused strength. It had not been long since Christian armies had been persuaded not to fight with each other without good reason, and some areas of Europe still faced the problem of armies fighting across their fields.

The situation can be neatly paralleled by Arthurian tradition. When Arthur came to the throne he had first to prove his supremacy in battle over the rival kings of Britain. After he had done this he engaged their services in policing the country. But when all the fighting is done, when there are no more bold, bad barons to discomfit, no more black knights hoving at fords, and when all the dragons are dead, then the famous Round Table Fellowship begins to be lethargic and to exhibit some of the traits they are vowed to overcome. Then, as the whole court is teetering in the balance, when the scandal of Lancelot's illicit passion for the queen is about to break, the Grail appears, leading to new and wondrous opportunities for growth and adventure.

So, too, the Crusades appeared at the right moment to harness the combined strengths of Christendom into a single spearhead of power. Unfortunately, the parallel holds good when we come to look at the course of the Crusades: great deeds were achieved, but great evils unloosed as well; those who approached the Grail quest unworthily may well have wreaked worse damage than if they had stayed at home. In the Arthurian Tradition the appearance of the Grail heralds the ultimate break-up of the Round Table; so too we must view Urban's call to Christendom, for it undoubtedly set up a chain reaction which we still feel today. Ownership of the Holy Lands, the division between Catholic and Orthodox churches, and many other issues which still trouble us may be seen as originating with the Crusades.

THE CRUSADER CUP

The chief object of the Crusader armies was to liberate the Holy Sepulchre, in the same way that the goal of the Quest Knights was to seek the Grail. But a problem soon emerged: when the Crusaders finally beheld Jerusalem in 1099, there was not a dry eye in their ranks. Hardened killers wept at the sight of their

God's tomb, which was, after all, merely the temporary resting place of Christ's body prior to the Resurrection. The dilemma had still not struck them. The tomb was empty; their victory hollow. It was not until the leaders of the First Crusade began supervising the removal of bodies from Jerusalem, whose streets had been purged of every last Moslem, Jew and, for that matter, some Christians sympathetic to Islam, that they began to wonder – what next?

Christendom retained its tenure in Jerusalem until 1187, when it once again fell into Moslem hands. But, just as no one can appropriate heaven as a personal possession, neither could the Crusaders establish an earthly city as a heavenly enclave. It was not long before wrangling began; religious and secular leaders were chosen, after long dispute, and a kingdom of Jerusalem created, known as Outremer. It remained a bone of contention as claimants came thick and fast on the death of any king careless enough to leave doubtful successors.

The Crusades brought many changes to Christendom. Coffers were emptied to send forth vast armies of men who returned to find themselves homeless. Disillusioned by fighting and religion, they roamed through Europe, begging for food or forming themselves into gangs who terrorised the land. The strengths of Christendom were found to have their weaknesses also; the holy images were blackened by smoke and slaughter. All save one – the Grail, which instead of being weakened by the souring of the great enterprise, seemed to be strengthened.

Chrétien de Troyes, who as we saw wrote the earliest known Grail text, *Le Conte du Graal*[13] was himself in the service of one of the most renowned Crusading families, that of Philip of Flanders, who Chrétien declared had given him the source for his poem from a book he had obtained in the Holy Land in 1177. This date certainly tallies with Philip's movements at the time, and even if he did not bring back an actual text, he could certainly have carried home an account of several sacred objects discovered by the Crusading armies.

Among these was the Sacro Cantino, a green glass dish about 40cms across, which was found during the sack of Caeserea in 1101 and carried by the victorious troops to Genoa, where it remains in the cathedral to this day. It was believed to be the gift brought by Sheba to King Solomon, and to have been made of emerald (sic!). Archbishop Jacapo da Voraigne, writing in the late thirteenth century, gives a first hand account:

That vessel is made in the likeness of a dish, whence it is commonly said that it was the dish out of which Christ . . . ate at the Last Supper. . . . Now whether this be true, we know not; but since with God nothing is impossible, therefore we neither firmly assert nor deny it. . . . This, however, must not be passed over in silence; that in certain books of the English it is found that, when Nicodemus took down the body of Christ from the Cross, he collected His blood . . . in a certain vessel of emerald miraculously presented to him by God, and that vessel the said English in their books call *Sanguinalia*[26].

THE STONE FROM HEAVEN

This is still not quite the Grail, but it is near enough to it. The description of the cup as an emerald is also worth noticing. As such it appears in another major Grail text, the *Parzifal* of Wolfram von Eschenbach[92], possibly the most intricate and symbolically loaded of all the versions – and the one most clearly indebted to Eastern ideas. Wolfram, indeed, claims that he took the essence of his great poem from a book by one Kyot of Provance, who in turn had it from an unexpected source: an Islamic teacher named Flegitanis, who was wise in the wisdom of the stars and who wrote of the great war in heaven between the angels. Lucifer, whose name means, significantly, the Light Bringer, and who had not then been associated with the Christian idea of the Devil, wore in his crown a great emerald. At some juncture, either during the fighting or in his fall from the height of heaven, this became dislodged and, according to Flegitanis, as reported by Wolfram, fell to earth, where it became known as the *Gral* or Grail. Unlike all the other versions of the story, where the Grail generally takes the form of a cup or dish, Wolfram makes it a stone. In *Parzifal* he describes it thus:

A stone of the purest kind . . . called *lapsit exillas*. . . . There never was human so ill that if he one day sees the stone, he cannot die within the week that follows . . . and though he should see the stone for two hundred years it [his appearance] will never change, save that perhaps his hair might turn grey[92].

This description has given rise to a great deal of speculation ever since the work appeared. The Latin is inaccurate and cannot be translated exactly. It may be that Wolfram meant to write *lapis lapsus ex caelis*, stone fallen from heaven, which would certainly square with the story of its falling from the crown of Lucifer. Other interpreters have felt themselves to be on the right track by identifying Wolfram's 'Gral' with the *lapis philosophorum*, the Philosopher's Stone which is the central image for the Alchemical Great Work. This is born out somewhat by the following quotation from the work of one of the greatest of the Alchemists, Arnold of Villanova, who in his work on the *lapis*, written not long after Wolfram's poem, writes:

Hic lapis exilis extat precio quoque vilis
Spurnitur a stultis, amartur plus ab edoctris.
(This insignificant stone is indeed of trifling value,
It is despised by fools, the more cherished by the wise).

The concept of the stone's lack of worth is typical of the symbolism of alchemy, which went out of its way to hide the true meaning of the Great Work in a cloud of impenetrable symbols used in an endlessly changing pattern. The real nature of Alchemy is not, as so many people have been lead to believe, a form of early chemistry in which the Alchemists sought to turn base metal into gold. The element with which they worked was called the *prima materia*, the 'first material', and was indeed more concerned with the human spirit than with the earth, mud, spittle and faeces (among other ingredients!) which supposedly made up the recipe for the creation of the Philosophers Stone.

Working with the element of the spirit they sought rather to transmute *this* into heavenly gold, to perfect Creation, and especially man. This is, of course, very much a function of the Grail, which transforms those who go in search of it into spiritual beings. Christ himself addresses the Quest Knights in Malory's *Morte d'Arthur* in words which make this clear: *See John Steinbeck on Malory.*

My knights, and my sergeants, and true children, which be come *out of deadly life into spiritual life*, I will now no longer hide myself from you, but ye shall see now a part of my secrets and of my hidden things. . . (Bk XVII Ch 20. My italics.)

Alchemy is about 'exchange' and 'transformation'. As in the Grail legends there has to be a meeting point between the Divine and Human, the former reaching down as the latter reaches up. The nexus point of meeting is the Centre, the World, the pivot of the cup shaped Grail. The stuff of humanity, thus encountering the matter of divinity, is transformed. Galahad, as we saw, looks into the Grail and is transfigured into another realm. Arthur, at the end of his first tenure on earth, as Malory says 'changed his life'. Thus in Alchemy, which is a far too vast and astonishingly rich subject to deal with in these pages, the baser elements of humanity are transformed into spiritual gold. Man himself, in the guise of every individual seeker, becomes the *lapis philosophorum*, the *lapsit exillas*, the 'fire-tried stone' which is renewed and set in its rightful place in the crown of heaven.

> Alchemy is fundamentally involved with a mystery; and, though it is not identified so simply as saying it is the mystery of life itself, and man in this place of creation, it is almost that mystery. It *is* that mystery not in the abstract but as an ongoing series of exercises man must carry out in order to fulfil a destiny his mere existence, his 'magical emergence' from sperm and egg in uterus, already fulfils[31].

The *lapis* remained only a stage in the creation of the Great Work, just as the Grail itself is but a symbol of the interior quest for human perfection and oneness with God. To those who came across Alchemy for the first time its strange and often bizarre symbolism seems to have struck a deep chord. It is possible that Wolfram encountered it in the writings or conversation of one of the many travellers returning from the East – especially the Spanish city of Toledo, where Moslems, Jews and Christians rubbed shoulders in uneasy truce, and which became a veritable melting pot for the teachings and beliefs of the major faiths.

It may have been here that certain concepts of the Judaic mysteries entered into the story of the Grail. Certainly there are recognisable elements of Qabala, that most impenetrable aspect of the ancient mystery schools, from the thirteenth century onwards.

Qabala itself seems to have grown out of a certain difficulty among the Jews in comprehending or entering into relationship with God. Forbidden to mention his name, driven to using synonyms, unable to make a likeness of their deity, the Qabalists evolved a way of coping with the limitations thus imposed upon them not unlike the methods adopted by the Alchemists. They understood God in terms of the Tree of Life, an abstract diagrammatic structure, which allowed symbolism and often anthropomorphic representation of the workings of Creation. While they did not seek to overthrow the accepted tenets of faith, they were lead further and further into areas of speculation about which orthodox Jews were far from happy. They tended, again like the Alchemists, to practice in small groups that kept their activities quiet. But it is from this highly eclectic and secretive source that the next strand of Grail tradition appeases.

THE BRIDE OF GOD

The study of the Qabala (the name means 'from mouth to ear') is based on the revealed Biblical texts and a more shadowy personal revelation which accompanies its exegesis. The Tree of Life represents the plan of God for man – a series of paths and spheres (called Sephiroth) which he must traverse in order to attain union with the Godhead. The journey is the course of life, with all its sufferings and joys, a quest very similar to that of the Grail, but without its Christian bias. As J. C. Cooper notes in *An Illustrated Encyclopaedia of Traditional Symbols*[14], 'The book is connected with tree symbolism and the Tree and the Book can represent the whole cosmos. In Grail symbolism the book can also typify the Quest, in this case for the lost Word.' The paths of the Tree of Life thus offer a multitude of possibilities for every seeker after hidden meaning. The lost Word of the Grail is that uttered by the Solar Logos at the beginning of time, and which will be spoken again at the end. The Grail, like Christ himself, is the Alpha and Omega of creation.

One of the most important mysteries within the intricate system of Qabala is that of the Shekinah, the compassionate Presence of God, who when Adam and Eve were exiled from Paradise, chose to accompany them into exile. This presence of the Shekinah has never been seen by orthodox Jews as a feminine element of the Godhead, but to the Qabalists she was just this, so that they personified her as a woman and as the indwelling soul of Israel – and therefore, of each person. Man is understood as being in captivity, relegated from his perfect state within God but, because he is accompanied by the Shekinah, is enabled to attain it once more. In the same way the Presence of God remains with the Israelites in exile because Moses causes the Ark of the Covenant, which is the 'dwelling place of God' – and therefore of the Shekinah also – to be housed in a sanctuary while they are still pursuing their wandering path through the world.

There is a tradition which says that no one may set out to liberate the Shekinah, or even set out with that intention, because God will choose one to do this, someone who does not know his destiny. This reminds us that Perceval, in the Grail story, does not know his destiny, never in fact intends to seek the Grail when he leases his forest home yet he is chosen, and in all but the latest texts, is the successful candidate.

The Shekinah is also described as the Veil of God, protecting mankind from His awful presence; but she also stands for the Compassion of God. It is she who broods upon the face of the waters

55

when the world is created. She may also be seen as a paradigm for the Grail – the vessel of honour which stands as a covenant for all of God's mercy and richness, a presence to be sought, a love which prompts mystics to journey in perpetual quest until union or realisation is achieved and the world redeemed at last.

In later, Lurianic Qabalism, the concept of the *shevirah*, or 'breaking of vessels' which held the light of God's emanations, was brought about by the lack of harmony between the masculine and feminine elements of the Tree of Life. A similar conclusion may yet be drawn in our study of the elements of the Grail tradition, for the Grail symbolises all that is fertile, liquid, hopeful. It is a totally feminine symbol of God's love which, apart from that of Christ, is noticeably absent from exoteric Christianity. The Grail as Shekinah, as vessel of hope, is not totally without foundation if we look at the parallel examples of the feminine in other religions.

The idea of a feminine counterpart to God, or at least a feminine agency within the Godhead, is too common to be ignored. In Judaism we have seen the Shekinah; within Islam, and particularly within the esoteric tradition of the Sufis, we encounter the Sakina. This form of the word seems to have been taken straight from Jewish sources and adapted to the needs of Islam. It seems to signify angelic withdrawal, a quietude or moment of understanding and bliss such as comes to all who seek the Grail, sooner or later.

Islam also knew of the Gnostic figure of Sophia, the Bride of God, and made use of the symbolism she afforded. For this figure permeated the whole of Western civilisation, beginning with the Platonic world-soul, which in time became inextricably linked with the idea of Wisdom personified as a woman, and thus spread into other forms of belief. The Shekinah, as we have seen, was implicit in Jewish mystical understanding, as was the person of Wisdom as help meet of God in the Biblical books of wisdom. In early Gnostic thought, as this grew up within the Fertile Crescent and interfaced with the ancient Classical Mystery religions, Sophia was considered to be a divine emanation, one of the causes of creation and of the redemption. The early fathers of the Church rejected this idea, deploring the dualism suggested in such a theory. Thus the idea of a compassionate, feminine force descending from the Godhead was neglected. *Thank God?*

Despite this, the figure of Sophia and her function became associated with the actions of the Holy Spirit – as though this was itself a feminine aspect of the creator – in Christian iconography represented as a dove. It is thus significant that the dove has always represented a feminine, maternal watchfulness who is seen as 'deploying her strength from one end of the earth to the other, ordering all things for good' (The Book of Wisdom 8.1.). We must not forget, either, that the dove is the symbol of hope to the Grail guardians in Wolfram's poem; and that in the same work the Grail messenger, Kundrie, comes to announce the Lordship of the vessel to Parzifal, dressed in a hood of black samite, on which 'gleamed a flock of turtle-doves finely wrought in Arabian gold in the style of the Grail insignia'[92]. *But of course* ".! ?

The feminine quality of the Grail is more than apparent in the section of *Parzifal* in which this reference appears. Ferefiz, Parzival's half brother, is a pagan and, because of mixed parentage from Europe and the East, is pied white and black. The Grail is born among the company and Ferefiz announces that he sees no Grail, only an *achmardi*, a word generally used to describe the cushion on which the sacred stone is carried, but which also has the meaning of an emerald, thus linking the Grail further with the stone from Lucifer's crown. Ferefiz is transfixed, not by the Grail itself, but by its bearer, Repanse de Schoye. He is willing to be baptised so that he may marry her. *Totally off the wall* "!

Repanse appears to have all the attributes of the Shekinah – she bears the vessel of love for all mankind; she shares the sufferings of humanity so that 'her looks have suffered'[92]; she wears the crown of sovereignty or wisdom, like the queen of Israel, or the Queen of the Sabbath in Jewish tradition. Of all the company, only Ferefiz recognises her quality, and desires to marry her. In the baptism which follows, the significance of this salvation and transformation is shown when the font, tipped towards the Grail, miraculously fills with water.

From this union of West and East comes a line of Grail kings, of which more will be said in Chapter 4. We see in her the union of pagan and Christian, black and white, male and female: a cosmic mystery of such importance that it transcends the esoteric and exoteric and reunites them in a primal unity. It is the completion of a strand of the Alchemical Great Work, and it shows the Grail as Divine Sophia, symbolising the ability of man to regain paradise by means of her help. *Org + Bauf!*

THE WAR BETWEEN LOVE AND FAITH

Another strand of history which had a most profound effect on the history of the Grail, and which likewise drew its strength from Eastern sources, concerns the history of two groups of people who were much concerned with love – though in what might be seen as mutually exclusive ways. These were the Troubadours, those wandering singers of songs and tellers of stories, and the Cathars, a break-away group of Christians who were swiftly declared heretical when their teachings became widely known and increasingly popular.

Both were concerned with love, as has been said; and the acts of the Grail are also the acts of love. But to understand how this is so we need to examine the way in which the message contained in the stories grew out of an ancient gnosis, re-interpreted by Medieval man and joined, in his mind, with a triple response towards the teachings of Christianity.

On the one hand, there was *agape*, divine love – of man for God and God for man – represented by the doctrines of the Roman Church and dispensed by the orders of monks: Benedictine, Cistercian, and Franciscan, who interpreted the teachings of the God of Love by means of sermons and commentaries on the Scriptures.

Against this, at the other end of the scale, stood *eros*, profane love – of the flesh rather than the spirit – a dangerous way celebrated by the Troubadours, whose cult became one of the strongest alternatives to the morality of the Church and the piety of its monks, and whose writings, so closely allied to the creation of the first Grail texts, reflect the mingling of Eastern with Western doctrines of love.

Between these two opposing (though not necessarily irreconcilable) points stood the sect known as the Cathars, who harnessed something of each to their own complex beliefs. This lead them to follow a way which taught that the flesh was evil and that only by living a pure and spiritual life could the divine spark of humanity be reconciled with God. To this end they chose to call their priests *perfecti*, 'perfected ones', who followed a way not unlike that of the Grail knights of Muntsalvache in Wolfram's *Parzival*.

Despite appearances to the contrary, these widely differing approaches to love are *not* mutually exclusive, but are linked by the Grail mystery itself, and by the character of Sophia, (Divine Wisdom) on whose role we have already touched.

To begin with the Cathars, it is necessary first of all to correct the popular view of them as life hating fanatics. They were indeed dedicated to reaching the highest possible goal of human achievement – that is, in the spirit – and to this end they saw no alternative but the exclusion of gross matter, concentrating instead on the inner reaches of the soul rather than procreation and the acquiring of worldly goods. In this they were no different from the monks who sought God in the desert, and donned hair shirts to remind themselves constantly of the evils of the body, and lived lives as bereft of comfort as possible. Both were followers of agape and both sought to know God interiorly and to arrive at a point of spiritual union with Him which they believed could only be achieved through abjuring the flesh and living a simple existence. Indeed, the more one reads in the annals of Medieval philosophy the more one is forced to believe that the differences in aim between the orthodox Christian and the Cathar heretic were marginal. They may have differed in the description of the God with whom they sought to be re-united, but they shared a deep-rooted desire to return to a state of innocence and purity from which both believed they had been cast out. *And, so they has been!*

And, they shared another belief – that a part of God had gone willingly into exile with them, and remained there in the person of the figure variously refered to as Sophia, Divine wisdom, or the Shekinah. Beyond this, it is the points of divergence which stand out.

For the Cathars the God of Israel was false, a Demiurge who invaded creation and warped the design of the true God, imbueing matter with a taint of evil from the start. In this they show their origins as basically Gnostic, or as stemming from that subtle blend of gnosis which flourished in the second century AD under the name of Manichaeanism. But as Sir Stephen Runciman points out in his study of *The Medieval Manichee*, [77] 'the origins of Gnosticism remain obscure', though he adds that it is partly to be sought in 'the age-long magical tradition' as well as Hermetic and Egyptian doctrines. Its part in the mysteries of the Grail will become clearer as we proceed.

In essence then, what did these early challengers of orthodoxy believe? It could be said, without excluding anything of major import, that their chief concern lay in the definition of good and evil, their own part in the origin of the world, and the continuing battle for redemption which resulted. Acknowledging the existence of evil, their solution to the problem, as Runciman puts it 'was to take from God the responsibility of having made the visible world' *Ha Ha, Ha, O Ha.* (ibid). Instead they propounded a distant First Cause, God the Father of Light, of whom the Demiurge, the actual creator of our world, was only a fragmentary representation. In this act of false creation, some of the original, primal light became trapped in the bodies of the first men, and thereafter the greatest single objective of the Gnostic (as of the Cathar) was to bring about the freeing of that 'divine spark' and of bringing about its reunion with the true God. In this they had help from Christ, who while he never became man as in orthodox belief, was nevertheless seen as a Son of the True God, sent into the world of matter to aid in its redemption.

So humanity began, almost by accident, with grains of original light trapped within him, each of which must spend itself trying to be reunited with God. Thus the drama of exile, which was to be played out again in the orthodox story of Eden, was firmly founded. In due course, the Grail became a key which lead back to the original, lost state of innocence, a gateway between the worlds of matter and spirit, darkness and pure light.

Thus light and darkness are shown as interpenetrating within the world of space and time, at the nexus of the two worlds (that same nexus which for the orthodox was manifest by Christ's birth in human form, and for the followers of the Grail in the cup itself), and a cosmic struggle began which is seen as continuing throughout time.

In various other Gnostic texts, as well as in many other books of esoteric wisdom, Lucifer, the Prince of Light, is seen as the principle hero of this struggle, fighting, as his name would suggest, to bring light into the darkness of the wrongful creation. In this he becomes a type of Christ and though it may take some effort to accept the fusion of two characters normally opposed to each other, we will find that if we do so the nature of the Gnostic story becomes clearer, and the part played by the Grail in all this takes on a surprisingly central role.

Lucifer, worshipped as a sun god in the Zoroastrian religion, does battle against the legions of darkness. In the words of a modern Gnostic text, which embodies much earlier beliefs,

> With his green wings wide open, transported by his own inner fire, followed by a host of faithful angels, he makes for the centre of the world; his sword of green light, straight in front of him, is in the grip of his powerful hand . . . [2]

At the centre of the world squats the Beast, the embodiment of evil, which Lucifer must destroy. But all he succeeds in achieving is the dislodgement of his adversary, who falls even deeper into matter, while the heroic Lucifer remains trapped in the heart of the visible world. Evil's place is taken by '. . . the most beautiful and ardent and potent of the Angels of the Father, the light bearer, the beautiful Lucifer . . . . He stayed there, where he is now, in the invisible centre of our universe.' (ibid.) But the sword of green fire (green being the colour traditionally associated with Lucifer in all the myths) falls from his grasp.

60

[It] crossed . . . space and lost its power and light. . . . Obeying the law of concentration . . . it grew denser and denser. At last it became a stone, a wondrous emerald shaped like a cup, and it fell on the surface of the sidereal body. . . because it was pointed it became concave; because it was formed to split, to dissolve, to blast, it became adapted to collect, to unite, to mould; because it was a sword it became a vessel. (ibid.)

Here we see clearly the actions of the Grail. Lucifer's sacrifice is a humane act, made at great cost. This, surely, is the secret hinted at in Wolfram's *Parzival*, where the Grail is a glowing green jewel fallen from heaven or the crown of Lucifer, carried on a green *achmardi*, becoming a talisman for the guardians of the hidden temple.

But there is still another interpretation of this story. A 'Jewel from the crown' can mean more than a stone. It can also be an aspect of personality, a presence of light who in this instance chooses to remain voluntarily in exile in order to transmit a rumour of that light to mankind. In the Biblical story of Eden this is retold anew – when Adam and Eve are driven forth into exile, part of the light of paradise goes with them. In Judaic tradition, as we have seen, this is the Shekinah, Sophia, Wisdom of God, and in Qabala she is called *lapis exulis*, or materialised Shekinah, the shadow bride of God who is called the stone of exile – a much closer approximation of Wolfram's *lapsis exilis* than any of the other possibilities we have so far examined. In a certain sense this figure stands for the mystical heart of the Church, the esoteric strand of Christianity of which the Grail is also a part. BuLL⁰.

THE 'PERFECT' MEN

Many of these ideas became enshrined in the beliefs of the Cathars, who established a firm foothold in a part of France known as the Languedoc. There, centres of learning, of music, medicine and philosophy (based largely on those of the East, with which trade was well established) flourished. There existed a thriving industry in the translation and study of Arabic manuscripts and Qabalistic learning. Eastern medicine, philosophy, science and alchemy were openly taught and discussed. Carpets, richly inlaid weapons, silks and jewels poured into Europe through these channels.

A period of political, economic and religious flux existed at this time, and the Cathar priests were able to wander far and wide, consolidating their hold over the people of the South and extending their sphere of activity into Italy and parts of Germany and Spain. Word of this began to reach the ears of the Pope, Innocent III; and Bernard of Clairvaux, who was later to have a profound effect on the history of the Grail, harangued the population, claiming that their churches were empty and that they had no true priests. He met with a mixed reception, cheered in some places, booed in others, and soon returned to his monastery.

A new order of monks, lead by the Spaniard Dominic de Guzman (later St Dominic) began tramping the roads in pursuit of the *perfecti*. At first, they attempted to persuade their followers by gentle speech, but soon they began to mount open verbal attacks on the Cathars.

When this failed to have any noticeable effect, stronger measures were sought, and when in 1208 a papal officer named Peter of Castelnau was murdered, at the behest, it was said, of Raymond IV, Count of Toulouse, a known supporter of the heretics, this was all the excuse Pope Innocent needed to raise a crusade against the Cathars. He found the nobility of Northern France only too willing to wage 'holy war' against their neighbours, and the Pope was too concerned to stamp out Catharism to look too closely into the motivation of his allies.

There is no space, and neither is it desirable to chronicle the horrors of the Albigensian Crusade in detail. Others have done so fully[73]. Thousands perished on the swords of the Crusaders, or in the fires laid by Dominic de Guzman – who once addressed a crowd of chained heretics with the words; 'When you heed not the blessing of the Church, you shall heed the stick. We will stir up against you princes and prelates. Towers shall be destroyed and walls broken down, and you shall be reduced to slavery'[51].

It has not yet been possible to prove one way or the other that the Cathars possessed any secret knowledge of the Grail, though there is a strong tradition which suggests that they did. There are however, several points which indicate a very close similarity of intent with the nature of the Grail's message.

Shortly before he was to die in the fires of the Inquisition, a Cathar Bishop named Girard of Montefiore remarked that: 'It is not I alone whom the Holy Spirit visits. I have a large family on earth, and it comprises a great number of men on whom, on certain days, and at certain times, the Spirit gives light'[51]. Such words could have been spoken by the Grail king in almost any of the texts, and could have refered to the family of the Grail, visited indeed by the Holy Spirit 'on certain days and at certain times' – as in Wolfram's poem, where a dove descends to lay a sacred Host on the stone of the Grail.

Certainly the notion that the Cathars in some way possessed inner knowledge of the Grail became a generally accepted fact, as is shown in an incident which took place during the final siege of Montségur, the great Cathar citadel in the Pyranees, which held out longest of all against the invading armies of the North.

Montségur, whose name so closely resembles Muntsalvache, the name of the Grail mountain in Wolfram's poem and the *Titurel* of Alberecht von Scharfenburg[74], was ruled over by the Countess Esclamonde of Foix, perhaps the most famous of the many women *perfecti*. Indeed, so revered was she, that many refused to believe in her death, shortly before the destruction of Montségur, believing her to be sleeping until doomsday in the caves which riddled the mountainside beneath the castle. Many besides identified her with the Grail maiden Repanse de Schoye.

It was in these circumstances that the incident mentioned above took place. During the final long siege of Montségur, a member of the family of Esclamonde, the flamboyant Roger of Mirepoix, dressed himself in white armour and appeared on the walls of the citadel with a golden-hilted sword held on high. At this sight many of the besieging army fled in terror, believing that the Knight of the Grail himself had come against them.

Another story, probably apocryphal, describes how the original Cup of the Last Supper was hidden in the cave of San Juan de la Pena in 713 (though it is not suggested how it came there) by an Aragonese Bishop named Audebert. When Aragon was threatened by the Moors at the beginning of the twelfth century, the sacred Cup was removed and taken to the Pyranees, where it was entrusted to the Cathars. When they were destroyed, the Cup was smuggled back into Spain and hidden in the cave again, this time under the protection of Don Martin L'Humain, the then King of Aragon. In later years the Cup was identified with one kept in the Cathedral of Valencia, but which had now further acquired the identification with the vessel given to Solomon by the Queen of Sheba. Wildly improbable though this story may seem at first glance there is a ring of authenticity about it. Nor should one overlook the fact that it is to the Cathars that the precious object is entrusted.

In due course, Montségur fell; its defenders were killed or burned, without trial, below the walls. To this day the place has an atmosphere of horror to which many bear witness. If this was the home of the Grail, it has retained none of its sanctity. However, the story is told that on the night before it fell, four of the *perfecti* escaped over the walls and thence into the mountains, taking with them their Holy Books and other secret treasures, among which was believed to be numbered a certain cup.

Whether or not they bore the Grail is not important for the purposes of our argument. If some of the *perfecti* escaped, as seems more than reasonable, they took with them the secrets of their faith. For every hundred heretics who perished, half as many again escaped into the mountains and beyond, into Italy and Germany, where their treasures were probably scattered.

But their doctrines and beliefs lived on, and their continuance can be traced through widespread traditions of esoteric knowledge, according to which some of those Holy Books found their way into the hands of Rosicrucian adepts, carrying the knowledge of the Cathar Church, the *Eglise d'Amour*, or Church of Love, as it was called by them, into the centuries which followed[35].

Into the Grail texts themselves, elements of Cathar belief filtered widely. In Chrétien de Troyes '*Lancelot*'[13]. One of the foremost works embodying the new ethic of Courtly Love, the Knights of King Arthur, after communion, give each other the kiss of peace, according to the custom of the Eastern Rite, and which the Cathars took over in their rite of the *manisola*, the Love Feast, which itself suggests both the imagery of the Last Supper and the banquet of the Holy Grail.

The Cathars, for all their belief in the evil nature of the flesh, their desire to transcend their humanity and to find oneness with the true God of Light, were true adepts of love – not the profane sensual love celebrated by the Troubadours – but a spiritual *agape* which differed hardly at all from that of the orthodox Christians. They were filled with a burning anguish of spirit, which drove them to the greatest possible endurance (in fact the Cathar rite, called the *endura*, involved many hours of fasting – sometimes to the point of death – in which they purified themselves to become vessels of light). This they did out of love of God, the Light; and it this, rather than any possible truth in their having possessed the Grail, which makes them one with its universal brotherhood.

The Cathars understood perhaps better than any the message of the Grail of Love, which above all involves service and dedication to the Light. They carried with them always the one Gospel in which they found expressed a true knowledge of that Light – the Gospel of John. Therein they read the Divine Mandate that God was Love, and that to be with Him was to dwell in love.

64

THE SINGERS OF LOVE

All this was understood by the Troubadour poets also, though in a very different manner. Their way was through the adoring of the Feminine Principles, one of whose names is also Sophia, and there is evidence too that the troubadours were by no means ignorant of Cathar beliefs. Their operation in the same area of France alone makes this more than likely; but there is besides, much more evidence, much of which has been collected by Denis de Rougemont in his famous study *Passion and Society*[21].

De Rougemont has, for example, pointed out that one of the first, as well as foremost, of the troubadours, Pierre Vidal, wrote a song in praise of hospitality, which though on the surface looks innocent enough, becomes less so when it is known that all the castles and hospices mentioned were either actual Cathar strongholds or were situated in areas where they were particularly active.

De Rougemont goes on to list some of the other similarities between Cathar and troubadour ways of life, that they:

> ... extolled (without always practising) the virtue of chastity; that, like the Pure, they received from their lady but a single kiss of initiation; that they distinguished two stages in the *domnie*, [service to ones lady]... as the Church of Love distinguished between Believers and Perfect. They reviled the clergy and the clergy's allies, the members of the feudal caste, They liked best to lead the wandering life of the Pure, who set off along the road in pairs[21].

The one problem which does seem to preclude any close identification between Catharism and the Troubadour ethic – the hatred of physical love of the one against its celebration by the other – vanishes when one accepts that the Troubadours celebrated not actual, physical love at all, but rather an abstract, distanced worship of womankind, even of the Divine Feminine itself. Troubadour songs abound in sentiments which exhibit this symbolic attitude, with Love as an imperious Queen, reigning over her subjects with Goddess-like power. She is at once an earthly sovereign, and, by extension, every woman addressed by the practitioners of Courtly Love. At the same time, she also represented Mary, the Heavenly Queen, behind whom stood Eve, the first woman, and Sophia, the semi-divine symbol of Wisdom.

Courtly Love, as well as possessing an actual court, with all the rules and etiquette which were part of this, was also seen as a semi-religious order, a true *eglise d'amour*, with its own laws and rules for worship.

Thus, a man might look at a woman, might woo her, desire her, and might vocalise that desire in endless panegyric – but he was expressly forbidden to do more. Actual physical congress was never permitted – at least, not by those who obeyed the Rule of Love, as set out in tracts such as *The Art of Courtly Love* by Andreas Capellanus[21], which may accurately be described as the Troubadour's bible.

Nor were the ideas expressed in Andreas' book new. In the East, as early as 1022, the Arabic poet Ibn Hazm had written his *Tawq al-Hamana* (The Dove's Neck-Ring) in which he spoke of a chaste love which was a sign of the highest natural attainment of a noble man. Andreas, as well as the greater body of his contemporaries, took up this idea, and others like it, and embroidered them into a Western Courtly system designed for the seeker after love. The Provencal word *jois*, which has no precise rendering in English, but can be said to mean something like 'blissful joy', was coined specifically to describe the object of the quest – the whole purpose, means and end of which are summed up in one tremendous line, written by the thirteenth century Troubadour Uc de St Circ:[1] 'To be in love is to stretch toward heaven through a woman.' Whether we choose to see this woman as Mary, Sophia, or simply as the Eternal Feminine, we must believe in the force with which such statements are made.

From this point it is not difficult to see that what binds the Troubadours and the Cathars together in an underlying unity of spirit, is their feeling for the 'femininity' of God. The singers and poets of Provence, exposed to the words of the wandering perfecti, worshipped at the throne of the Divine Feminine, whether addressed as Lady Venus, Mary or Sophia, the Shekinah of the world. The Perfecti, abdjuring *eros*, sought the underlying principle of *agape*, personified again as Sophia, the sacred vessel of knowledge, a figure inherited from Gnosticism.

The Gnostics themselves had encountered at some point the influence of Eastern thought in the form of Sufi doctrines. Here again the theme of chaste love was found, turning towards a search for *spiritual agape*. From this tremendous mingling, or as Denis De Rougemont puts it, 'the final confluence of the "heresies" of the spirit and those of desire . . .[21] arose the Courtly ethic, which in turn gave rise to the impulse of the Grail narratives, both known and unknown. From this we can see that there is a natural debt of succession devolving from the Gnostics to the Troubadours and Cathars, finally emerging in the matter of the Grail which binds all these threads together in the vast monolith of the Arthurian epic cycles – the natural outcome of a hunger for original truth, face-to-face contact with the Deity, and a longing to return to the first home, Eden or Paradise or Heaven. *Or WHATEVER?*

EXERCISE 3: THE GREEN STONE

Close your eyes and imagine you are standing before a great round church capped by a magnificent dome. Above this rises a great golden crescent which catches the sun and gives back its light with powerful radiance. The walls are ornately carved with intricate patterns, and two vast doors stand open to admit you into the cool depths beyond.

Within, all is dimly lit and echoing. As your eyes grow accustomed to the light, you see that the building is truly of mighty proportions, the soaring dome seeming to stretch up to heaven itself, while the walls are lined with colonnades of pillars ornately carved. From four small openings in the roof, beams of sunlight filter down, illuminating a point towards the centre of the building. You are drawn to go forward to that spot, and notice for the first time that the floor is of beaten earth, with none of the magnificent tessellated flooring you might have expected in such a place.

At the centre, where the four beams of light meet, is a rough, conical mound, in which is a low, narrow opening large enough to admit one person at a time. Peering in, you see a small chamber, lit with torches. You enter and find yourself in a room with bare, earthen walls, in the centre of which is a low altar. On this is set a great faceted jewel, an emerald more bright than anything you have ever seen before. In its thousand surfaces you catch glimpses of many things; your own image, and other images that seem to move and turn within the heart of the stone. In one you see the figure of a wounded man, lying upon a bed, in another a knight kneels with a shining cup in his hands. Another facet shows you three mailed riders pursuing a brilliant star. Yet another holds a perfect rose, which emits light . . . .

For a long time you watch spellbound as the light of the torches plays across the surfaces of the Green Stone, showing you many things. But at last your trance is broken by a movement in the chamber. Two men have entered, one clad in chain mail with a white cloak on which is emblazoned a red cross; the other, clad in a plain robe of white, carries a leather-bound book. These two take up their places at either end of the altar, and facing towards each other begin a chant which rises and falls in measured cadences, filling the room with sound. The words seem to be in Latin, with some that may be old French, but you seem able to understand them despite this . . .
(PAUSE.)

The sound and the meaning of the words fill your mind, and you feel at peace with the world and with your life as you have perhaps not done for a long time. You are given the grace to forgive yourself whatever faults you may feel you have committed; whatever hurt or sorrow lies within you is slowly dissolved. In the presence of the Green Stone and its guardians you feel only joy and an overflowing sense of well-being which transcends all the outward shape of your life . . .

At length the song finishes. In the silence of the chamber you hear a sigh which you know is the sound of all fears, doubts, and uncertainties being expelled from you and from the place of the Stone. Light hearted, you emerge from the chamber like one new-born and walk through the great dim church to the doors. Outside, all is brilliant sunlight, and you go forth into the world renewed and strengthened . . .

Slowly bring yourself back to the place in which you began this meditation. Its memory will remain with you for many days to come, and you will find that merely recalling the song and the joy you felt then will continue to irradiate your whole being with light.

PART TWO:
INITIATIONS

4 · THE FAMILY OF THE GRAIL:
GUARDIANS AND GODS

THE HOLY BLOOD

Those who go in search of the Grail are following the impulse of their
spiritual blood. The description of the Grail in certain texts as *San
Greal* (Holy Grail) in others appears as *Sang Real* (Holy Blood), the
changing of a single letter describing a wholly different concept. The
idea of the existence of a Grail 'Family', chosen to act as guardians of
the sacred vessel, seems to arise from this, and in the works of Robert
de Borron and the Vulgate *Queste*[55], Joseph of Arimathea does indeed
establish a line of Grail Kings who, in their turn, have to keep the Grail
securely and administer its secrets to each one of their successors.
These secrets have been inviolably guarded throughout the ages, each
Grail author commenting obscurely upon them, or else refusing tacitly
to discuss them. Wolfram von Eschenbach's theory is expounded by
the hermit Trevrizent, who after a long disquisition on the meaning
of the Grail itself, tells Parzifal the true nature of the Grail Family:
'Maidens are given away from the Grail openly, men in secret, in order
to have progeny . . . in the hope that these children will return to serve
the Grail and swell the ranks of its company'[92].

Wolfram here speaks of a fleshly succession, but he also indicates
that the dispersion of the Grail lineage is a secret known only to the
angels. Earlier in the text he had spoken of the troop of angels who

71

had left the Grail on the earth to ensure that 'A Christian progeny bred to pure life had the duty of keeping it. Those humans who are summoned to the Grail are ever worthy.' (ibid.)

Robert de Borron, in his *Joseph d'Arimathea*[64] gives an account of the company who sailed from the Holy Land under Joseph's leadership, experiencing many adventures along the way. Here the Grail Family is presented in a fully rounded form. Joseph receives the message of the Grail directly from Christ, who visits him in the tower where he has been imprisoned after the disappearance of the Saviour's body: 'he spoke to [Joseph] holy words that are sweet and gracious and full of pity, and rightly are they called Secrets of the Grail.' (Trans. by Margaret Schlauch *Medieval Narrative* Gordian Press, 1969.) Thereafter Joseph is kept alive by the power of the Grail, which provides him with food just as it later provides materials for his ancestor Titurel to build the Temple of the Grail.

Released from prison by the emperor Vespasian, Joseph is instructed by the voice of Christ. He sets up a new Table in imitation of the one at which the Last Supper and the first Eucharist was celebrated. One place represents the place of Christ, another, which is to remain empty until the rightful Grail knight appears, stands for that of Judas. When Joseph's followers are seated there they 'perceived a sweetness which was the completion of the desire of their hearts.' (ibid.)

For a time the company of the Grail remain somewhere in Europe until a desire comes upon them to divide their number. One Petrus, named, we may safely assume, after the disciple Peter, sets off for 'Avaron', a land to the West which can only be the Celtic Otherworld of Avalon, or perhaps Glastonbury in Somerset, where legends of Joseph's coming and the Grail still abound.

Another of the Grail lineage, Bron, whose name so closely echoes that of the Celtic God Bran the Blessed, and who becomes known as the Rich Fisher after he feeds the company from a single fish in emulation of Christ's feeding of the 5000, becomes Joseph's successor and the new guardian of the sacred vessel. Joseph is bidden by the Voice of the Holy Spirit to relinquish the Grail into the keeping of Bron, who will take it to a safe place and there await the coming of his grandson, Perceval.

And when that son arrives, the Vessel shall be given over to him, and do thou tell him and command him to charge him with its keeping thereafter. Then shall be accomplished and revealed the significance of the blessed Trinity which we have devised in three

parts . . . . And when thou hast done this thou shalt depart from
this world and enter into perfect joy which is My lot and the
portion of all good men in life everlasting. Thou and the heirs
of thy race . . . shall be saved . . . and shall be most loved and
cherished, most honoured and feared of good folk and the people.
(Trans. Margaret Schlauch, ibid.)

So Joseph does as he is bidden, assembling the whole company and
relaying to them all that the voice has instructed him to do, '. . . saving
only the word that Christ spoke to him in the dungeon. This word he
taught to the Rich Fisher, and when he had said these things he also
gave them to him written down.' (ibid.)

THE GRAIL TEMPLE

Thus the Secrets of the Grail are passed on, from father to son, until
the time came for the Quest for the Grail to begin in earnest. Until
then it was kept in a safe and secret place, a temple where it could be
reverenced until such time as mankind was deemed ready to be told
of its existence, shown its miraculous powers, and offered the chance
to go in search of what it represented.

From the start certain features appeared fixed. The temple usually
stood at the top of a mountain, surrounded by either impenetrable
forest or a stretch of wild water. Access, if any, was more often than
not by way of a narrow bridge (though other variants are possible), and
this bridge often had a sharp edge, from which it became known as
the Sword Bridge. Sometimes, to make the entrance even harder, the
Temple would revolve rapidly, so that it was necessary to judge the
moment exactly before leaping for the single entrance as it flashed by.

One of the most detailed pictures of the Grail Temple appears in
a thirteenth century poem called *The Younger Titurel*[74], composed
around 1270 by a poet named Albrecht von Scharfenburg. He drew
widely on Wolfram's *Parzifal* and devoted altogether 112 lines of his
work to a description so specific in detail that it seems more like an
actual description than poetic fancy.

The story runs thus: Titurel, who is the grandfather of the famous
Grail knight, Parzival, was 50 when an angel appeared to him and
announced that the rest of his life was to be dedicated to serving
the Grail. He was then lead into a wild forest from which arose a
mountain called the Mountain of Salvation, or Muntsalvach. There
he found workers recruited from all over the world who were to help
him to build a castle and temple to house the Grail, which at that time
floated in the air over the mountain, held there by angelic hands. So

Titurel set to work and levelled the top of the mountain, which he found to be made from solid onyx, and which, when polished 'shone like the moon'. Soon after, he found the ground plan of the building mysteriously engraved on this fabulous surface. It was to take thirty years to build, but during this time the Grail provided not only the substances from which the temple was built, but also food for the workmen. At length it was complete, and it is at this point that we find the following description, which is worth quoting in full:

The Temple arose as a wide and high rotunda, bearing a great cupola. Twenty-two chapels stood out in octagonal form; over every pair of chaples stood an octagonal bell-tower, six storeys high. At the summit of each tower was a ruby surmounted by a cross of white crystal, to which a golden eagle was affixed decorated by many goldsmiths. At its summit was a carbuncle, which shone forth at night. Should any Templar return late to the castle, its glow showed him the way . . .

Two doors lead into each of the chapels. Each one contained an altar of sapphire, which was so placed that the priest should face to the east. The altars were richly decorated with pictures and statues; over each one a high ciborium. Curtains of green satin protected them from dust . . . . In the east stood the main chapel, twice as large as the others. It was dedicated to the Holy Spirit, who was the patron of the temple. The chapels to either side of it were dedicated to the Holy Virgin and St John.

On the wall between the chapels were golden trees with green foliage, their branches filled with birds. Golden-green vines hung down over the seats; roses, lilies and flowers of all colours could be seen . . . . Over the vines were angels, which seemed to have been brought from paradise. Whenever a breeze arose they came into movement like living beings.

The portals were richly decorated in pure gold and in every kind of precious stone which was used in building . . . The windows were of beryl and crystal, and decorated with many precious stones, among them: sapphire, emerald, three shades of amethyst, topaz, garnet, white sardonyx and jasper in seventeen colours . . .

The cupola rested on brazen pillars, into which many images were graven. It was decked with blue sapphire, on which stars of carbuncle shone forth both day and night. The golden sun and silver-white moon were pictured there . . . cymbals of gold announced the seven times of day. Statues of the four Evangelists were cast in pure gold, their wings spread out high and wide. An emerald formed the keystone of the cupola. On it a lamb was depicted, bearing the cross on a red banner.

In the midst of the temple was a rich work dedicated to God and the Grail. It was identical in form to the temple as a whole except that the chapels were without altars. In this the Grail was to be kept for all time. (Trans. J.& D. Meeks.)[24]

Here the magical vessel was kept, watched over by a select body of knights drawn from the Family of the Grail. Wolfram called them *Templiesen*, Templars, and while it is possible that he meant simply 'guardians of the temple' by this term, few would doubt that he is making a more than casual identification of the Grail knights with an actual body of men, whose history, like that of the Cathars discussed in Chapter 3, was tragic and wrapped in mystery.

THE WARRIORS OF GOD

In 1118 a Burgundian knight named Hugh de Payens, together with eight companions, all Crusaders, founded a new order of chivalry, dedicated to poverty, chastity and obedience and established specifically 'in honour of Our Lady' and to guard the pilgrim routes to the Holy Land. This was something wholly new in the Western world, though similar orders existed in the East. The idea of combining the piety of a monastic way of life with the rules of Chivalry must have seemed as startling as it was original. Yet little is known about the man who founded the order except that he described himself as 'a poor knight', and held a small fief at Payens, only a few miles from Troyes, where Chrétien wrote the first Grail story some sixty-two years later.

The other significant fact about Hughes de Payens is that he was related to Bernard of Clairvaux, one of the most famous theologians of the age and the founder of the Cistercian order. It was to Bernard that Hughes now wrote, begging him to sponsor the new order and to give them a Rule by which to orient their lives.

After some hesitation Bernard took up their cause, and it was largely due to his influence that the order was ratified at the Council of Troyes in 1128. They were permitted to wear a white robe with a red cross emblazoned on the right shoulder, and were given, as their headquarters in the East, the building believed to have been the Temple of Solomon in Jerusalem. From this they received the name by which they were ever after known – the Knights Templar.

75

The say it all.

From this beginning grew the single most famed military organisation of the Middle Ages. The Templars became the permanent 'police' of the tiny war-torn kingdom of Jerusalem, They fought with utter dedication and became feared by Moslem and Christian alike. St. Bernard's Rule was a harsh one, binding the knights to forswear home and country, to fight at need to the death for the holy places of Christendom. For the sake of chastity they had to sleep fully clothed in lighted dormitories; nor were they permitted to receive private letters – any communication had to be read out aloud before the company. They must attend mass at least three times a week wherever they were, accept every combat that came their way, despite the odds, and neither ask nor give quarter.

Despite this, Bernard's sponsorship alone was sufficient to swell the ranks at a rapid rate. Soon the order began to build a network of castles, called 'commanderies', across the Holy Land, as well as in France and England and elsewhere in Europe. Their power and strength increased, and their wealth grew accordingly. Though each individual forswore personal possessions, they gave freely of their goods to the order, and began also to win much treasure in their battles with the Moors. In time they became so wealthy and of such good standing that they virtually became the bankers of Europe, lending huge sums to help finance the Crusades. And, as their political power grew, so their enemies increased. Finally, the miserly and avaricious King of France, Philip the Fair, plotted with a renegade Templar to bring about their downfall – for the most astonishing of declared reasons.

Philip charged the Order with heresy, and in a single night had the greater part of their number taken prisoner. They were tortured, and under pressure admitted to every kind of crime, from sodomy to spitting on the Cross. The last Grand Master of the Knight's Templar, the saintly Jacques de Molay, was executed on 19 May 1314, bringing the order effectively to an end one hundred and ninety-six years after its foundation.

Such are the historical facts. Behind them lies an even more remarkable story, one which is closely linked to the inner history of the Grail.

There are several facts about the Templars which bear notice. Firstly there is their name, which though it is said to derive from the Temple of Solomon is also reminiscent of the *Templiesen* of Wolfram. Then there is the connection with Bernard of Clairvaux. As well as the Rule he wrote at the request of Hughes de Payans (to whom he dedicated it) *A Treatise on the New Knighthood*[5] in which he speaks of the Order in terms which are easily applied to the Grail knights. He wrote:

See: the Free Masons!

It seems that a new knighthood has recently appeared on earth, and precisely in that part of it which the Orient from on high visited in the flesh. . . . It ceaselessly wages a twofold war both against flesh and blood and against the spiritual army of evil in the heavens.

The idea was something wholly new. Though the Church had long seen itself as the army of God, this had never been taken to the extreme of actually arming its priests. The idea seemed mutually exclusive. Yet this is precisely what the Templars became, priests and soldiers 'doubly armed' writes Bernard, so that they 'need fear neither demons nor men'. Adding that 'these are the picked troops of God', and exhorting them that

precious in the eyes of the Lord is the death of the holy ones, whether they die in battle or in bed, but death in battle is more precious as it is the more glorious. . . . If he [the knight] fights for a good reason, the issue of this fight can never be evil. (ibid.)

Yet these men, who as Bernard says will be 'in company of perfect men' (how reminiscent of the Cathar perfecti), are later reviled, their order discredited and destroyed. Why should this be so?

Among the list of crimes, both sacred and secular, of which the Templars were accused, are listed the harbouring of the Cathars and of friendship to the Islamic sect of the Ismaelites – their nearest equivalent in the East. Both accusations are possibly true, at least in part. The order did offer sanctuary to wrongdoers, provided they forswore their former lives and obeyed the Templar rule. The period of testing was lengthy however, and discipline strict. It is also more than likely that certain of the Cathars, fleeing from the South, did find their way into the Order, and may even have influenced it from within. At any rate it is interesting to note that the Templars were widely known to accept men with a past, and that records exist which suggest a curious form of absolution for such men. It is said to have taken the form of the following words: 'I pray God that He will pardon you your sins as he pardoned them to Saint Mary Magdalene and the thief who was put on the Cross'[51].

The Templar who vouchsafed this, Galcerand de Teus, under torture was persuaded to admit that the 'thief' referred to here was to be understood as Christ (rather than one of the thieves traditionally supposed to have been crucified alongside Jesus). He added that at the moment the Lance of Longinus pierced the side of the doomed Messiah he 'Repented that he had said he was God the King of the

Jews, and having in this way repented concerning his sin, he asked pardon of the true God and thus the true God spared him . . .' (ibid.)

This remarkable 'confession' is startlingly like the stated beliefs of the Cathars, as well as harking back to earlier Gnostic teachings. It is significant also that it places the incident at the moment of the piercing of Christ's side with the Lance, which was later identified as the Grail spear. While to the Inquisition it offered a further instance of Templar heresy, it also may be seen as a link between the Order and the Cathar movement.

As to the suggestion that the Templars were friendly with the Islamic sect of the Ismaelites, this is also likely enough. Though the order began with the avowed intention of destroying the infidel and of winning back the Holy Sepulchre permanently for the Church, constant encounters with the Arab way of life had a transformative effect on the relations between East and West.

THE HEAD IN THE DISH

· It has been suggested that the Templars may also have been the guardians of a relic of such importance that it even outshone the Grail – though in fact the two were connected. According to the argument put forward by Ian Wilson[91] and more recently by Noel Currer-Briggs[17] both of whom offer considerable documentation, there is every reason to believe that the object known as the Mandylion passed through the hands of the Order during the height of its power, and that this same object, which seems to have been a piece of cloth, folded several times and stretched between frames of wood, may have been the shroud of Christ, apparently lost to the world during the siege of Constantinople in 1204, but possibly disguised in this form to prevent it falling into Moslem hands. It is this same relic which is nowadays to be found in the Cathedral of Turin, and is the subject of continuing controversy and world-wide scientific investigation.

If Wilson and Briggs are right, and there is no reason why they should not be, then not only does this present the Templars as possessing a sacred relic, it also goes some way towards explaining another of the 'blasphemies' of which they were accused.

This concerned the worship of a graven idle called Baphomet (usually accepted as a corruption of Muhammad) and described as a bearded head wearing a crown. This could easily be a garbled understanding of the Mandylion, which was folded so that only the bearded face of Christ, marked with the wounds caused by the Crown of Thorns.

In both the *Perlesvaus*[6] and the Cistercian-inspired *Queste del Saint Graal*[56], which was part of the Vulgate Cycle composed at St Bernard's monastery at Clairvaux, there are echoes of this mysterious image. In *Perlesvaus* King Arthur himself witnesses the Grail mass, and when he looks towards the altar: 'It seemed to him that holy hermit [who was officiating] held between his hands a man bleeding from his side and in his palms and in his feet, and crowned with thorns. . . .'[6] While in the *Queste* we find Galahad at Mass in the Temple of Sarras, the Holy City of the Grail, where the vessel is kept in an Ark standing upon a silver table – an image that reflects both the Temple of Solomon, and also the model of the Holy Sepulchre found in every Templar commanderie throughout the world, where their most sacred rites were performed.

So we have the Templars, based at the site of Solomon's Temple, guarding a sacred relic, holding a special devotion to the Virgin, supported by St Bernard – elements all recognisable from the Traditions of the Grail. Approved by the Pope, their rule written by one of the foremost churchmen in the Western world, they became for a time the highest standard of earthly power. The whole of Western Christendom had grown used to the idea of the knight. The Templars were super-knights, combining the skill of fighting men with the spiritual fervour of the priesthood. We should not be surprised if many of the Grail writers took the Order as a model not only for the Grail chivalry, but also for the Round Table.

And here too the notion that too much power carries its own built in law of self-destruction is apparent. Might can be harnessed for right; but when there are too many wrongs to right, when the Kingdom of Jerusalem had been secured, however uneasily, the Templars, like the Round Table, fell apart. Accumulations of wealth and power served only to provoke jealousy and fear. The earthly Jerusalem was only a symbol of the heavenly city after all – discontent bred of by heaviness of time and stale custom shook the high purpose with which the Crusaders had set forth. In consolidating an earthly kingdom they had lost sight of the heavenly one. A scapegoat was required, and the Templars provided it.

And so, by a supreme irony, the Warriors of God, whose order had been founded to uphold the highest ideals of Christendom, as well as of knighthood; which had been blessed by the foremost churchmen of the time, were themselves accused of the very same evils which had only recently been levelled at the Cathars – the denial of God, the defamation of the Cross, the worship of false idols, and the practice of unnatural vices.

So close, indeed, are the accusations, that one is almost led to believe that behind the garbled confessions, extracted by torture, confessions of things only half understood (by both sides), lies a body of teaching which would make the Templars the truer inheritors of the Cathar heresy, their aims and beliefs the same, yet perverted and twisted by the change from passive to active roles in the world.

THE CAUSE OF LOVE

Perhaps we may look to the part played by St Bernard for further illumination. Just as, within the disciplines of love, there were three approaches, so outside this area there were three ways: that of love itself, that of knowledge and wisdom, and thirdly, the way of action. It was to this third way that the order of the Knights Templar dedicated themselves, becoming first and foremost, despite their innate spiritual trend, a military order. From Monks of Love they became Monks of War, and in some senses at least Bernard of Clairvaux was responsible for this.

It is easy to see why, as more than one commentator has observed, Bernard came to see his own order, the Cistercians, as a superior force in the struggle against the heretics in the South. Several of his sermons are given over to a bitter attack on the Cathars of Germany, whom he had never even visited. With the advent of the Templars, he saw the strength of this Christian force as directed 'against a spiritual army of evil in the heavens'. Perhaps he was trying to reconcile love and war, by embracing both.

Henry Corbin, the great authority on Eastern and Western religions, made the point in his book *The Fight for the World-Soul* (1952), that there is a battle for the soul of the world going on continuously, and that St Bernard was aware of this and tried to defuse the situation from both sides by harnessing love and war together. His chief agents in this would have been the Templars, and it is perhaps this as much as anything which hastened their demise. In fighting against the heresy of Catharism they were fighting their own inner impulse.

There was always an inner court within the order, consisting of the Grand Master and eight others – a tradition which sprang from the original founder and his companions. If there were any secret activities, beliefs or practices within the Order, these men would have been directly responsible for it. They would almost certainly remain silent even under torture, and the jumbled fragments which were extracted from the lesser members of the order would be no more than half understood pieces of a much larger whole. It is unlikely that we shall ever know the truth. What does seem certain is that the Templars are the most likely candidates for the transmission of the Grail message from the Cathars to the mysteries of Alchemy and the parables of the Rosicrucian adepts.

THE HIDDEN KINGS

The Temple of the Grail, wherever it stood, whether in the realm of fancy or of fact, was established in the minds and hearts of the Medieval Grail seekers. Whoever its true guardians may have been, they continued to carry out their appointed task – as they surely continue to do today. Of those whose names rise to the surface from the mists which surround the inner Tradition of the Grail, certain figures stand out. We might name Melchizadek, the priest king of Salem, who in Biblical tradition made the first offering of bread and wine long before the Eucharist was celebrated in the Upper Room in Jerusalem. Solomon himself, master of Wisdom, seems to have held the Cup, or at least the symbolic powers it contains, for a time, and to have passed it on to others of his line. Even Jesus, who prayed that the cup of his agony might pass from him, may be in some senses a Grail guardian. While Joseph of Arimathea, and the line he founded, carried the mystery into the age of Arthur and beyond. Perceval's part-coloured half-brother Feirefiz, wedded to the Grail princess Repanse de Schuoy, begot of her a son who was named Lohengrin, and he in turn sired an even greater figure of mystery and might.

The first mention of this character, little more than a rumour, comes in a medieval chronicle which for the year 1145, relates how a certain Bishop Hugh of Cabalah visited Rome and was told how, some years previous to this,

> ... a certain Priest and King named John, who lives on the further side of Persia and Armenia, in the remote East, and who with all his people were Christians ... had overcome the royal brothers *Samiardi*, Kings of the Medes and Persians, and had captured Eckbattana, their capitol and residence. ... The said John advanced to the help of the Church of Jerusalem; but when he had reached the river [Tygris] he had not been able to take his army across the river in any vessel. He had then turned North, where he had learned that it was all frozen by the winter cold. He had lingered there for some time, waiting for the frost, but because of the wild weather ... [was] forced to return home after losing much of his army because of the unaccustomed climate[79].

With a touch of colour the chronicler adds that Prester John is 'said to be of the lineage of the Magi who are mentioned in the Gospel, and to rule over the same people as they did, enjoying such glory and prosperity that he is said to use only a sceptre of emerald. . .' (ibid.) We are reminded by this of the emerald Grail – this is not surprising when we consider its bearer's lineage.

But what was the truth behind this extraordinary account? We have to remember that at the time the threat of invasion from the East hung over the West rather like that of Atomic war in the twentieth century. The perilously slender hold of the Crusaders over the Kingdom of Jerusalem was constantly in danger of failing, with a consequent inrush of Muslim armies expected to follow. News of a crushing defeat 'in the furthest East' was a morale booster comparable to hearing that Hitler's forces had been turned back by the Russians during the last war. Thus we must admit at once that there is a strong element of wish-fulfilment behind the various references to a 'Christian king in the East'.

Be that as it may, in 1165 there appeared a mysterious letter, copies of which found their way to Pope Alexander III, the King of France, the Emperor of Constantinople (Manuel Commenius), and the Holy Roman Emperor Frederick II – the spiritual and temporal rulers of Western Christendom. The letter purported to come from no lesser person than Prester John himself, and it is a most intriguing document.

The letter begins:

> Prester John, by the Grace of God most powerful king over all Christian kings, greetings to the Emperor of Rome and the King of France, our friends. We wish you to learn about us, our position, the government of our land, our people and our beasts. . . . We attest and inform you by our letter, sealed with our seal, of the condition and character of our land and men. And if you desire. . .to come hither to our country, we shall make you on account of your good reputation our successors and we shall grant you vast lands, manors, and mansions[79].

The letter continues in this style for some twenty pages, describing a land overflowing with goodness and riches, ruled over by the benign Priest King, whose crown is the 'highest. . .on earth', and whose sway extends over forty-two other Christian kings. The writer then goes on: 'Between us and the Saracens there flows a river called Ydonis which comes from the terrestrial paradise and is full of precious stones . . . and of each we know its name and its magical power.' (ibid.) The letter ends by exhorting the rulers of Christendom to put to death 'those treacherous Templars and pagans' and is signed 'in the year five hundred and seven since our birth'.

The letter is a forgery, of this there can be no doubt. The style, as well as the contents, clearly derive from identifiable sources – mostly Eastern – an ironic fact when we consider that Prester John was set up as a bitter foe of the Muslims! What we do have in the text of the letter is a description of the Otherworld, a semi-attainable, paradisial place filled with wonders, offering spiritual as well as temporal pleasures. Rather like the country of the Grail in fact, as much of the text bears out. Indeed, we should hardly be surprised to find the extraordinary Temple of the Grail from Alberecht von Scharfenburg's poem to appear in this setting. Both are the product of the same impulse, the desire to return to our home, the Earthly paradise from which Adam and Eve were driven forth.

Prester John, as here presented, is a recognisable archetype, belonging to the race known as 'Withdrawn Kings', once great and noble beings who have withdrawn to an inner plane of existence, from where they watch over the progress of humanity and occasionally take a direct hand in historical events. Merlin is another, as are Melchizadek, the Biblical Enoch, King Arthur, and the angelic Sandalphon. John, whose title means simply 'Priest-King' is the product of several vague historical personages, half remembered accounts of Alexander the Great, various kings of Ethiopia and more than one Tartar lord.

But he is something more than this. Whether Wolfram found a reference to Prester John as the offspring of the Grail knights, or whether he made up the connection, he touched upon a deep nerve. John represented all that was best in Christendom. He suffered none of the traits of corruption or heresy which hung over much of the West like a dark cloud. He was all powerful, all good, and he was the guardian of a great secret – the Holy Grail. Dauntless!

THE WORK OF THE GRAIL FAMILY

The descent of the Grail lineage is thus a metaphysical one. It includes mystics, seekers after truth, alchemists, magicians, Kings, and many more. Whatever its provenance, it remains a symbol of man's desire for union with God, the return from exile on earth to a home in Paradise. *This is found only three belief in Christ*

Lancelot at the Chapel of the Grail by Evelyn Paul

Certain individuals are assigned to this task of restoration – some with a specific duty and goal in mind – others who have no clue as to their errand but who together share in the Family of the Grail. They make up what we might term the Tribe of the Grail, a tribe drawn from no earthly lineage, with no specific racial descent; a tribe which has no territorial boundaries, no common basis for belief other than the symbol which reunites all opposites – the Grail itself.

As one of the greatest modern commentators on the Grail Tradition, Walter Johannes Stein, wrote, as long ago as 1928:

The Grail race has the mission of expanding to cosmopolitan proportions all that belongs to the narrow group, of enlarging separate interests to world interest. In our time this mission lies no longer with the family group. How the present day faces the impulse will only become clear as through our consideration of the ensuing centuries, we step by step draw nearer the problem[80].

THE TABLES OF THE GRAIL

We have seen how Joseph of Arimathea set up a Table which became a symbolic expression of the Table of the Last Supper, having twelve places plus one, and one which remained empty in token of the betrayer Judas – a place which would only be filled when the chosen Grail knight arrived who could sit in the Perilous Seat without danger.

This was the second Table of the Grail. The Round Table, made by Merlin 'in the likeness of the world' was the third. Together they make up a triple emanation of the Holy Spirit which is the central Gnosis of the Grail. Each succeeding emanation is further from the point of origin, but containing the essence of the rest.

Thus, all who sit at the Table of the Grail inherit the fullness of the earlier Tables, for there has come into being a fourth table, where all who are engaged upon the great Quest find themselves led inevitably in the end. Some set out with no specific task in mind, like Perceval; others feel they are acting on the impulse of the Divine Will, as Galahad does. And there are those who become lost in the webs of a labyrinth of conflicting interests who never arrive at the place intended for them – those who seek an earthly city, a physical relic, and who will never achieve the Grail until they understand that not by deeds of arms, nor feats of endurance, will they gain their heart's desire. Instead they must seek a subtler form of alchemy which unites human and divine. *That is CHRIST! Enough said!*

There are those who may discover their Grail in a nearby place, where they had not thought of looking; the rejected stone the *lapis exillas*, is transmuted into the sacramental stuff of life by a simple act of love, or of devotion. The transformations taking place at the altar of Divine Love is every bit as valid as the transmutations of the psyche achieved by magical means.

In the end, all become part of the Grail Family. They meet in the circular Temple so reminiscent of Templar churches and chapels. And they discuss the actions of the Grail in the world: how its operations work towards the healing of the planet, and of the great divide in the human psyche which lead to the dualism of the Gnostics and the Cathars. In so doing they learn. The lessons of all who go in search of the divine are taught to them and they either listen to or ignore them. Finally, they are caught up, transmuted, changed out of all recognition; they become one with the divine impulse and walk in the great places of the Spirit which have so many names:

Eden, Paradise, Avalon, Shambhala. In time they may be sent out again, openly or in secret, to spread the word of the Grail to the rest of humanity. *field!*

This is the work of the Family and it is not always easy. Opposition, as we saw in Chapter 4, will almost certainly be encountered along the way. That this may be overcome, or itself transmuted, is one of the gifts of the Grail which are available to all who seek it out. In the end it becomes more than a symbol, more than an idea; becomes instead a life giving force which permeates the whole universe, until it glows with the fire of divine love and light.

EXERCISE 5: JOINING THE FAMILY OF THE GRAIL

We have already seen something of the importance of the direct links between the Grail guardians of each age. In the two-part pathworking which follows you are led into the world of two such guardians: Prester John and Sophia Aeternitas. These two represent the masculine and feminine elements of the Grail tradition, and once contact with them is established the work of the seeker will be much enhanced. The two parts of the meditation should preferably be done on succeeding days, or at least with no more than a week separating them, but preferably not on the same day. The gifts and knowledge imparted will become increasingly important as you progress on the path of the Grail.

PART ONE

As you begin to relax, breathing slowly and evenly, the room in which you are sitting slowly fades, and you find that you are standing in the open air, high up on top of a range of hills, with a view of much of Britain spread out below you. A little to your left is a low mound, not unlike the old Prehistoric burial mounds, and in it is a heavy wooden door let into the side at the Eastern end. You approach the door, and as you do so it opens before you. All is dark at first within, but as you enter you become aware of a soft glow which lights your way. Inside, the mound seems much larger than it did from outside, and you see that a tunnel opens out from it, sloping away into the earth. It is lined with very ancient looking blocks of stone which look as though they have always been there.

As you follow the path downwards the slope grows steeper, though never too much to walk comfortably along it, and the gentle light remains steady and unchanging. In a while you come to another door, much like the one by which you entered, and this too swings open to the touch. You pass through and find yourself in a hall of vast proportions. You can only dimly see the roof far above, and the walls on either side recede into darkness. The floor of the hall is paved with huge blocks of masonry, fitted so exactly together that they are perfectly smooth and even to walk upon.

As you proceed across the floor of the great hall you become aware that the light ahead of you is brightening, and you begin to see where two great thrones stand, carved out of rock and decorated with the likeness of strange beasts. Seated in the left hand throne is the figure of a man who appears to be deeply asleep. He is tall, regal and bearded, and wears a crown of three tiers, surmounted by a dome. His robes are of deepest blue, with elaborate letters in silver embroidered on them. These seem to move and change subtly as you look. In his arms the figure holds cradled a sceptre carved out of emerald, on top of which is set a silver rose.

In the second throne is a figure who appears at first much like the first, so that they might be brothers. He also wears a crown, this time with four tiers with a great cross surmounting it. He is robed in scarlet with designs in gold which seem like stars and suns, always moving in an endless dance. He carries a sceptre carved from red jasper, tipped with a cross of gold.

In front of the two thrones is a low table made from a single block of marble, and on it stands a small bronze bell suspended from a dark wooden frame. Hanging from the frame is a striker, and you understand that you must go forward and strike the bell once, but no more. (PAUSE.)

With the first sound of the bell, which echoes softly in the huge hall, the figure on the left stirs, though he does not yet open his eyes. But now the bell continues to reverberate, even though you have laid down the striker, and with the second reverberation the figure on the right also begins to stir. Thereafter, with each echo of the bell the two become progressively more awake, until at last they are fully conscious and gaze smiling down upon you.

Now you become aware that while you were engaged in your task with the bell, the hall behind you has filled up with a multitude of people. People who are dressed in the fashions of many ages, from the furthest days of the Neolithic and Bronze Ages, to the most recent times. They are of every race, colour and creed, Indians, Arabs, Chinese, Slavs, all these and many more. Some appear careworn and sad, others afraid, but all have a look of dawning certainty and assurance as they stand before the two figures in their great stone chairs.

As you look at the two we have awoken, they seem to grow blurred to your eyes, and slowly they merge with each other. As your sight clears, you see that there is now only one figure on the left hand throne, and that his crown is of seven tiers, domed and surmounted with a cross of gold and emerald. His robes are now of purple, with patterns of sun, moon and stars, and letters inscribed of gold and silver upon them. The sceptre he bears is of emerald, tipped with a golden cross in the centre of which is a silver rose.

As you stare in awe at this mighty figure, a great cry comes from the crowd which now seems to fill the hall. They are calling out many names in many tongues, but you hear only one. It is PRESTER JOHN, the name by which the figure is known to you from the writings of the wise in your own land.

Now he beckons you to approach, and when you stand before him offers you a gift, either in the form of a message or an object of some kind. Remember what is said or given to you. (PAUSE.)

After a time you find that you are again standing before the throne of Prester John with the great crowd, who now begin to come forward to speak with the Priest King in turn. Many days will pass before all have spoken with him, and many more will enter the hall who may yet know nothing of this place. But for you the time has come to depart. Salute the figure in the throne and then turn away and retrace your steps across the great hall, through the tunnel and outside again onto the hillside overlooking most of Britain. Slowly let the images of earth and sky fade until you find yourself once more where you began. The memory of what you have learned will remain fresh in your mind and may lead you to further explorations into the inner realms.

PART TWO

As your senses adjust to the state of meditation visualise yourself as standing on the deck of a ship which is already at sea. A strong wind fills the sails and the ship moves swiftly through the water. In the distance ahead you see a line of tall cliffs which grow gradually closer until you are able to see the details of lichen and birds nests along the cliff edges. The ship enters a narrow channel between dark rocks and soon you arrive in a sheltered inlet which forms a natural harbour. The craft docks against a jetty constructed of massive blocks of stone, and stepping ashore you walk inland through deep woodland filled with the noise of streams that trickle down to the sea on every side.

Emerging from the wood you find yourself in a narrow valley at the head of which a waterfall plunges down from the cliffs far above into a deep pool. On either side of the waterfall are two giant stone chairs like the thrones of ancient kings, and standing between them are two angelic figures, the one on the right dressed in green, the one on the left in red. They are the guardians of the valley and all that lies within.

To the right of the waterfall is a narrow crack in the face of the cliff, wide enough at the bottom to admit one person at a time. The angel in red indicates that you should enter, and this you do. Within is a dimly lit passage, and it is only a short distance to a pair of doors of ancient dark wood, which open at a touch, admitting you into a vast hall, the walls of which lead off to right and left, vanishing in shadow, and the roof of which is too far distant to see. A gentle light allows us to see where we are. The floor is made up of huge stone blocks, set smoothly together so that the cracks hardly show.

As we proceed the light grows stronger and you begin to see glimpses of mighty stalagmites hanging from the roof, each one pulsing with its own inner radiance. Then ahead you see two great stone chairs, their backs towards you. They are smaller than the vast carvings you saw outside at the feet of the mountains, but of the same kind. As you pass the chairs and come round to the front you realise, with something of a shock, that this is the same hall you have visited before, in which you first met the great figure of Prester John. Once again you see him seated in majesty, in his purple robe emblazoned with sun, moons and stars, and bearing a sceptre carved from a single emerald.

The throne next to him is now occupied by the figure of a woman, dressed in a robe of red. She is veiled and carries a white sceptre tipped with a carved red rose. Upon her robe are embroidered the letters S A. Both the figures seem lost in meditation, sitting unmoving with indrawn sight.

In front of the two thrones is a cubic altar, upon which is set a golden stone, emitting sufficient radiance to touch all who stand before it. You should respond to this as you wish, letting it sink deeply within you as you stand in silence before the King and Queen.

As before you become aware of a bell in a wooden frame, which stands upon the altar beside the golden stone. This time however the bell is of silver, and as you lift the striker and touch its side to the bell a sweet ringing tone is emitted which continues to reverberate through the vast hall. At its first sound the two figures stir, looking down upon us from the two great thrones. They indicate that you should approach, choosing whether you will stand before the mighty figure of Prester John, or before the veiled Lady whose initials are S. A. They will have a message or an instruction which you should remember . . .

When you are returned to your place you become aware that, as before, the hall is now filled with a great multitude from every race and time that have filled the world. But, where before their faces seemed care-worn or fearful, now they are filled with radiance and joy. Turning again to the great King and Queen you see that they have risen from their thrones, and together with the multitude you bow your head for a moment in homage.

Looking up again you see the mighty archetypal figures hold out their hands in blessing above the throng; then together they descend and, hand in hand walk slowly from the hall, vanishing at last behind a curtain which hangs to one side of the thrones. In the silence which follows their departure the great multitude of people from all ages begins to disperse, vanishing silently back into the shadows of the great hall. A small group remains about the altar however, and these now invite you to take hands with them in a circle. You do so and all begin to dance slowly around the golden stone. As if in answer its light grows brighter, filling your ears and heart and mind with a golden glow . . .

At last this begins to fade, and with it the shape of the hall and the people with whom you danced fades also. You awaken to find yourself back where you began this journey.

5 · WASTE LAND AND WOUNDED KING:
HEALING WITH THE GRAIL

GRAIL KINGS AND ANTI KINGS

There is an ancient (and admittedly dualistic) saying that all things have their opposites. Thus just as there is a Grail, and Grail Kings, and Grail Knights, so there is a black Grail, anti-Grail Kings and evil knights who seek the ruin of the kingdom of the Grail. *Whoopee. Bingo.*

These things are seldom spoken of, or written about, in our time, though the medieval writers knew of their importance. But they remain a necessary part of the mystery, providing a balance to the darker side of the myths. At the nexus point, in the heart of the Grail, is a point of harmony, of resolution, of polarity, which is brought about through the *interaction* of the darkness and light which surrounds the Grail.

To avoid the darker side of these stories is to close our eyes to a very real problem. There is a great deal of casual-seeming cruelty in the Quest texts – the casual slaying by Gawain of pagans in a city which had become Christianised is one such example, though it would have seemed perfectly normal and proper to a medieval audience; or the episode where Bors is about to go to the rescue of a woman in distress when he sees his brother Lional, tied naked to a horse and beaten with a thorn twig by an evil knight who is carrying him into captivity. Bors has to make a choice between brotherly love and his knightly vows, and being the staunch Quester that he is he opts for the latter. But the woman he rescues is herself a demon in disguise, and although his brother is rescued by Lancelot, when the brothers next meet there is such anger on the part of Lional that they almost kill each other.

The Quest by William Ernest Chapman

This kind of situation is common throughout the Quest, and we are likely to encounter the same kind of thing on our own journey – not literally the same of course, but no less difficult or painful because of that. What we must never expect is that the Quest will be easy, or that we will become miraculously sorted out people before we begin. Many, if not all the Grail mysteries are about self discovery, hence the emphasis on questions. The Quest is a journey inward as well as through the lands of the Grail.

For this reason it is useful to know about some of the adversaries the Quest knights encountered, so that we can recognise their like if, and when, they crop up.

THE DOLOROUS BLOW AND THE MAIDENS OF THE WELLS

Two themes which appear continually in the texts relating to the Grail are the Wounded King and the Waste Land. These are inextricably linked because the former is generally the cause of the latter. There are several stories which deal with this in detail, but for the moment we will look at just two of them. In Malory's *Morte d'Arthur* we find the following description of what is known as 'The Dolorous Blow'.

Balin le Sauvage is following the track of an otherworldly woman, and along the way he finds himself in the company of a friendly knight. But this man is murdered by an unseen foe, and Balin soon learns that he is called Garlon, and that he rides under a cloak of invisibility. Balin arrives at the castle of King Pellam of Listenesse, who is about to hold a great tournament, and there he discovers Garlon, who is pointed out to him as 'he with the black face; he is the marvellest knight that is now living, for he destroyeth many good knights, for he goeth invisible'. Observing Balin watching him, Garlon strikes him in the face and in a moment of fury Balin takes out his sword and strikes him dead. 'Anon all the knights arose from the table to set on Balin, and King Pellam rose up fiercely, and said, "Knight, thou hast slain my brother, thou shalt die therefore or thou depart."' In the fight that follows Balin's sword breaks,

> 'And when Balin was weaponless he ran into a chamber for to seek some weapon, and so from chamber to chamber, and no weapon he could find, and always King Pellam after him. And at last he entered a chamber that was marvellously well dight and richly, and a bed arrayed with cloth of gold, the richest that might be thought, and one lying therein, and thereby stood a table of clean gold with four pillars of silver that bare up the table, and upon the table stood a marvellous spear strangely wrought. And when Balin saw that spear, he gat it in his hand and turned him to King Pellam, and smote him passingly sore with that spear, that King Pellam fell down in a swoon, and therewith the castle walls brake and fell to the earth, and Balin fell down so that he might not stir foot or hand. And so the most part of the castle, that was fallen down because of that dolorous stroke, lay upon Pellam and Balin three days.' (Bk XVI. Ch.15.)[52]

The spear is the lance of Longinus, with which he had struck a blow into the side of Christ on the Cross. Used thus to defend and wound, rather than to protect and heal, it causes a hurt that cannot be healed until the coming of the Grail knight.

Before we look at the second example, we should notice two things about this version. Firstly there is the way in which the blow comes to be struck – not just through Balin's impetuous actions, but ultimately because of Garlon, the Invisible Knight. Secondly that the effect is local rather than general. It is the Fisher King Pellam's lands which are laid waste rather than the whole kingdom of Arthurian Britain.

93

The second text is called the *Elucidation*[22]. It was intended as a kind of prelude and explanation to Chrétien's *Conte Del Graal*, although in fact it does very little to make things any clearer, not at first sight anyway. The beginning of the story goes like this:

'Now listen to me, all ye my friends, and ye shall hear me set forth the story that shall be right sweet to hearken unto. . .[of] how and for what cause was destroyed the rich country of Logres whereof was much talk in days of yore.

The Kingdom turned to loss, the land was dead and desert in suchwise as that it was scarce worth a couple of hazel-nuts. For they lost the voices of the wells and the damsels that were therein. For no less thing was the service they rendered than this, that scarce any wandered by the way. . . but that as for drink and victual he would go so far out of his way as to find one of the wells, and then nought could he ask for of fair victual . . . but that he should have it all. . . .The damsels with one accord served fair and joyously all wayfarers by the roads that came to the wells for victual.

King Amangons, that was evil and craven hearted, was the first to break the custom, for thereafter did many others the same according to the ensample they took of the king whose duty it was to protect the damsels and to maintain and guard them within his peace. One of the damsels did he enforce, and to her sore sorrow did away her maidenhead, and carried off from her the cup of gold that he took along with him, and afterward did make him every day be served thereof. . .thenceforth never did the damsel serve any more nor issue forth of that well for no man that might come thither to ask for victual.' (ibid.)

Afterwards, we are told, was the kingdom laid waste 'that thenceforth was no tree leafy. The meadows and flowers were dried up and the waters were shrunken, nor as then might no man find the Court of the Rich Fisherman. . . .' The Damsels of the Wells, in whom we may see a memory of a female priesthood who guarded the mystery of the Grail and its healing springs, serve no more. The land is dried up, and cannot be restored until the coming of the Grail knight, who in other texts is called 'He Who Frees the Waters'.

Here we have a quite different version of the events which caused the Waste Land, but once again it is the actions of an anti-Grail character, Amangons, that is the direct cause.

There is evidence to show that the names Amangons and Garlon derive from a single etymological source, and that a third name,

Klingsor (or Clinschor), applied to the black magician in Wolfram von Eschenbach's *Parzival*, also derives from this same source. ✓

If we look for a moment at this third figure we will begin to see more. Klingsor is described as a mighty sorcerer of the line of Virgil (in the Middle Ages the famous Roman poet had achieved the reputation of a magician), who rules over Castle Mortal or the Castle of Wonders, an evil fortress which stands in opposition to the Castle of the Grail. Dark stories are told of him.

> There was a king of Sicily called Ibert, and the same of his wife was Iblis ... Clinschor became her Servitor till she rewarded him with her love. ...The King found Clinschor with his wife, he was asleep in her embrace. If his was a warm bed he had to leave a deposit for it – he was levelled off between the legs by royal hands. ...The King trimmed him in his body to such effect that he is unserviceable to any woman today for her sport. Many people have had to suffer as a result[92]. *Oy vey!*

Here Klingsor's evil is partly attributed to his emasculation, for which he takes revenge on all who come within his sphere of power. A darker tradition indicates that he practised self-castration in a magical operation which gave him a terrible strength. He is thus seen as diametrically opposed to the Maimed King whose wound, also a sexual one, is caused by the hand of another.

By looking at these three texts we arrive at a kind of composite portrait of an Anti-Grail King, a dark aspect of the actual guardian. In the case of Garlon, he is described as Pelles' brother, and there is a suggestion that the same relationship once existed between Klingsor and Anfortas, the Grail King in *Parzival*. Amangons, though not related to Arthur by blood, functions as a kind of opposing force before the coming of Mordred later in the stories.

Each of these characters is then, in some sense responsible for the advent of the Waste Land, which, from a purely localised event, becomes more widespread and generally felt in the later Arthurian texts. So that by the time we get to the thirteenth century story of *Perlesvaus*, the failure at the heart of the Arthurian kingdom, which is illustrated by the Waste Land, has become more directly linked with the actions of Arthur himself, whose failure to take the initiative in the Quest – leaving it to his knights instead – is to be seen as a failure of will and the empowerment of his sovereignty.

In this sense the Waste Land has become indicative of a more general malaise – the heart of the Kingdom, its King, is ailing, and until both are healed, by the finding of the Grail, the sickness will not be cured.

This is an important theme which runs throughout all the Arthurian tales, and in those which deal with the Grail is particularly central. Throughout the earlier part of his career Arthur plays an active role – fighting battles, getting the sword Excalibur from the Lady of the Lake, setting up the Round Table. At one point, he even experiences the mystery of the Grail directly, though he does not seem to do anything about it, and already there are indications of a certain malaise. The passage in question is found in *Perlesvaus*, and contains one of the most vital clues to the inner meaning of the Grail.

> Now, the story tells us that at that time there was no chalice in the land of King Arthur. The Grail appeared at the consecration [of the Mass] in five forms, but they should not be revealed, for the secrets of the sacrament none should tell save he whom God has granted grace. But King Arthur saw all the transubstantiations, and last appeared the chalice; the hermit who was conducting the mass found a memorandum upon the consecration cloth, and the letters declared that God wanted his body to be sacrificed in such a vessel in rembrance of Him. The story does not say that it was the only chalice anywhere, but in all of Britain and the neighbouring cities and kingdoms there was none[6].

After this Arthur almost disappears from the scene, the attention of the stories moves to the Quest and we hear scarcely any further mention of him except as a titular figure-head. Only with the end of the Grail quest and the gradual decline of the Arthurian court which ends with the breaking of the Round Table Fellowship, does Arthur move back to the centre of the stage. It is almost as though he falls asleep for the duration of the Quest, waiting like some enchanted being for the magical word or talisman that will awaken him.

And this, of course, is exactly what happens. Although it is never spelled out in any of the texts, Arthur is himself a wounded king – Pelles, Anfortas, Titurel are only surrogates who bear the wounds of the King as their own.

We get a hint of this again in *Perlesvaus*, where Arthur has actually gone on an adventure of his own, and meets with a chastening experience. Taking part in a tournament, he wins a golden crown and a war horse. But the knight who offers him the prizes does not recognise him. He says:

> Sire, you have won in combat this golden crown and this war-horse, for which you should rejoice indeed, so long as you are valiant enough to defend the land of the finest lady on earth, who is now dead. It will be a great honour for you if you have

strength enough to protect that land, for it is great and rich and powerful indeed.

'To Whom did the land belong?' asked the king, 'And what was the name of the queen whose crown I see.'

'Sire, the king's name was Arthur, and he was the finest in the world, but many people say that he is dead; and the crown belonged to Queen Guinevere, who is now dead and buried, which is a grievous pity[6].

Arthur is not really dead, but the sickness which afflicts all the land had affected its people too, so that they believe the king has deserted them.

Another text, *The Didot Perceval*, attributed to Robert de Borron[78], makes it even clearer. Merlin prophecises, in words that seem to apply to Arthur as much as to the Grail King, that:

The...king has fallen into a great sickness and into great infirmity, and know that [he ...] will never be cured ... until a knight foremost those who are seated at this table has done mighty deeds of arms, of bounty, of nobility ... and when he will have asked what one does and whom one serves with the Grail, the...king will be cured ... and the enchantments will fall which at present are in the land of Britain[78].

Arthur does not *seem* to be physically wounded it is true, but if one remembers his connection with Bran the Blessed, discussed in Chapter 1, and who does possess such a wound, then the identification is further strengthened.

The point is, indeed, that Arthur *has* to be the Wounded King. Nothing else will satisfy the need to explain the Waste Land, which though it is only a part of his kingdom, extends symbolically over the whole of the land.

If we then list the points as they appear from a reading of the texts we find that:

1. Arthur had once played a more central role in the Quest for the Grail, leading, as we saw in Chapter 1, a raid on the Otherworld to bring back the proto Grail.

2. In the later stories his role has become passive or inactive, and that he remains at home awaiting the return of the knights from the Quest.

3. In the older, Celtic stories, the figure of Bran the Blessed occupied a position similar in many respects to that held by Arthur *and* the Wounded King, and who was also held in a state of suspended life awaiting a ritual act that would free him.

For though the Entertainment of the Noble Head is seen as having

a negative outcome – the return of the Company and the burial of
the Head at White Mount – there is another way to see this; as the
inevitable working out of a series of events which culminates in the
installation of Bran as Guardian of the Land.

Arthur, as we saw, later dug up the head, thereby assuming the
mantle of that guardianship himself. If we need any further evidence
we have only to look at Arthur's own end as Malory describes it in
the *Morte d'Arthur*:

> More of the death of King Arthur could I never find, but that
> ladies brought him to his burials; and some such one was buried
> there [in Glastonbury] that the hermit bare witness to . . . but the
> hermit knew not in certain that he was verily the body of King
> Arthur . . . . Yet some men say in many parts of England that
> King Arthur is not dead, but had by the will of our lord Jesu
> into another place; and that he shall come again. . . . I will not
> say it shall be so, but rather will I say, here in this world he
> changed his life. But many men say that there is written upon
> his tomb this verse:

> HIC JACET ARTHURUS REX,
> QUONDAM REXQUE FUTURUS.
> (Book XXI. Ch.7.)[52]

In this 'other place' Arthur was to remain, perhaps in perpetual sleep,
until such time as his country needed him again – at which time he
would come forth in splendour, accompanied by all the panoply of
Faery, to defend the Land.

In other words Arthur, like Bran before him, was a Sacred King, a
guardian of the land itself to which he was so closely connected that
he could not even leave it, even in death. And in this he was not
only like Bran, but like the Wounded King also. In fact, he was the
Grail king, to all intents and purposes. This was why he remained
in Camelot awaiting the news that would signal the end to his own
torment. The inner realm of Britain, which in all the stories is called
Logres, was also the Waste Land of the Grail texts. Even its name,
which is a corruption of the French word *orgueilleuse*, proud, makes
sense in this context. Logres, Arthur's kingdom, is the Proud land
indeed, and suffers because of it.

The medieval writers never bothered to set this down because to
their audiences the mystery was no mystery at all – they knew
Arthur was the Wounded King and that the wound was, like the

food of the Grail, of the spirit. And because of it the whole land lay under enchantment, it was wounded by the wounding of its Lord, and awaited his healing so that it, too might be healed.

In the same way, we have to cure our own inner ailments; our divided selves must be reunited just as, to speak for a moment in Gnostic terms, the innate goodness of the human soul desires to be reunited with its higher self – God. Not for nothing is Perceval refered to as 'the Good Knight' – like the Gnostically-inspired Cathars who called themselves *parfaits*, good men, and who carried their part of the Grail mystery into the heart of Medieval Europe, (see Chapter 3). He is a distillation of the human condition. His tests and trials, his agonies, are ours, to a greater or lesser degree according to the depths of our involvement in the Quest.

Above all else the Grail Knights strive to reconcile the opposing forces which surround the object of their search. The Grail is a symbol of unity and reconciliation, and as such it requires that we lay to rest the ghosts of our own inner malaise. As one writer puts it:

Imagine yourselves always in your spirit, as pure, deep, luminous vessels, open to the cosmos, standing on the earth but firmly closed against the outer world. The cosmic and divine streams flow into your cups and make the divine spark within them luminous and glowing. This luminosity then penetrates outside and streams as blessings upon all life. It is a wonderful ceaseless giving and taking, an eternal circulation which must never be disturbed by your own damaging thoughts, because only if your heart is pure all this can take place for the blessing of all life[70].

If the Waste Land is to be healed and the Courts of Joy, which are its opposite and cure, are to be built we must each find a way to heal the wounds we ourselves bear. As the same writer just quoted puts it:

Your thoughts and feelings, whether good or bad, the earth on which you live absorbs and digests. You provide her nourishment – if you love the earth and think kindly and divinely the earth is health and radiates. If you do not love her, and have dark and destructive thoughts, she becomes sick and dark, and one day her wounds break open. (ibid.)

Thus is the Waste Land caused, by our neglect and our 'dark and destructive thoughts', which are externalised in the form of characters like Amangons, Garlon and Klingsor.

As we said at the beginning of this chapter, as there is a Grail of light so there is a black Grail. This is a statement which requires qualification. The Grail is the Grail is the Grail and can be nothing else – but there are always those who would misuse its power, which is neutral rather like the power of the neutral angels who, according to Wolfran von Eschenbach, first brought the Grail to earth. And here again we see the paradox: the Angel of Light falls, is renamed Satan, the Devil; yet from his crown comes a fragment of the original, pure light he at one time omitted.

The Grail is thus as much within the keeping of the anti kings as it is in that of the Grail Family – Joseph of Arimathea and his kin. It is in our care also, and we must learn to use its power wisely.

All of which is just another way of saying that the Quest is unlikely to be easy and demands a level of service that is of the highest kind. But, once that initial commitment is made, once the first steps – however halting – are taken on the road through 'the Grailless Lands', then *already* the rewards are prepared. It is up to us, finally, whether we overcome the negative aspects of the Quest within ourselves, the anti Grail kings and their servants, and have in the end the satisfaction of seeing the dual aspects of the search united in one – the ultimate mystery of the Grail.

THE TIMES ADVENTUROUS

Although the enchantments, the magic and the phantasmagoria of the Times Adventurous in which the knights of Arthur sought the holy vessel are on another plane to that where we live today, there is no lack of continuity between the two worlds, which overlap at all times and in all places eternally. As a recent Grail seeker has unforgettably put it:

[throughout] these untoward adventures, told in all sincerity, there pierces a higher truth. Historic verity obtains in the descriptions of warring creatures, in the clash of monk with initiate, of priest with pagan, of devotee with druid. In the forests, on wild wastes, by hills and vales for ever unexplored, this subtle conflict rages unceasingly. It is not otherwise in the Quest of the Holy Grail, whose battleground is our own soul [or our own world], that 'realm of Logres' whose frontiers no man can define. Blessed indeed is he who has seen the Grail or felt the Divine Presence in outer vision and inner consciousness; his feet are already on the Way. The Times Adventurous await him[76].

As, indeed, they await all the members of the Family of the Grail who follow the thousand and one paths through the forest, across hill and dale and mountain, river and sea, as Tennyson put it: 'following the Gleam'.

EXERCISE 4: THE FIVE CHANGES

The five changes through which the Grail passes, constitute, as we have seen, one of the most mysterious aspects of the Grail Tradition. In the following meditation the energies represented by four of the five aspects are gathered together and channelled through the fifth into the heart of the earth and from there to the seven great continents which form the greater part of the planet. This is a healing ritual of great power and efficacy if performed with the right degree of intent.

To begin imagine that you are standing on the Northernmost pole of the planet. This is not the magnetic pole, but the pole of the earth's axis, around which it spins. Above your head, therefore, be aware of the constellation of Polaris, with the great beacon of the Pole Star at its heart, and around it the constellations of the Great and Little Bears and the coiling form of the Dragon, Draco.

Here, there is no real horizon, no cardinal points to the compass, so that references to East, South, West and North are relative, referring to the true points from which influences pour in from the distant constellations.

With eyes still closed, stand up and face the East. You are looking across the vast sea of space, lit by a million stars. Amongst them you are able to pick out the silver shape of the Bull, the constellation of Taurus. At its centre, like an eye, is the star Aldebaron, a smoky red point of energy sometimes called The Eye of God.

Within this starry form you gradually become aware of another shape, that of a great circular Dish, which catches the light of the stars and reflects it towards us. This light surrounds you and is drawn into your heart centre, where it is gathered up and projected downwards, through the centre of your body, through your feet, and on down in the earth beneath.

From there it branches out towards the points of the Equator, and then inward towards the core of the planet. There, in the very centre of the earth, you see a great crystal Cup, shaped so that it catches light both from above and below and is able also to emit light in either direction.

Now it catches the light you send, the concentrated force of the great Dish, which is that in which you make an offering of all your intentions, and sends it raying out in all directions, striking upwards through the earth until it reaches each of the seven Continents: North America, Asia, Europe, Africa, Australasia and Antartica. Each of these becomes ringed by a line of brilliant light, which remains glowing as you make a 90° turn to the right . . .

You are now facing true South, and ahead across the depths of space you see the constellation of the Lion, whose heart is the bright star Regulus, also known as the Little King. As you look you see that sitting astride the back of the Lion is the bright shape of a radiant child. This is the Divine Youth who will grow to carry the light for all men into the world. Now he raises both hands and throws a long shaft of light across the gulf which separates him from you. Once again it is gathered into your heart centre and from there channelled down into the planet, raying forth beneath our feet to the Equator and then inward to the receptive Cup of the Grail. From there it rays out on all sides, striking upwards into the land masses of the seven continents, islanding them in a second band of light.

Now make another 90° turn towards the West where, across the depths of space, you see the constellation of the Scorpion, a creature sacred to the Goddess Isis. There, you see another dark red star, known as Antares. And, in the midst of the Scorpion, a glowing cube of light, each face of which represents one of the elements of which Creation is formed. As it turns, it rays out a great beam of light towards you, and you catch it and gather it into your heart centre, from where it flows through and down into the body of the planet which is still called by us 'Mother Earth'. There, as before, it reaches the points of the Equator on either side and is channelled inward to the great crystal Cup at the centre of the world. Caught up and sent forth again, it passes upwards until it reaches each of the seven continents, surrounding them in a third band of light, which glows ever brighter.

Turning once more 90° to the right, you now face true North, where you find the constellation of Piscis Australis, the great Cosmic Fish, in whose mouth glows the bright star Formahalt. Below the outline of the fish is the shape of a great Spear, the weapon which, in the story of the Grail was used to wound, but which now sends forth healing light towards you. You capture and distil it forth again from your heart centre, through your feet and into the earth, where the crystal Grail, the final shape it assumes in the the mystery of the Five Changes, waits to catch, and then send forth again, the light you perceive as passing through the earth and then outwards again to each of the seven great continents, building a fourth barrier of light around them.

For a moment hold these images as clearly as you can: see the outlines of the continents islanded in light, and know that this will bring harmony and peace to all who live there, and that the light binds all into a singly unified whole which is the earth. In this way the healing power of the Grail in each of its fine forms, is given back to the world a thousandfold, and you also, as a channel for its light, gain benefit from it.

Slowly now, as you watch, the light begins to fade from your sight – though it will continue to shine out in the inner world and do its work for the healing of the planet . . .

Become gradually aware again of your surroundings and awaken gently from the work of the meditation.

6 · THE LIVING HALLOWS:
KNIGHTHOOD FOR TODAY

A TIMELESS MYSTERY

What makes the Grail such an enduring symbol for the inner search is its continuing value for each and every age which has followed upon its first appearance in the world. Men and women have been seeking to plumb the mystery ever since, with varying degrees of success. We have seen something of the outer as well as the inner course which the stories have taken; now it is time to look in more detail at the reality of the experience which the Quest entails, first through the adventures of the original Quest Knights, and then through some contemporary accounts.

The Hallows of the Grail are living symbols of a very real Quest, in which many men and women are at present involved. This new knighthood is every whit as true and valid to the original precepts of chivalry, honour and the search for meaning as were the knights of the Round Table.

THE THREE WHO ACHIEVED

By the time of the *Vulgate Cycle*[56], the many stories relating to the Quest had been synthesised into a more detailed and specific set of allegories. This natural winnowing process left five major characters: three who were successful (though in a qualified way), and two who

The Hallows by William Ernest Chapman

failed (though spectacularly). The three successful questers were Galahad, son of Lancelot and the Grail Princess; Perceval, the 'oldest' of the three in terms of the Tradition; and Bors, who perhaps possesses the most human qualities. The pair termed unsuccessful are Lancelot and Gawain. The best way in which to arrive at the impact felt by the individual seeker for the Grail is to examine the roles of each of these five in turn.

GALAHAD

Galahad is a direct descendent, through his mother's family, of Joseph of Arimathea. He is, from the start, destined to achieve what no other knight of the Round Table could – to take the Grail in his hands to the Holy City of Sarras, and there to receive from the hands of the Grail's True Master the food of divine sustenance – at which point he dies, in what used to be termed 'an odour of sanctity', from the sweet aroma supposed to issue from the dead bodies of holy Saints. He had accomplished the work he was born to do and there was no longer any reason for him to remain.

But what are Galahad's special qualities, and how can an understanding of them help the modern seeker? First of all it is important to understand that Galahad is very much a product of the Middle Ages, of the cult of Saints, and of the deeply mystical approach to religion which typifies the age. Once this is properly understood much that appears strange or inhuman in the character of Galahad becomes surprisingly ordinary. Like Bors, he shows a single-minded determination for the task he has been bred for. No physical attack can overcome him, no temptation of the flesh beset him. It seems as though he could have walked straight into the Castle of the Grail without opposition and finished the Quest there and then. But, as has already been suggested, Galahad is seen as an aspect of Christ, and in this he shares a function of teaching by example – whether it consists of a buffet from the flat of a sword or an act of piety and Christian chivalry.

Thus he must accomplish the mysteries of the Quest as Christ accomplished those of his ministry. He is a clear case of someone who believes implicitly in their own destiny – as very few do today – and partly for this reason his path is the hardest to follow. Yet here is also a living embodiment of Divine Love (Agape) in operation: his perfection, as great as any earthly man can be expected to attain, is born out of a love for all of Creation. He needs to cure the wounds of the Fisher King and the Waste Land before he can enter into the higher mysteries of the Grail.

Galahad is, when all is said and done, little more than a cipher. As the Arthurian scholar Jean Frappier noted, he is 'the culmination of the desire to fuse Chivalry with Religion'[47]. His path is as clear as it could be: his coming, attended by signs and portents, his acquiring of arms, first sword and then shield of a special kind; his adventures, in which he proves himself the superior, both physically and spiritually, of his peers – all these mark him out as the destined Grail winner. Yet when he has done, when the great acts of affirmation, of healing and restoration have been accomplished, there is nothing left for him to do but die – his quest is crowned by this personal apotheosis which, though many might aspire to emulate it, few would actually meet with such whole hearted acceptance.

Thus, when he has partaken of the last mysteries, he takes leave of his companions: 'therewith he knelt down before the table of the Grail and made his prayers, and then suddenly his soul departed to Christ, and a great multitude of angels bore his soul up to heaven, that his two fellows might see it . . .' (Malory, Bk XVII. Ch. 23.)

Not many would attempt this route to the Grail; but lest we dismiss Galahad as a proto Saint, let us remember that his last thought is to ask his companions to 'remember me to my father Sir Lancelot and as soon as you see him bid him remember this unstable world', a message from which we might also benefit if we take the time to understand it. For Galahad the world is more than a cloak of flesh soon to be put off. It is a beautiful and rare place through which he moves with grace and

honesty and as much love as he can muster. It is a place worth dying
for. But he is his father's son also, direct and powerful and to the point
in all that he does. Behind the facade of this pious knight stands a very
human figure, from whom, if we wish, we can learn much.

PERCEVAL

Perceval, of course, was brought up in the depths of the forest, in
ignorance of such creatures as knights, or concepts such as chivalry.
But this was one of the characteristics which enabled the young hero
to come so near the centre of the mystery, so much so that he becomes
a future Guardian of the Grail. The other particular feature was his
simplicity – some would say his foolishness – which earned him the
title of the 'Perfect Fool'. This innocence of the world and of worldly
matters makes him impervious to the kind of temptations undergone
by both Galahad and Bors – to him women are like flowers, brightly
coloured creatures designed by nature to care for his needs and make
him laugh. He has, in fact, something of the primal innocence of our
first father, Adam.

His battles with other knights have a dreamlike quality, as though
such pursuits are of little importance to him – as is perhaps the case.
Indeed, like both his companions, he has a single minded approach
to the Quest which cuts across the various trials set before him almost
as though they were not there. It is as though Perceval lived always a
little bit in the otherworld.

This same absent-minded innocence gives rise to such incidents as
the 'blood in the snow' episode told by Chrétien de Troyes[15]. Here
Perceval becomes fascinated by the red blood and black feathers of
a bird which has made a kill in the snow. To the young hero they
are a reminder of his lady's colouring, her red lips, black hair and
white skin. He is so completely enraptured that he absent-mindedly
swipes several attackers from their saddles without even looking up.
Later on, in the episode where he arrives at the Grail Castle and fails
to ask the important question, he does so out of a curious mixture of
politeness and absentia.

It is this which constitutes much of Perceval's success. His chivalry
is both of this world and the other: he is a bridge between the worlds,
able to see into the mists and mysteries of the Faery realm as well as
into the harsher realities of daily life.

And this is indeed a most important function of the would-be
Grail seeker. To be able to relate the realms of the everyday and the
otherworldly into some kind of unity is to move close to the central

107

mystery of the Grail, the ability of which to do the same thing in non-finite terms is one of its greatest gifts. To have one foot in both worlds, the infinite and the mundane, is a blessed state and one which only the truly innocent generally attain.

One could even say that it is necessary to learn how to become truly 'foolish' before one can begin the Quest, for as long as we are enamoured of the 'serious reality' offered by the outside world, we can hardly begin to step outside ourselves in the manner necessary to perceive the Grail. Perceval's ability to do just this makes him a worthy successor to the line of the Grail Kings, and thus, after the achievements of Galahad and the temporary withdrawal of the mystic vessel, he is to be found once more entered into the Castle of the Grail. Here he takes up the role of the Fisher King until such time as a new seeker arrives with the keys of innocence and experience in his or her grasp — at which time Perceval, like his forebears, will step down, leaving the position open to the next initiate.

BORS

For various reasons there has been a tendency to overlook Bors in discussions of the successful candidates. He is generally considered the least romantic of the three, and as Lancelot's cousin lives always in the shadow of his more famous sibling. Also, he is the only one of the three who is actually married, with a child, at the time of the Quest. (Perceval marries later, when the Quest is over.) But Bors thus understands the nature and mystery of human love, of desire and procreation, in a way that neither of his companions ever can.

He is, then, in the world where they are only of it. This gives him a special degree of insight into the mystery as a whole which makes him the natural choice to be the one who returns to Camelot after the Quest is over, to relate all that has happened to Arthur and the rest of the world.

Bors, then, represents *earthly* chivalry, where Perceval stands for unearthly and Galahad for purely spiritual chivalry. He is the ordinary man whose aims are neither so high nor so lofty as his companions, but who is nonetheless raised by the power of the Grail to a position from which he may witness and experience the greater mysteries. As the poet Charles Williams put it:

Malory . . . does not say he was married. But he does say that he has a son by another Elayne (not the Grail Princess) . . . . But if we allow Sir Bors his marriage and his work in the world and his honest affections, see how perfect the companionship of the three lords becomes! There is the High Prince (Galahad), wholly devoted to his end in the Grail; and there is Perceval with his devout and selfless spiritual sister; and there is Bors with his wife and child. These are functions each of the others. The High Prince is at the deep centre, and the others move towards him; but also he operates in them towards the world. These are three degrees of love. Their conclusion is proper to them . . . Bors returns to Camelot, joins Lancelot, is made king, goes on a crusade, and in the last sentence of [Malory's] book dies . . . 'upon Good Friday, for God's sake'[90].

To carry this a step further, we may see the three knights as aspects of Christ. Bors is 'He that has come to bear witness to the truth', to the mystery itself; Perceval is 'He upon whom the Mystery shall be founded'; while Galahad, quite simply, undergoes the great transformations of the Grail in a manner that is the nearest any human being can come to sharing in the Crucifixion and Resurrection of the body. When he first goes aboard the Ship of Solomon, which is to carry him to the country of the Grail, he lies down on the bed made from the wood of the true Cross, thus emulating Christ in symbolic fashion even before he comes to the celebration of the mysteries at Sarras.

Bors, the witness, the 'man in the street', watches and observes everything with a kind of open mouthed wonder, almost bewilderment. He does not know why he has been chosen, or not even what he has been chosen for – yet he accepts, willingly, and treads the path of the Grail along a road which is often far harder for him *because* he is less spiritually-oriented than his fellows.

For this reason perhaps, his temptations are always more rigorous and produce the most dramatic effects. In Malory for example he is already feeling overwhelmed by being faced with a grim choice – that of rescuing his brother or a lady who was being carried off against her will. Bors had chosen the latter and as a result earns the bitter enmity of his brother. Now he is tested yet further when he comes to a castle where he is gently treated, given food and wine and then introduced to 'the richest lady and the fairest of all the world . . . more richly clothed than ever he saw Queen Guinevere or any other.' She is surrounded by fair ladies of her own who tell Bors that she will have no other man but he to be her champion. But there is more to it than this, for the lady then declares that she has always loved him, will do anything for him, so long as he does her will. But Bors is steadfast.

'Madam' said he, 'There is no lady in the world whose will I can fulfil in this way . . . ' 'Ah Bors', said she, 'I have loved you long for the great beauty I have seen in you, and the great strength I have heard of you, that needs must you lie with me this night, and therefore I pray you grant this to me.' 'Truely' said he, 'I shall not do it by no means.' Then she made such great sorrow as though she would have died. . . . And she departed and went up to a high battlement, and lead with her twelve gentlewomen; and when they were above, one of them cried out: 'Ah, Sir Bors, gentle knight have mercy on us all, and suffer my lady to have her way, for if you do not we must all suffer death by falling from this high tower. . . .' Then Bors looked up, and they seemed all ladies of great estate and beauty, and he had of them great pity, but he counselled himself that it were better for them to loose their souls than that he should loose his. . . . And with that they all fell down upon the earth, and Bors crossed himself . . . and anon he heard a great crying, and he saw neither tower or ladies, or castle, for all had vanished away as though they had never been.' (Malory, Bk XVII. Ch. 12.)[52]

This is, admittedly, an extreme example, and one which hardly puts Bors in a sympathetic light. He seems indeed far more concerned with his own well being than that of the supposed lady and her companions. Yet this is typical of his approach to the wonders and tests which happen to him: he comes to them with a solid, clear-eyed sensibility. He knows what is right with a kind of inner certainty, and he does his best to recognise it.

Such an approach may seem old-fashioned and moralistic; yet it shows a single-minded devotion to the Quest which puts Bors firmly among the three Grail winners because he is virtually *unable* to fail. He is typical of the kind of person who proceeds, steadily and cautiously, towards a goal he or she may be scarcely aware of; who follows the code of 'earthly chivalry' to the letter. He may seem unsympathetic – but then so does Galahad, who often follows the dictates of his faith so blindly that it is to the cost of others. What he, Bors and Perceval ultimately show us is that one has to trust to the inner directives of the Quest whatever the cost, and often without knowing for a long time after if one really did choose wisely. But then, the Quest is not expected to be easy, and neither are the tests which its participants undergo.

LANCELOT

So much for the successful candidates; but what of the two who failed? It is difficult not to feel greater sympathy for these, who seem

110

altogether more human and down-to-earth than their peers. Both, Lancelot especially, aim high, throwing their not inconsiderable abilities into the effort to be Grail winners. Lancelot, according to the Christian tradition in which the texts relating to his failure were written, is a 'fallen' man, one who has become very deeply enmeshed in the glamour of the world, and has allowed an image of human perfection (Guinevere) to supplant the image of God. Thus, his open heartedness, his willingness to set all his earthly desires aside to climb the spiritual heights of the Grail mountain, where the temple of the mysteries is situated, but where so few ever come, is not enough.

Throughout texts such as Malory's Morte d'Arthur[52] or the Queste[56] this point is laboured again and again. As, for instance, when Lancelot, early on in the quest, comes to a cross road and poses to rest there:

'. . . and so he fell asleep; and half waking and half sleeping he saw come by him two horses all fair and white; bearing between them a litter, in which lay a sick knight. And when he was close to the Cross, he paused. All this Sir Lancelot saw for he slept only lightly. And he heard the knight say: 'O Sweet Lord, when shall this sorrow leave me? And when shall the Holy Vessel come to me, through which I shall be blessed? For I have endured long without committing any evil. . . .' Then Sir Lancelot saw a candlestick with six lights come before the cross, though no one brought it there that he could see. Also there came a Table of silver, and the Holy vessel. . . . And the sick knight sat up and held out his hands and said: 'Fair Sweet Lord, who art here with this vessel, take heed of my need that I may be made whole'. And he went on his hands and knees to the vessel and kissed it, and immediately he was made whole and gave thanks. (Bk VIII. Ch.18.)

All this Lancelot sees but is unable to move or speak, so that he cannot tell if he is dreaming or not. But apparently the sick knight can see something which remains hidden from Lancelot, which enables him to be healed. He then comments to his squire that the knight lying close by (Lancelot) must be a great sinner since he is unable to do homage to the Grail. Then, lacking either sword or helmet of his own he takes Lancelot's, along with his horse, which is a better mount than his own.

'Then Sir Lancelot awoke, and sat up, and considered what he had seen and whether or not it was a dream. And then he heard a voice that said 'Sir Lancelot – more hard than the stone, more bitter than the wood, and more naked than the leaf of the fig tree art thou: therefore go hence and withdraw from this holy place.' (ibid.)

So Lancelot departs, and discovers that his horse, sword and helm are gone, from which he understands that it was no simple dream that he experienced. And he realises that he is too sinful to achieve the Quest because, in his own words: 'All my great deeds of arms, I did for the Queen's sake, and for her sake I did battle were it right or wrong, and never did I battle only for God's sake, but to win worship and be the better beloved.' (ibid.)

All Lancelot's strength has been channelled towards winning greater fame or attracting the attention of Guinevere; of acts done for their own sake or out of love for God he knows nothing. Thus, even when he does attempt an act of selfless goodness for the most honest of reasons, he is struck down.

This adventure takes place late in the Quest – for he does not give up, even though he now doubts his own abilities. Like many before and since he continues his course without hope of success, and thus comes close to achieving his desire. He reaches the very door of the Grail chapel and looks within. . . .

Then looked he to the middle of the chamber and saw a table of silver, and the Holy vessel, covered with red samite and with many angels about it. . . . And before the altar he saw a good man dressed as a priest, and it seemed he was celebrating the Mass. . . . And it seemed to Lancelot that there were three men there, and two put the youngest between the Priest's hands, who lifted him up high. . . . And then Lancelot marvelled that the Priest could hold up so great a load . . . and when none came forward to help him . . . he entered into the chamber and came towards the table of silver . . . and there came a great breath of air, all mixed with fire, which smote him . . . so that he fell to earth and had no power to rise, and lost the power of movement, and of hearing and of sight . . . (Malory, Bk. XVII. Ch. 15.)

Even then, out of a desire to help, Lancelot is not permitted to approach the holy things; good intentions are not enough for the Grail seeker, it is necessary to believe, to an almost terrifying degree, in the Quest itself, and to exclude all other things, however honourable, from the mind.

But Lancelot is given a kind of forgiveness. It is his son, Galahad, who finally achieves the Quest. Indeed it is hard to forget, once one has read it, the description of the meeting of father and son on the mysterious Ship of Solomon, where they are permitted to spend some time together and to talk as father and son should.

From that point onwards one knows that Lancelot will never reach a successful conclusion in his search, but that Galahad is destined to succeed, in some way, for him. And this is surely one of the most astonishing and moving parts in the whole story – for we must remember that Galahad is begotten upon the Grail Princess Elaine through Lancelot's being made to think she is Guinevere! Even out of the depths of Lancelot's fault comes healing, the child who will one day outshine his father in the greatest adventure of all.

GAWAIN

Gawain is a different matter. For him, except in a single version of the Quest story, there is scarcely even the chance of achievement. Yet there is a reason to believe that Gawain was once the original Grail winner, in the time before it became Christianised. Then, as I have shown elsewhere[63] Gawain was the Knight of the Goddess rather than of the Virgin as he later became. This places him in a unique position as one who bridges the gap between the Christian and Pagan images of the Grail, and makes him especially important as a subject for deeper study on the part of modern day questers.

In the version of the story given by Chrétien de Troyes, Gawain does indeed find a way to the enchanted castle where the Grail is kept, but like Perceval before him he fails to ask the question which will set in motion the healing of the Waste Land and the Wounded King. Yet he still achieves more than Lancelot, for he does remark upon the Spear which drips blood which is carried in the Grail procession, and this is sufficient to undo some of the harm done to the land through the striking of the Dolorous Blow.

But Gawain still fails to ask more and is deemed unworthy to succeed further. Instead his quest becomes one for the sword of Judas Maccabeus, or sometimes for that which beheaded John the Baptist. But the sword is always broken, and Gawain's task is to discover how to unite the two pieces of the blade. Only after many adventures is he able to do so. For Gawain's fault is impatience, the kind of behaviour which results, right at the beginning of his career, in his beheading an innocent woman who had begged for his help. Thereafter, perhaps not unrelatedly, Gawain is plagued by women, and gains the reputation of a libertine. Yet this is actually an unfair judgement, since he was also famed for his courtesy towards all women, and through his service to the Goddess saw all aspects of the feminine as representatives of deity.

Time has done a considerable disservice to this great knight, who once occupied a place superior to that of Lancelot, and may well have been the Queen's champion before him. A nephew of King Arthur, he was brave, honest and a great fighter in the cause of right. Yet at some point he fell from popularity, perhaps because of the lingering association with paganism, and thereafter literary judgement relegated him to a subordinate position which he never wholly lost.

Thus in Malory's version we find him, late upon the Quest, riding with Ector de Maris, Lancelot's brother. Both complain that they have met with no good adventures, or indeed seen anything of the wonders and marvels promised at the start of the Quest. They arrive at a ruined chapel and decide to rest there. Both have a dream-vision which tell us a good deal about the nature of their failure and the success of the other three.

> Sir Gawain seemed to come into a meadow full of herbs and flowers, and there he saw a herd of one hundred and fifty bulls, that were proud and black, save for three of them, that were all white, and one had a black spot, but the other two were so fair that they might be no whiter. . . . And the black bulls said, among themselves, 'Let us go forth to seek better pasture', and some went and came again, but they were so thin they could hardly stand; but of the three bulls that were white only one returned. . . . And Sir Ector saw himself and his brother Sir Lancelot getting upon their horses, and one said to the other, 'Let us go seek that which we shall not find'. And then he seemed to see that a man beat Sir Lancelot, and despoiled him and put old and torn clothing on him and set him upon an ass. And so he rode until he came to a well, but when he would have drunk from it, the water sank down and he could get no sustenance. (Malory, Bk XVI. Ch.1–2.)

This is straightforward allegory, and tells of the working out of a prophecy made by Merlin at the founding of the Round Table – that many would search for the Grail but few find it. And when asked how this might be he replied:

> . . . that there should be three white bulls that should achieve it, and the two should be maidens, and the third should be chaste. And that one of the three should pass his father as much as the lion passes the strength of the leopard. (ibid. Bk XIV. Ch. 2.)

Merlin is of course referring to the three successful knights, two of whom, Galahad and Perceval, were considered sinless and virgin, and

Bors, who is chaste but married. Galahad is the lion who surpasses his father the leopard. But of Gawain there is once again no mention.

DINDRAINE

No consideration of the Grail seekers would be complete without some mention of a fourth character, who also made the journey to Sarras with the Grail, and who was with the knights who carried the miraculous vessel to its final destination. This is Perceval's sister, sometimes referred to as Dindraine. Her story is simple and brief. Brought up, like her brother, in ignorance of the world, she joins the three knights on the Ship of Solomon when they already have the Grail on board and are journeying to the Holy City. On the way they stop at a castle where the custom is that any virgin who travels that way must give some of her blood to heal the lady of the castle, who is sick with leprosy. The Grail knights would have defended Dindraine to the death, but she willingly offers her own blood as a sacrifice – for such it becomes with her subsequent death. The lady of the castle is healed however, and we can see here a foreshadowing of the healing actions of the Grail itself.

Much can, and has, been written of this episode. Some have chosen to see it as an allegory of Christian sacrifice[44], others have sought deeper anthropological or psychological meanings in menstrual customs or the right of women to serve at the rite of the Eucharist[61]. It is perhaps more appropriate, in the context of the story, to see her as the embodiment of feminine wisdom, completing the quaternity of Grail winners and representing the ability to create new life.

As a recent commentator has put it, this: 'hints at the inner identity of the woman's menstrual blood, which tells her that she has not yet conceived, with the blood of the wounded Grail King, bleeding because he cannot bring to life the [dead land]'[61]. *Arg + Barf*

There is much in the story of Dindraine that is mysterious beyond even the Grail itself, which touches upon the role of the Divine Feminine in the mysteries. It will repay considerable meditation by those who undertake the path to the Grail, and it is of course particularly important in that it demonstrates that the new knights do not have to be male. *Ha Ha, Ha! ~~1990~~ the date? 1987-90? Says quite a bit Zero!*

THE GRAIL EXPERIENCE

When one has looked at the image from every angle, meditated upon it, read the texts and travelled the inner roads, looked in depth at the way in which the individual knights approached the quest, it is, finally, the individual experience which matters most. No matter whether it is apocalyptic or personal, each encounter is relevant in some way to the work of the Grail in the world. There follow two very different reports of such experiences. It is hoped that these accounts may give an idea of the scope of realisation and healing which can come from working with the Grail.

The first report comes from a young woman who had suffered for most of her life from overshadowing memories of her childhood. Things finally reached crisis point, where she felt no longer able to continue with her life as it then was. What followed is told in her own words.

CASE HISTORY ONE

'Previously I had been to Butleigh, near Glastonbury and had had a very vivid experience. This entailed looking at my whole past with a cold but clear eye. I knew that archetypally this corresponded to looking at the Gorgon's face which might turn me to stone or make me mad. I nearly did go mad because things that had happened to me in my childhood were really horrific. I felt that I was standing at the eye of the storm, the very centre of the Wasteland. I felt absolutely desperate. I also knew that Butleigh was the centre of the Glastonbury Zodiac [see Chapter 1] and thus that it must also be the centre of balance and home of the potential Grail. I felt very strongly that this was a place where all worlds were accessible – the hub of the wheel.

'I could see no way out of my extreme unhappiness but to call upon St Michael as "judger of souls", either to let me die or find the Grail. Being in a way one of the raped Well-Maidens [see Chapter 1], sexually ravaged and also "heart-broken", there was no way out. I was very aware of the reality of the Wasteland, and that I could not even commit suicide in order to rest, as I would take my torment with me.

'I went back to London, and there had a Grail experience of an unusually sustained and vivid kind (for me). I saw the door of a church, which I recognised as being at Eweleme in Oxfordshire. I had visited it several times and always felt it contained a mystery, but had not even thought of it for a couple of years. I went inside, and the interior was full of light. In front of the high altar stood St Catherine ablaze with white and golden light. In one hand she held a white sword, her other rested upon a blazing wheel. Beside her stood St George, in white and silver, but passive. Above St Catherine was suspended a rose cup surrounded by golden light.

'Suddenly a massive black hand smashed through the East window. Instinctively I put a seal on the window, banished the hand and moved the "Grail" away into the centre of the church. I did not understand what it was, and thought of a negative, outside force trying to steal the Grail.

'St Catherine handed me the sword, and I knew this meant that I could use it from then on to defend myself – to keep negative forces away from the Grail. St Catherine pointed to the West end wall. On it was a painting of a green cross with golden drops in the background. I recognised this as the emblem of St Helen – the living cross with drops of honey amber. (Afterwards I found it was also the emblem of Joseph of Arimathea.) At the centre of the cross was a rose, which I knew was also the heart of the Grail. Then the black hand smashed through the wall again and grasped the rose.

'I tried to understand what this meant, and decided it must be a symbol of dark, archaic forces, so must be accepted and acknowledged rather than banished. As soon as I had mentally done this, the black hand divided into two, which cupped the rose. Then a dove flew out and upwards and the wall-painting changed so that it now depicted a withered, blackened tree. I knew this was a symbol of me and my life; that my roots, both in this incarnation and in many past ones, were rotten; that rather than heal the "rape", I had attracted the same pattern again and again, thus doing more damage.

'I can't remember quite what I did next. Somehow I mentally released the negativity, made an affirmation of willingness to change. At one point I remember the church door opening and faery people coming in, one in the form of a badger which dug out the roots of the blackened tree. The whole wall then crumbled and fell down, revealing a green, flowering tree behind.

'Then I was outside in the churchyard, sitting on the grass, earthing myself. All around me were animals and faery people. I felt at home, released.

'Two days later a friend told me that "death had gone from my face" and that there was now "a Grail in my heart". I saw the experience as meaning that I do still have a potential chance of happiness and love which I did not have before, rather than some great spiritual achievement. I remembered seeing my own right hand as black for the last few months, and had been worried that I was going to get a disease or that it would somehow be damaged. And I remembered drawing a picture of the Lady of the Grail after I had seen a vision of her in the lane behind Eweleme church years ago. She was woman rather than maiden, as usually depicted – fulfilled rather than virginal.'

117

The next report comes from an experienced practitioner of the inner magical path, who demonstrates in this account how deeply the imagery of the Grail can strike, and how much can be learned from it.

'In the Spring of 1983 I undertook a series of meditations which took the form of colloquies with an Inner guide. After the dialogue stage came the envisioning. As anyone who has ever meditated will know, this last process is often stubbornly non-productive and boring.

'On 19 March, the day of this particular meditation, I was aware of St Joseph of Arimathea, who shares with St Joseph the Carpenter, this feast-day in the church's calendar. St Joseph of Arimathea is credited with bringing the Grail, or rather more traditionally, two cruets containing the blood and sweat of Christ: the "blood and water", which came from his side at the crucifixion when his side was pierced by Longinus' spear.

'The image was drawn into the meditation wherein I was told that "we must combat the unleashed wildness in the blood". With these words came a picture of chaotic upheaval, of presumptuous pride and unregenerate influences. In short, I was aware of a video of the Fall of Atlantis running in my head. This event, whether one sees it as a mythical or historical happening, lies behind the esoteric tradition as the great admonitory story, just as the Judaeo-Christian Fall is at the basis of orthodox spirituality as a reminder that we continually fail to take responsibility for our actions and must abide the consequences.

'I asked my Inner guide, "How are we to control these influences?" He replied: "Firstly recognise these influences in your own lives. Then transfer them to the receptacle of the Moon Ark of the Grail."

'As I registered these words, I was aware of a feeling so deep, so piercing, that it was as though a child had taken root in my womb. Most mothers will know what this feels like: it is the almost indefinable yet unmistakable presence of life within one's own body. It was a moment as precious to me as the Blessed Virgin's Annunciation by the Angel of the Holy Spirit. The feeling preceded the image of the Moon Ark itself.

'It appeared to me as a pair of hands cupping an orb which pulsed with liquescent, luminous light which was also a singing harmony. I was in no doubt that I was in the presence of the most ancient symbolic appearance of the Grail itself.

'All meditators will testify that such experiences come in a great knot of image, perception, recognition and unfolding which is like a lightening flash of supra-normal comprehension. All artists perceive their creative impulse in a similar way: they see it fully manifest, completely achieved, even though they may not yet have fashioned it with their hands. It was so that the following understandings were clear to me: in a moment of illumination, though the writing down took a little longer.

'The Moon Ark was an energy transformer, a purifier which acted as clearing house for psychic debris. As it had originated in the Moon Temple of Atlantis, which never suffered from the corruption which had sent that mythic civilization plunging to the depths of the sea, it was a vessel of supreme purity. Within this vessel, the life-force, bearing the spark of divinity, could be transferred to each newly-engendered soul. This explained why I felt I had physically conceived. I gathered that this symbol had been ritually used in meditation by priests and priestesses over many generations and that, by virtue of this symbol, they understood the mysteries of engendering. There was nothing sinister or smacking of eugenics about this understanding: theirs was profound guardianship of the seeds of life. And now I had had the same experience, I was changed and charged with purpose. As in the Gnostic teaching story, The Song of the Pearl, where the soul takes flesh and descends into incarnation in a series of didactic experiences, so the Moon-Ark was a perfect paradigm of initiation into the spiritual mysteries. As the Platonic form of the medieval Grail, it was a vessel of regeneration more powerful than anything I had ever imagined.

'I meditated upon it frequently over the following months, visualising it as a shallow, crescent-shaped bowl with a round disc hovering over it. I came to see that it was a profoundly simple symbol with staggering implications. As I sat in meditation before its visualised image, the Moon Ark taught me many things. It worked by the power of exchange of energies: whatever went into it came out transformed. It was no good just sitting and looking at it, being totally passive. One had to have an exchange.

'It was Caryll Houselander, a Catholic mystic of the forties, who pointed out that for Christ to work miracles he first of all required the raw material with which to work: using spittle to make paste with which to cure a blind man, an affirmation of regret and repentance in order to heal the afflicted. It is so that the Grail works: Perceval, instructed that it is impolite to ask questions, fails to ask the all-important Grail question by which the Wounded King and the Waste Land will be healed in one stroke, just as they were originally wounded by the Dolorous Blow. The Grail Question is the antithesis of the Spear Which Heals and Wounds. So it is with the Moon-Ark. One must give in order to receive. One must be healed before one can heal others. This is the service of the Grail.'

THE QUEST

Having looked at the nature of the Grail Questers, successful and otherwise, let us now look at the Quest itself as it appears from a contemporary perspective.

It is possible, as has been the case throughout this book, to view the search for the Grail as necessary. It was, after all, active in restoring the Waste Land and the Wounded King, who are really symbols for the wounds in Creation itself, made waste by our inability to understand the Divine purpose. So the argument goes. But we must also be able to see it all in another way – as neither necessary nor indeed desirous. In this way it is possible to see fresh aspects of the stories which may have been obscured by a natural reverence for the subject of the Quest.

So let us not forget that the Quest for the Grail resulted in the deaths of many of its seekers, the humiliation of others; or that it hastened the breaking of the Round Table fellowship by giving its adversaries opportunity to fill the empty places at the Table with their own supporters; and that the Quest ultimately broke the spirit of men like Lancelot and Gawain, so that they were no longer able to resist the tide of darkness which swept in upon them from all sides, and perhaps raged within them as well. For them the Grail was hardly a good thing at all.

Again, Galahad's victory was a purely personal apotheosis; He is able to ascend to heaven, as Malory says 'with a great multitude of angels', while Perceval remains to take up the burden of guarding the Grail, and Bors returns to his old life as though, in some way, nothing had happened. Furthermore, if Perceval does indeed return to the castle of the Grail to become its new warden, then in effect the Quest has been for nothing . . .

This point is raised not to shock but to indicate the different ways in which it is possible to view the Grail Quest, and to show how we may learn something more from a mingling of such approaches. Yes, we can say, the Quest was a failure; it brought destruction in its wake and did nothing for the general good of more than a few people. Or we can look at it another way and say again: the Grail is for all time, and by choosing not to work more than an occasional miracle or so, it leaves the Quest open, a challenge to all who come after.

Obviously the second answer is the one we should prefer. But is it, finally, any more valid than the first? The Grail is a mystery, as few would deny. As one commentator (Joseph Campbell) put it: why should one need to go in search of God (or the Grail) when he was present on every altar of every church in the land?[10] But the Grail is not common only to Christian belief: it is sought, in different guises, in many other parts of the world as we have seen. It is there to be sought, even though it eludes discovery – perhaps until the end of time.

It is time which is important here. It goes with the realisation that there is a right time and a wrong time to go in search of the Grail. Arthur's time, the age of the Round Table, whether we take that as an inner reality or a reflection of the ideals of chivalry, was the wrong time. The apparitions and wonders of the Quest are activated by the seekers themselves, as much as by the high powers which control the Grail. Their experience, even their defeat, if such it was, is not wasted. We can learn from it just as we can learn from any great spiritual teaching. Indeed we might think of it as a sublime example from which we can all learn – from both success and failure.

Like all inner impulses – and the Grail, however else we may see it, is most certainly this – it has its own purpose, which we may not always recognise. One aspect only of this may be see in the transformative energy of the Grail, its ability to make things other. No one who goes in search of it remains unchanged, and if it had no greater purpose than this it would be sufficient to fulfil its existence.

One further quotation sums up the direction which the Quester sooner or later seems to take. It comes from a Gnostic text, the Gospel of Thomas, translated by Gilles Quispel:

Let not him who seeks cease until he finds,
and when he finds he shall be astonished.

It is that degree of astonishment, of surprise, which above all else marks out the Grail mystery. If you have not yet come upon, it is hoped that you will do so, and that it will be as great a reward as you could wish for.

EXERCISE 6: WORKING WITH THE GRAIL

How can we best work with what we learn from the Grail? The exercises throughout this book are designed to promote a direct and personal experience of the mysteries we have been discussing.

They are, however, only a beginning. There are groups throughout the country working with the Arthurian and Grail streams. The present author, together with Caitlin Matthews, gives regular courses every year at Hawkwood College in Gloucestershire, and there are plans to produce a Grail Course in the near future. (For further information write to: BCM Hallowquest, London WC1N 3XX.)

The following exercise is part of a body of received material given at a course for the Wrekin Trust in March 1989.

One of the most basic forms of sickness common to humanity is soul-loss. It is so common that few either know of it nor recognise it. Yet it is a fact that many people are without souls, they have lost touch with their true inner selves. In the same way the earth itself has suffered a wounding through the terrible afflictions which humanity have laid upon it, wounding it in the soul also.

The way towards healing lies first and foremost in the recognition of soul-loss and soul-damage. The Grail can help to restore both of these, on a planetary level and on a personal level. For a planetary level envisage the following: a Grail of light at the centre of the earth, which emits rays forming a penumbra, a soul-envelope around the planet. For personal healing from the Grail, envisage three aspects of the Cup one above the other and superimpose them upon the body. The lowest of the three represents the heart, the middle cup the mind, the highest the soul. When all three are brimming with light, and when the light pours over and irradiates the body, then healing will begin. Finally to unify the two aspects of healing, envisage the Goddess, in whatever form is most pleasing, standing at the centre of a maze of light, holding out her cupped hands which brim with water and light. Approach her and drink from her hands so that you imbibe wisdom, strength and joy from the wells which never run dry. For she herself is a Damsel of the Wells, is **all** damsels of the wells, and she ever continues to offer her Cup to all who are weary from travelling upon the road.

BIBLIOGRAPHY

(All titles were published in London, unless otherwise stated.)

1. Adolf, H. *Visio Pacis: Holy City and Grail* Pennsylvania State University Press, 1960
2. Ancorna, S.G. *The Substance of Adam* Rider & Co., 1934.
3. Ashe, G. *King Arthur's Avalon* Fontana, 1973.
4. Bernard of Clairvaux *On the Song of Songs* Cistercian Pubs., 1976.
5. Bernard of Clairvaux *Treatise in Praise of the New Knighthood* Cistercian Pubs. 1977.
6. Bryant, N. *The High Book of the Grail* D.S. Brewer, Cambridge, 1978.
7. Bryce, D. *The Mystical Way and the Arthurian Quest* Llanerch Enterprises, Llanerch, Dyfed, 1986.
8. Burckhardt, T. *Alchemy* Element Books, 1987.
9. Campbell, J. *The Inner Reaches of Outer Space* Alfred van der Marck Editions, New York, 1985.
10. Campbell, J. *Myths to Live By* Souvenir Press, 1973.
11. Campbell, D. E. Trans. *The Tale of Balain* Northwestern University Press, Evanston, 1972.
12. Cavendish, R. *King Arthur and the Grail* Weidenfeld & Nicholson, 1978.
13. Chrétien De Troyes, *Arthurian Romances* Trans. by D.D.R. Owen. J.M. Dent, 1987.

14. Cooper, J.C. *An Illustrated Encyclopaedia of Traditional Symbols* Thames and Hudson, 1978.
15. Cooper-Oakley, I. *Masonry and Medieval Mysticism* Theosophical Publishing House, 1977.
16. Cross, F.L. *Oxford Dictionary of the Christian Church* Oxford University Press, 1978.
17. Currer-Briggs, N. *The Shroud and the Grail* Weidenfeld & Nicholson, 1987.
18. Day, Mildred Leake, [Ed & Trans.] *The Story of Meriadoc, King of Cumbria* Garland, New York, 1988.
19. De Sede, G. *La Rose Croix* J'ai Lu, Paris, 1978.
20. De Sede, G. *Les Templiers* J'ai Lu, Paris, 1969.
21. De Rougemont, D. *Passion and Society*. Faber & Faber, 1955.
22. Evans, S. *In Quest of the Holy Grail* J.M.Dent, 1898.
23. Fortune, D. *Applied Magic* Aquarian Press, 1962.
24. *The Golden Blade* Issue No. 33. Rudolf Steiner Press, 1981.
25. Gantz, J. Trans. *The Mabinogion* Penguin Books, Harmondsworth, 1985.
26. Gardner, E. *Arthurian Legends in Italian Literature* Octagon Books, New York 1971.
27. Gerald of Wales *Journey Through Wales* Penguin Books, 1978.
28. Geoffrey of Monmouth: *The History of the Kings of Britain* Trans. by Lewis Thorpe, Penguin Books, Harmondsworth, 1966.
29. Geoffrey of Monmouth: *The Vita Merlini* Trans. by J.J. Parry, University of Illinois, 1925.
30. Gogan, L.S. *The Ardagh Chalice* Brown & Nolan, Dublin, 1932.
31. Grossinger, R. (Ed.) *The Alchemical Tradition* North Atlantic Books, California, 1983.
32. Gryffydd, W.J. *Math vab Mathonwy* University of Wales Press, 1928.
33. Gryffydd, W.J. *Rhiannon* University of Wales Press, 1953.
34. Guest, Lady C. *The Mabinogion* John Jones, Cardiff, 1977.
35. Hall, M.P. *Orders of the Quest: The Holy Grail* The Philosophical Research Soc., Los Angeles, 1976.
36. Heinrich von den Tulen *The Crown* Trans. D.W. Thomas, University of Nebraska Press, Nebraska, 1989.
37. Johnson, P. *History of Christianity* Peregrine, 1978.
38. Jung E. & M.-L. Von Franz *The Grail Legends* Hodder & Stoughton, 1971.
39. Karr. P.A. *The King Arthur Companion*. Chaosium Inc., Albany, 1983.

40. Kennedy, B: *Knighthood in the Morte d'Arthur* D.S. Brewer, Cambridge, 1986.
41. Knight, G. *The Secret Tradition in Arthurian Legend* Aquarian Press, 1983.
42. Lacy, N.J. & G. Ashe *The Arthurian Handbook* Garland Publishing Inc. New York, 1986.
43. Lambert, M.D. *Medieval Heresy* Arnold, 1977.
44. Lang-Simms, L *The Christian Mystery* Allen & Unwin, 1981.
45. Lievegoed, B.C.J. *Mystery Streams in Europe and the New Mysteries* Anthroposophic Press, New York, 1982.
46. Lindsay, J. *The Troubadours and Their World* Frederick Muller, 1982.
47. Loomis, R.S. *The Development of Arthurian Romance* N.Y. Norton, 1963.
48. Loomis, R.S. *Celtic Myth & Arthurian Romance.* Columbia University Press, New York, 1927.
49. Loomis, R.S. *Wales & the Arthurian Legend* University of Wales Press, 1956.
50. Macgregor, R. *Indiana Jones and the Last Crusade* Sphere, 1989.
51. Magre, M. *The Return of the Magi* Sphere Books, 1957.
52. Malory, Sir Thomas, *Le Morte d'Arthur* University Books, New York, 1961.
53. *The Mabinogion* Trans. by Lady Charlotte Guest, The Folio Society, 1980.
54. Marie De France, *Lais* Trans. by G. S. Burgess and K. Busby, Penguin Books, Harmondsworth, 1986.
55. Markale, J. *King Arthur King of Kings* Gordon Cremonesi, 1977.
56. Matarasso, P. *The Quest of the Grail* Penguin Books, Harmondsworth, 1969.
57. Matthews, C. *Arthur and the Sovereignty of Britain* Arkana, 1989.
58. Matthews, C. *Mabon and the Mysteries of Britain,* Arkana, 1987.
59. Matthews, C. *Elements of Celtic Tradition* Element Books, 1989.
60. Matthews, J. *An Arthurian Reader* Aquarian Press, 1988.
61. Matthews, J. *At the Table of the Grail* Arkana, 1987.
62. Matthews, J. *Elements of Arthurian Tradition* Element Books, 1989.
63. Matthews, J. *Gawain, Knight of the Goddess* Aquarian Press, 1990.

64. Matthews, J. *The Household of the Grail* Aquarian Press, 1990.

65. Matthews, J. *The Grail, Quest for Eternal Life* Thames & Hudson, 1981.

66. Matthews, J. *Taliesin: Shamanic Mysteries in Britain and Ireland* Unwin Hyman, 1990.

67. Matthews, J. & C. *The Arthurian Tarot: A Hallowquest*, Aquarian Press, 1990.

68. Matthews, J & Green, M. *The Grail Seekers Companion* Aquarian Press, 1988.

69. Matthews, J. and Stewart, R.J. *Warriors of Arthur* Blandford Press, Poole, 1987.

70. Morduch, A. *The Sovereign Adventure* James Clarke, 1970.

71. Morizot, P. *The Templars* Anthroposophical Publishing Company, 1960.

72. Newstead, H. *Bran the Blessed in Arthurian Romance* Columbia University Press, New York, 1939.

73. Oldenbourg, Z. *Massacre at Montsegur* Weidenfeld, 1961.

74. Pearshall, L.B. *The Art of Narration in Wolfram's Parzifal & Albrecht's Jungerer Titurel* Cambridge University Press, 1981.

75. Pultarch, *Moralia* Trans. by F.C. Babbitt. Heinemann, 1957.

76. Rolt-Wheeler, F. *Mystic Gleams From the Holy Grail* Rider, 1945.

77. Runciman, S. *The Medieval Manichee* Cambridge University Press, 1969.

78. Skeeles, D. *The Romance of Perceval in Prose* University of Washington Press, Seattle, 1966.

79. Slessarev, V. *Prester John: The Letter* University of Minessota Press, Mineapolis, 1959.

80. Stein, W.J. *The Ninth Century and the Holy Grail* Temple Lodge Press, 1989.

81. Steiner, R. *Christ and the Spiritual World, and The Search for the Holy Grail* Rudolph Steiner Press, 1963.

82. Stewart, R.J. *The Prophetic Vision of Merlin* Arkana, 1986.

83. Stewart, R.J. *The Mystic Life of Merlin*, Arkana, 1986.

84. Topsfield, L.T. *Chrétien de Troyes: A Study of Arthurian Romance.* Cambridge University Press, 1981.

85. Travers, P.L. *What the Bee Knows* Aquarian Press, 1989.

86. Walker, G.B. *Diffusions* The Research Publishing Co. 1976.

87. Waite, E.A. *The Holy Kabbalah* University Books, New York, 1972.

88. Ware, K. *The Orthodox Church* Penguin Books, 1963.

89. Weston, J.L. *From Ritual to Romance* Doubleday, New York, 1957.

90. Williams, C. *The Descent of the Dove* Faber & Faber, 1939.

91. Wilson, I. *The Turin Shroud* Gollancz, 1979.

92. Wolfram von Eschenbach *Parzival* Trans. by A. Hatto, Penguin Books, Harmondsworth, 1980.

See Green Glass dish = Emerald?

INDEX

Page 51 - green glass dish

When Did It Start for You?

how a car becomes a legend, by the fans of america's sports car

When Did It Start for You?

When Did It Start for You?

how a car becomes a legend, by the fans of america's sports car

Effingham, Illinois

When Did It Start For You?
By Mid America Direct, Inc.

Published by
  Mid America Direct, Inc.
  One Mid America Place
  PO Box 1368
  Effingham, IL 62401-1368
  (217) 347-5591
  E-mail: mail@madvet.com

Library of Congress Catalog Number: 00-100770

ISBN: 1-930613-00-8
Production Editors: Jennifer Altstadt and Cam Benty
Cover Design and Page Layout: Kim Deters

Table of Contents

When Did It Start for You?

Acknowledgements

Thanks to each and every one of this publication's 90 authors. Your active participation in the hobby and strong enthusiasm have brought "When Did It Start for You?" Volume I to life. The undying passion expressed within these pages has created a world-class sports car.

Supporters of the Corvette hobby, along with all of our fellow enthusiasts deserve similar recognition.

Cam Benty of Benty & Associates should also be acknowledged for both his editing resources and publishing references, along with Mid America's own Creative Team.

Thank you all!

Mike Yager

When Did It Start for You?

Introduction

"I will always remember my first Corvette sighting. It was May, 1963, and I was in the eighth grade..."

Needless to say, this car made an impression on me that has lasted a lifetime. For over 25 years, I've based my career on it, accumulated a Corvette collection numbering 40+ and met some of the most noted Chevrolet/GM dignitaries in the life of America's true sports car.

First, let me back up and explain that with six older brothers, cars always played a big part in my life growing up. My first project car, a '26 Model T, initiated my overall interest in cars.

But it wasn't until that day in '63 that a car, a 1962 Corvette, would ignite full-blown passion.

I was with my older brother, Frank, who at the time was our family's Corvette fanatic, when we spotted that fateful 1962.

We were actually on our way home from St. Louis, but I can remember precisely where the sighting took place...by the Pillsbury plant along the eastbound highway we were traveling. In my small hometown, I had never seen a Corvette before this day, but from that point on the image would never leave my mind.

And so my Corvette obsession began...only to be fueled by any automotive publication I could find. In the meantime Frank had purchased a 1960 the fever was now at full throttle! My own first Vette was only a couple of years away.

In September 1970, I sealed the deal on a 1967 Corvette roadster - a small block with side pipes and a four-speed. This '67 also symbolically served as the very first headquarters for Mid America (Enterprises, as it was first named), where items were shipped and received for my burgeoning side business. At the time, I was a full-time tool & die maker in Effingham,

IL. By 1972 I had also started a local Corvette club, served as its president and represented it in the NCCC as governor.

As you can see, the Corvette had evolved into much more than a car for me...it was, and remains to this day, a lifestyle. In 1974, the passion took another bold turn with the official birth of Mid America Enterprises. Founded on a $500 bank loan, I was confident that Mid America would fill a void in the marketplace and that my passion would take us the rest of the way. The ingredients were there so in 1976, I quit my day job in Effingham to dedicate all my time to the Corvette aftermarket business.

Fast-forward a little over 2 1/2 decades, and Mid America Designs has become the world's leading supplier of Corvette entertainment. During this time, I've always contended that I don't have to go to work everyday...I GET to go to work everyday. Today, my wife, Laurie, my sons Michael & Blake and

I are all very much involved in the hobby. In fact, the "When Did It Start for You?" ad campaign, shown on these pages, featuring our boys, is the foundation for this book.

Special thanks go to each and every one of our customers who contributed. While your stories all spin their own unique tales, the central theme of each revolves around Corvette pride, passion and longevity. For myself, I like to think that 1962 is still cruising the highways...making its way thanks to great products and service from Mid America Designs!

Mike Yager, President
Mid America Designs

When Did It Start for You?

When Did It Start for You?

Dad's Dream

Chapter 1

The University of Okoboji Corvette Club

I have always been a car nut, having owned more than 92 different cars over the past 42 years. I guess it all started when Dad helped me customize my '50 Ford; it was the sharpest car in my hometown. But it really happened for me in 1992, when I got "Corvette Fever." Having never owned one, it was something to aspire to. At that time we were driving a '91 Shadow convertible. I heard about the University of Okoboji Corvette Club and the camaraderie it offered. Every year about 17 of them went to Spearfish, South Dakota, to the Black Hills Corvette Classic.

Well, it didn't seem right to drive my Dodge convertible in the caravan, so my wife and I started looking and praying for a beautiful Corvette. I really wanted an '88 35th Anniversary Model, as we were so partial to white. We even purchased one in Indiana, but we couldn't go across state lines at the time for financing so we started watching the papers and looking again.

Well, one day in the Sioux City, Iowa, newspaper I found a beautiful '92 red Corvette coupe with 18,000 miles on it for what sounded like a very reasonable price at a Ford dealership in Ponca, Nebraska. My wife and I drove over to look at it in our '93 Ford Escort wagon (white, of course). I knew when I saw it out front from a block away that I had to have it. What a beautiful red shiny car it was! We traded our Escort wagon for it and headed home in the fog. I was so afraid of wrecking it, we drove home going 40 miles out of our way. On that 1992 night, it was like flying a fighter plane because it was so beautiful inside. We went to the Black Hills Classic with the University of Okoboji Corvette Club that year and had a ball with it autocrossing. I got second place in the novice class.

We drove the '92 for about a year and put on about 29,000 miles. I saw another ad in Pipestone, Minnesota, for a 40th Anniversary Corvette, so again we drove the '92 red Corvette up there just to look. Well, we ended up driving the '93 40th Anniversary Corvette home and now have put 31,000 miles on it. We can't say enough how much we have enjoyed the camaraderie that goes along with owning and driving a Corvette.

Dr. James Roberts
Estherville, IA

3

In Memory of My Dad

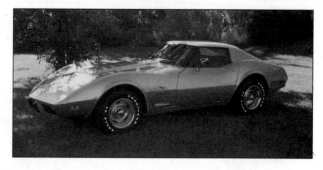

One July day in 1989 my father came home in a '77 L-82 Corvette with 24,000 original miles on the odometer. I was only 14 years old and had never seen a car so beautiful in my life. It was a bright sunny day and the silver metallic paint shined like nothing I had ever seen. With the T-tops off, my father took my two brothers and me each on our own special ride. It was the most exciting thing I had ever experienced.

My father's face had a particular glow on it; you could tell he was having the time of his life. He had always said he would own a Vette someday, and that someday was now. Three short months later, in October, he passed away very suddenly. But he had achieved his dream of owning an American icon, a Corvette. This car is still in my caring hands and I enjoy driving it as much as showing it. The odometer still only reads 28,000 miles and the Corvette remains in factory-original condition.

I would like to dedicate this in memory of my father,
Donald E. Wynkoop (1945-1989).

Dennis Wynkoop, Schererville, IN

Dressing Up for the Red Split Window

The pictures almost tell the story themselves. My mom still says, "It's all your dad's fault" about my love of the Vette. It all started in 1964, back when I was about one year old. My dad, who was a Chevy mechanic at the time, brought home a '63 red Sting Ray, a coupe with the split back window as you can see from the photo. I dressed for the occasion in matching red dress and tights. That was my first taste.

The '63 became an obsession as I got older. I started test driving new ones, used ones, it didn't matter. I'll never forget the day I drove a '91 Polo Green convertible 6-speed with suspension package. I hit the on ramp to the freeway feeling like a million bucks. Meanwhile, my husband was screaming, "Get the *%#!* off the freeway now!" and I was just hitting third gear.

A few years later I test drove a '94 burgundy coupe, 6-speed LT-1 with a wood grain dash. The Toyota dealership sales girl, who knew nothing about Vettes, came over to help. I told her I wanted to know what sixth gear did, and she said, "Let's go find out." We hit sixth gear in a state of extreme excitement that only a Vette owner understands, laughing and screaming with the radio blaring.

I've terrorized my poor husband for 11 years, yes, 11 years! I had a stack about two inches thick of business cards from different car dealers, and he still wouldn't let me buy one until recently, when we purchased the red one pictured in the photo below. Talk about the best day of my life! I could hardly stand it. Only a Corvette owner would understand that unbelievable feeling.

Sherri Rogers, Wheeling, IL

Living Out Dad's Promise

I couldn't really tell you when my love for the greatest automobile ever got started. But I can tell you that my wife and I have created a Corvette labor of love.

It began when I was a child growing up in the mountains of Boone, North Carolina. My dad and I were best friends. We went everywhere together.

He took me to car shows, pointed out antique cars on the road and taught me everything he knew about the automobile. I remember some of the best times we had together were under his old Chevy pickup or under Mom's wagon. When I got into my teen years my dad bought an old '57 Chevy Bel-Air rust bucket. Together we made that car a showpiece.

Even with a fine automobile like that, it still never satisfied his craving to own a Vette. I remember him saying to me, "Son, before I die, I will own my Corvette." My dad died at the age of 46 on November 20, 1988, 19 days after his birthday and exactly a month after I graduated from high school. My dad never owned his Vette, but I swore to my mother that I would own one in his memory.

Eight years later, with a wife, a little boy and little girl, I bought a '79 L-82 Corvette. My wife couldn't understand why I just had to have this car. I think it was my mom who finally told her the story. I drove the car about eight months when a rod started knocking. I parked my car until I got the funds to start fixing it. From that point on my wife has loved what she calls the "Batmobile" body style. My dad's favorite was the '63 split window. As for me, my choice would be the '96 Grand Sport.

Our plans are to fix the motor, change the weather stripping, change the interior from fabric to leatherette, put in a wood grain dash, new carpet, ground effects and paint. My wife has been doing the bodywork, and she's going to paint it my dad's favorite color, Metallic Wine Berry Red. On the back bumper, in airbrush, it will say "Daddy's Dream." The inscription engraved on the window will say, "In Memory of Richard Lee Offenbacker."

It's been nine years since my dad died and I have yet to return to his grave. When we finish the car, I hope to have the nerve to visit my dad in his Corvette. Then, finally, my wife can meet her father-in-law. I hope my mother can one day understand why I have yet to visit my dad.

That's how my wife came to love the Corvette. We are now leading our kids in the same footsteps my dad led me. Never underestimate the power of America's finest sports car!

Roy Offenbacker
Highpoint, NC

The '53 Corvette Poster

The year was 1953 and I was a seven-year-old boy anxiously awaiting my dad's return from an out-of-state business convention. I already had developed an eye for cars, which I think I inherited from Dad.

Finally Dad arrived, and he had brought presents for each of us! My present was a glossy black and white promotional photo of a white convertible, the likes of which I had never seen before. Dad had just picked it up at the unveiling of the new '53 Chevy Corvette. That car looked like it had come from outer space! The picture hung on the wall of my bedroom for many years, sort of as a target or goal. Life would never be the same!

Seven years passed before I got my first ride in a Corvette. My oldest sister's fiancee had just bought a new '60 model with two 4-barrels and a 4-speed. Would I like to go for a spin? A quick run through the gears put us over 100 mph with the wind blowing our hair. Life would never be the same!

Thirty-three years passed, including college, the military, marriage and fatherhood, before I finally owned a Corvette, an '89 coupe. Life will never be the same!

Russ Larsen
Fergus Falls, MN

When Did It Start for You?

Wishing For a White Corvette

When I was a young boy growing up in the late '60s/early '70s I used to drive around with my dad, pointing out Corvettes from the back seat of his '66 Chevy wagon. I remember bouncing up and down shouting, "Corvette!" and pointing toward the oncoming Vette as we drove down the road. At the early age of five years old I began dreaming of the day I would drive and own my first white Corvette. Back then, there were no BMWs or Mercedes to speak of and the coolest car on the road was the Corvette. On every birthday, I used to wish for a white Corvette as I blew out the candles on my cake!

As the years went on, I graduated college and began my first real job, with the luxury of driving a company car. For 13 years I never purchased my own car. (Even through high school, I always drove my dad's '66 Chevy wagon.)

Then, after 30 years of admiring other people's Corvettes (and blowing out several candles while wishing for my white one), my wife approached me and claimed she had found my dream car. I test drove a white '68 Corvette convertible and the rest is history. Now the car patiently awaits my approach with the key to start her up on a daily basis. Even if it's a short drive to the grocery store, I get such a thrill out of driving and living my "dream."

Ironically, this is the first car I have ever purchased (because I have always driven a company vehicle), and I think I might be the only 35-year-old person in America that waited so long to purchase his first car! Fortunately for me, my first automobile was my dream car, and for that I am sincerely grateful. I'll be cruisin' forever!

Timothy A. Katzinski
Redmond, WA

Stalking a '64 Coupe

I purchased my first Corvette when I was in my early 20s. It was a new '66 silver coupe. I swore that we would never part, but along came my son and the need for a down payment for our home and the Vette was gone. I always thought that someday I would again own a mid-year coupe, but it took approximately 20 years before it became a reality.

In the fall of '87 I was in my mid-40s and the kids were grown. We were on our way to Washington, DC, to attend our nephew's wedding. We stopped in Allentown, Pennsylvania, to visit relatives and the next thing I knew, we were all on Route 78 heading west to Fall Carlisle. I had never been there, and I always enjoyed looking at beautiful cars. Of course, I never expected the show to be as large as it was, so we tried to cover as much ground as possible in a period of a few hours. As we reached the top of one hill, there it was! I knew it as soon as I laid my eyes on it - there was the mid-year 1964 coupe for me. The car was gold, later to be clarified as Saddle Tan, with tan interior, 327/300 small-block with a 4-speed transmission. Just what the doctor ordered! My brother-in-law and I did the usual checks, asked the normal questions and I was convinced that it was a strong, presentable automobile.

I called first thing Monday. The dealership was in Ontario, Canada, so I had to wait an extra hour due to time zone considerations. That additional hour seemed like an eternity! Yes, the car was available and we agreed on a price. Keep in mind now, I had never even driven this car and my knowledge was limited to what I had heard at Carlisle. I did ask for the previous owner's name and address, as I thought it prudent to confirm what I had been told by the dealer. A quick conversation with Jim from Wallaceburg, Ontario, confirmed that he sold it to the dealer two months prior and that the car was original. On October 27, my wife and I flew to Detroit, were transported to Chatham, Ontario, by the dealer and consummated the deal. We then drove the car home to Poughkeepsie,

New York, approximately 700 miles away. The car ran well, although we encountered tense moments with some minor difficulties along the way.

My knowledge of correct matching numbers and the value of documentation was limited to what I had heard or read, which wasn't much at the time. One thing I did know was that I did not want to become one of those "nuts" searching for the correct nut, bolt or screw! I wanted to enjoy this car and drive it! That lasted about six months. I continued to read more and more about the importance and value of originality and documentation. I subscribed to several magazines, *Vette,* of course being my favorite, and joined the NCRS. I was off to the races, so to speak! The documentation task proved to be the more difficult of my projects. I was fortunate, especially considering the manner in which I purchased the car, to possess a totally original, matching-number car. Unbelievable, you say? I assure you it is true right down to the K-H knock-offs! These cars are out there. Either luck or knowledge has to be on your side and in my case it was the former.

But let's talk about documentation. Although it was initially the cause of the most frustration, in the end it was the most rewarding. Patience and perseverance are two extremely important virtues for this task. A call to the previous owner, Jim, netted a wealth of information. Jim told me he had purchased the car in June, 1976, from Michael L. in Connecticut, who had stored the vehicle for approximately seven years. He gave me the name of the restorer, Wes H., who was the next individual I called. Jim said he would check around the house to see if he could find any additional information.

Wes H. turned out to be a tougher guy to reach. I talked to his parents several times and finally reached him one day on his job at a local golf course in Ontario. Wes told me about the restoration he had performed on the car. It was evident that he was very proud of it. He provided me with a wealth of information, which I proceeded to document.

After a huge amount of tracking, I had the car documented back through November, 1967. Only three years of documentation were missing. At this time I left the project for a while, knowing that at some point I would resume!

One night I was reading one of my magazines and an article mentioned that Motor Vehicle Departments provide registration history. That was my next avenue of pursuit. I wrote a letter to the Connecticut DMV and waited with great anticipation. A couple of weeks later, I received the most significant piece of this entire documentation puzzle. The data not only confirmed what I had learned to date concerning previous owners in Connecticut, but provided me with the first registrant and dealer, both located in Hamden, Connecticut. I was absolutely ecstatic! Words cannot describe my feelings!

I immediately tried to call Edward F., the first registrant, but his phone was unlisted. I then wrote him a letter, then another. (Keep in mind here, I was using an address that was 24 years old!) One night, I received a phone call. It was Ed! He advised me that he had moved but that his nephew was living at the old address and had forwarded my last letter. Ed, of course, was extremely excited that the car, his car, was still in existence.

We talked several times, and he plans to personally "visit" the car and me next time I am in Connecticut for a show. Ed owned the car from March 1965 through November 1967, having purchased it from Partyka Chevrolet in Hamden, Connecticut. The car had approximately 2,000 miles on the odometer when he purchased it. It definitely was not a trade-in, which is substantiated by the fact that Ed was the first registrant.

After contacting the owner of Partyka Chevrolet and discussing several possibilities, we concluded that the car was either a dealer or factory demo. I haven't mentioned it yet, but on my owner's manual there are two very important signatures from Vette history, that of Z. Arkus Duntov and Dave McLellan. Could they somehow be tied to the original 2,000 miles on this automobile? I could fantasize about that forever, but to date have not found out why they autographed my manual.

That's my story. I've owned the '64 for almost 10 years now and couldn't be happier with the car and the people I've met at various events. The car has earned four NCRS Top Flight Awards, which speak for its originality and condition. Ed F., the original registrant, did join me at a Vette show in Danbury, Connecticut, several years ago to reacquaint himself with the car.

I still belong to the NCRS and a local Corvette club in Poughkeepsie, New York. The Corvette hobby has and continues to be a source of joy and satisfaction in my life.

Keith Convery
North Myrtle Beach, SC

Corvette Driver's Test

It started for me in 1955 when my dad bought a 1954 Corvette from our neighbor. I was 14 years old. I took my driver's license test ride in it, lucky examiner! We got a '57 in 1957. It only lasted a couple of weeks, until I totaled it, when a guy came through a red light and hit me. He was drunk and didn't have a license. We got another Corvette to replace the '57. In 1958 my dad got a '58 and in 1960 he got a '60. Of course, we only had one at a time! I bought a new '67 coupe with 435-hp after I returned from Vietnam in 1967. I traded it for a Caprice (can you believe that?) in 1969. Wish I still had it!

Now I'm 57 years old and just got a '95 coupe, red-on-black LT1, with 6,000 miles and not a mark on it. It's good to be back in the Corvette Club!

My wife, Peggy, and I went to ProTeam Corvette Sales, Inc. in Napoleon, Ohio, on January 23, 1997, just to look. What a great place! We ended up buying a '69 convertible. It's green with a tan interior and removable hardtop. It has a 350cid/300-hp engine with 4-speed. We're going crazy about Corvettes, but this has got to stop!

Wade Mertz
Avon Lake, OH

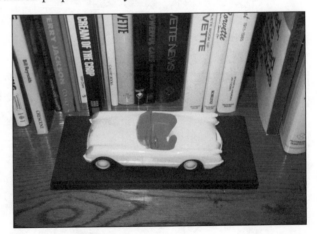

Corvette in the Mail

It's all my dad's fault! He is the reason I began
my association with Corvette.

I was 3 years old in 1953 and my dad was on a business trip
to Cleveland, Ohio. He would call every night to see how Mom and I
were doing. One night in my talk with him he said, "I mailed you a
Corvette." What he actually sent was a '53 Corvette promo, white with red
interior. I received the model several days later and kept it as one of my special toys. I still have it and it's in great condition. The only thing I've done is
apply a reproduction decal to the front. (These were available through *Vette
Vues* magazine a few years ago.)

The ironic part of this whole situation is that my dad, now 83 years old,
is not and never has been a car enthusiast. Yet he was the one who got me
started.

As I grew up, numerous Corvette kits were subject to my interpretation
of how the car should really look. The one that stands out in my mind is a
'62 convertible kit that I painted purple with a yellow interior. It had custom
wheels, spotlights and
other "Kustom Kar"- era
goodies.

In August 1974 after
high school and muscle
cars, it was time for a
real Vette. I bought a
used '69 coupe,
Riverside Gold, 427/390-
hp 4-speed. From then
on, I've always owned at
least one. The '69 was

When Did It Start for You?

followed by a '76, then a '79, next an '84, an '89 and then a restored '59. This March I took delivery of my '97, (red/black, 6-speed). I currently have the '59 (283cid/230hp, Powerglide), '84 (red/saddle, Z-51, automatic) and the '97. A look in my garage would confirm Jim Schefter's book title, *All Corvettes Are Red*. At least mine are!

Over the last 23 years, of Vette ownership, I've had the pleasure of belonging to a local club, autocross racing, being a member of NCCC, NCRS and a founding member of the National Corvette Museum. I've attended Bloomington Gold since '88 and have had two cars Gold Certified.

My wife has been tolerant of my hobby, and my two boys, 11 and 7, are as eagerly enthusiastic as I am about the car scene as we build models and attend many shows. My wife's tolerance was best tested when we built our current home and I had a late-model Corvette emblem incorporated into our driveway using exposed aggregate. Thanks for the opportunity to share my story.

Wally Grivna
Shoreview, MN

Campus Corvette

In 1957 my dad bought his first Corvette, which was a '54 beauty! I was not old enough to be impressed. During the summer of 1965, while I was attending college summer school, Dad let me borrow it to get around campus. Suddenly what had been obvious to almost everyone else became obvious to me! People I didn't even know stopped me to take a look and ask questions. It was one of the best summers I had ever had, and needless to say, that's when it started for me!

I didn't actually own my first Corvette until 1971, when I bought a '70. Since then, I've had a '73, '79, '84, '87 and '94, purchased not necessarily in that order! I currently own a '78 Silver Anniversary Model. There is nothing like the feeling of driving a Corvette! (Not even when driving my XKE V-12, a momentary lapse of judgment!) Sometimes I just go out in the garage and stare at my Corvette and wonder why everyone else doesn't own one!

Gayle Grigg, Phoenix, AZ

When Did It Start for You?

The Little Black '55

Dad was a traveling salesman. He was on the road from Monday through Friday every week selling and servicing foundry products throughout Ohio, Indiana and northern Kentucky. When I was a kid, it was a real treat to go with Dad for a few days, stay in a hotel, eat in restaurants, see the inside of the foundries and steel mills and meet the folks that Dad worked with.

When I was 9 years old, Dad got a new company car, a '55 white-over-gray Chevy 4-door sedan, and we took off for a week in southeastern Indiana and southwestern Ohio. My older brother was in Boy Scout camp, so Mom went with us, too. Dad had become friends with a gentleman he met through work, and we visited him and his family in Indiana. His oldest son had graduated from high school and gotten a job in the steel mill where his dad worked. He had just bought a brand new '55 Corvette. It was black with a red interior and never had a spot of dust upon it. My dad, of course, popped the hood on his 4-door and pointed out that it had the same engine, but the Vette's engine had a lot of bright work. The sound, that beautiful music that came from those twin pipes, was a world apart from Dad's sedan!

That little black '55 started a life's ambition to own my own Corvette. I married, we had kids and I worked a good industrial job while I made house payments, paid for braces for my daughters' teeth and drove used cars, station wagons and the mandatory "plain Jane" pickup truck to work.

With the daughters grown, married and educated, our financial lives were becoming easier when, in February of 1997, my mother passed away. Dad had died in 1983 and now I came into a small inheritance. After several months of shopping, I found a neglected but not abused '86 Corvette convertible. The paint was good and the car only had 54,000 actual miles on it, but the brakes and shocks were shot, two tires were worn out by being run out of alignment, the tail pipes had holes in them and her rag top lived up to its name. It was love at first sight! The last 18 months have been spent debugging my Vette, but I've learned to love every squeak and rattle.

After years of getting an occasional ride in the Corvettes owned by friends and relatives (including a great '69 convertible 427 4-speed that a brother-in-law once owned), I can now experience the top-down joy of my own Corvette. I like to think of my Corvette as the last present that my mother bought me.

David Stapf
Greenup, KY

17

Mid Ohio Racing

I'm 26 years old and my interest in the Corvette began at an early age. My dad used to take my two younger brothers and me to the races at the Mid-Ohio Sports Car Course during the late '70s and early '80s. My very first memory is of seeing the thundering loud Vette racers coming down the backstretch at 130-plus mph.

At first I didn't like the really loud cars, but as I got older, I relished their thunderous sound. My dad always did love that sound. Every time we went to the races, we would roll down the windows as we headed to the track, just so we could hear the cars at practice that much sooner.

As I grew older I started to notice the Sting Rays. I remember seeing a '74 orange convertible Vette and wondering what the heck it was. It looked so exotic! I thought that it was the neatest thing that I'd ever seen. It had to be fast and it looked like those loud racers at Mid-Ohio. That image was reinforced by the '78 Pace Car. I got a plastic model of one immediately after it came out.

My childhood as a Vette fan was frustrating. Mom and Dad always provided the best for us boys, but that left little extra money for sports cars. I thought a go-kart would solve my need for speed. I took my frustrations into my own hands in the early '80s when, after one especially thrilling weekend at Mid-Ohio with Dad, I took a hacksaw and red paint to that '78 Pace Car model. I cut the top off and painted it red to match one of the loud racers we just had seen. I still have that lump of plastic in my closet.

I took the ultimate step in providing a "red go-kart" for myself during the spring of 1995. I saved up a lot of money and after four months of searching found the red Corvette convertible that fit my first impression of the ultimate sports car. I decided that I wanted a red Vette with tan interior (to match the colors of my school, Indiana University, which were cream and crimson). I also decided it had to be a '71, which was my birth year. I could fix it up, take care of it and grow old with it.

I found the car at Mershon's World of Cars in Springfield, Ohio, and bought it. It had 60,700 miles on it, and all the numbers match. It still has the 350 small block, Rochester Q-jet, factory 4-speed and original radio. All of the vacuum lines work, overrides included, the fiberglass still has the Rockwell International stickers inside the body panels, and even the little light in the center rear storage compartment lights up. I haven't had to do a whole lot to it, just a few cosmetic things. The car was finished on January 8, 1971, and was in the dealership by my birthday, March 20, 1971.

The car, my fiance and I were participants in the 1996 Bloomington Gold

Silver salute to the '71 Sting Ray and were the center car in the 1971 Silver Salute panoramic picture that was taken. We got to lead the Road Tour that year and have since been participants in a variety of local and regional parades and shows.

As for the loud and thundering aspect of this Vette story, my buddy (who owns a '94 triple-black coupe) and I bought a tired '86 Z51 coupe this past spring. We rebuilt the engine, painted it Competition Yellow, installed MOMO race seats, Simpson seat belts, Grand Sport wheels, new brakes and have replaced the 4+3 transmission and almost every other reliability item. We raced it at Mid-Ohio this past August in the National Council of Corvette Clubs (NCCC) North Sectional. It was a Corvette experience that had come full circle! Now I've just gotta work on getting Dad into one!

Matt Davenport
Springboro, OH

Mom's Daily Driver

It really started because of my father. Back in mid-1964, he purchased a bright red coupe small block with red interior. He had to have that car and it became my mother's daily driver. She drove it to and from work every day (even in the winter) at GM Truck and Bus in Pontiac, Michigan.

On September 5, 1965, my mother went into labor with me. Dad, obviously wanting to get to the hospital in Royal Oak quickly, loaded her, her suitcase and some towels into the Vette and off they went. He sped all the way from Walled Lake to Royal Oak making record time, but on the way her water broke and I was born within the hour after reaching the hospital!

They kept that car until I was about five years old. At that point, I was getting too big to either ride on Mom's lap or in the back storage area. Dad sold the car to a friend and for many years laughed about how much he regretted it! Sting Ray (#40837S119676) was the only car I ever rode in for the first five years of my life. I still remember riding in the back with my feet up on the back window and also how the dashboard looked lit up at night.

The joke in our family has always been that I had fiberglass in my blood since birth! Corvettes have been a lifelong obsession for me. I was building Corvette models, playing with toy cars and reading *Corvette News* as a kid. It was simply a matter of time before I would have a Corvette of my own.

I currently own a '72 Elkhart Green coupe with an LS5 454 that I purchased September 18, 1985. Why this car? Well, actually, I think it chose me. I saw it at the Bob McDorman car show in Columbus, Ohio, and couldn't stop thinking about it. The Snap-On Tools regional sales manager owned it and had it displayed on a lift in the garage area. I went to Michigan State University and we Spartans are partial to green, so the color suited me well! The fact that it was a big block and needed a little fixing up made it more appealing because I was a closet gear-head at heart. A couple of weeks later, it was all mine.

What a thrill it was to finally fulfill a lifelong dream! I'll never forget the day in 1996 when I made the trek from home in Columbus back to Walled Lake, Michigan, to show Dad the car. I drove up the driveway and he was sitting on the front porch with the biggest smile I had ever seen on his face. I handed him the keys and said, "Come on, Daddy, let's go for a ride!" That was a day I will never forget! Because of that car, I now have Corvette friends all over the world and wouldn't trade my experiences in this hobby for anything in the world.

When Did It Start for You?

Only a couple of faded photos still exist of us with that red '64 coupe. Dad won't let them out of his sight, so enclosed is a photo of me with my '72. Thanks for letting me share my story.

Colleen M. Egan
Columbus, OH

The SCCA Tech Inspector

It started for me because I thought Corvettes were awful! In the '60s, my dad was a tech inspector for the SCCA. I was brought up on road races where "real" sports cars were European. I witnessed firsthand Corvettes being slaughtered by British-based Cobras. When I was old enough to drive, I owned a succession of MGs and (don't laugh) Corvairs.

In the late '80s, I had restored/created my own Yenko Stinger, but it wasn't living up to my expectations. In the '60s, the Corvair was a small car with exceptional handling. The technology had caught up and now the Corvair was a big car with merely satisfactory handling. I was looking to upgrade, but still had a place in my heart for the sports cars of my childhood.

The mid-year Corvettes were on my investigate list. I said to myself, "No way, chrome, white walls, hubcaps, styling gimmicks. Give me a break, this isn't a sports car." On the other hand, I knew the body wouldn't rust, it would be easy to get parts and repair, it would hold its value and it should handle as well as a Corvair.

Finally it dawned on me, the Corvette is an American interpretation of a sports car, it's supposed to be gaudy! Once I came to this realization, most of my objections disappeared. I started buying books and the trap was set. This is when it started.

When Did It Start for You?

As much as I liked the '67, the price was too much at the time. I never liked the gills on the '65s or '66s. That left the '63s and '64s, and it had to be a convertible. Finally the right car came along at the right time and at the right price. Do I need disc brakes to go cruising? No! Does the general public know the difference between a '63 and a '67? No! Do I get to look at the lovely Art Deco dashboard every time I drive the car? Yes! Does it draw attention? Yes!

Alas, as much as I love the car, it still has one failing. It's not a sports car in the handling department. Sorry, but I call it my 2-seat Impala! After a lot of money and a suspension package, the handling has improved. What did I expect from a 1960s-era American interpretation of a sports car? I can hear Duntov's engineers saying, "Roads are straight in America." The car goes like a scalded cat in a straight line. Maybe I'll buy a C5 in 30 years!

Derek Sutton
Falmouth, MA

The '70 Corvette Thrill Ride

In 1974, I was 3 years old and lay in the back of my dad's '70 Corvette convertible. It was somewhat dark, but looking between the seats and watching him shift that lever back and forth as the engine roared and my body lurched in every direction gave me the thrill ride of my life. I was in love. The only other memory I have of that car was the day he sold it, when the proud new owner pulled away from our driveway.

Since that time, my father has owned five Corvettes, his current one being a Pennant Blue '54 roadster on which he performed a nearly flawless restoration. I have owned six Corvettes. My first one, a very worn out '70 T-top, was purchased about a year before I had my driver's license. I bought it with the $4,500 I had saved working for my dad. I spent much of my life eating, sleeping and drinking Corvette.

It seemed as if I could never get enough of my obsession. I read, studied and researched every bit of Corvette material I could get my hands on. The day after I graduated from high school I got a job working at Paragon Reproductions, a major Corvette reproduction-parts supplier that was located about 45 miles from where I lived. During the short time I worked there, the owner of the company, Richard Fortier, gave me the Corvette information I had longed for. It was also at Paragon that I discovered the true love of my life, Angela. She was the first person to put Corvette at number two on my list.

It has been several years since Angela and I left Paragon, but the passion I have for the Corvette is still very strong. Angela doesn't share these feelings, but it was her idea to drive my uncle's restored black '57 in our wedding in 1994. I currently own a '68 convertible that I must sell in order to purchase what I consider to be the greatest Corvette ever made, the C5. I know my obsession drives my wife crazy and I love her even more for putting up with me, but the Corvette has played a major role in my life. It's amazing a car can do that!

Jeff Lemke
Swartz Creek, MI

When Did It Start for You?

Blame it on Your Uncle

Chapter 2

Uncle Gilbert and the Orlando Junkyard

1957 was a memorable year for me. It was the year I not only touched my first Corvette, but got to take my first ride in one as well.

My mother's Uncle Gilbert owned a junkyard in Orlando, Florida, long before Disney World ever existed. In 1956, at the request of the Highway Patrol, he towed in a '56 Corvette (in 1956) that had been in a rollover. The owner never claimed the car, so one year later Uncle Gilbert decided to get the damaged Corvette fixed and drive it.

And drive it he did!

In the summer of '57 he visited our home in Pittsburgh, Pennsylvania. I was four months short of my 12th birthday when I fell in love with that Corvette. The photo I've enclosed shows me proudly leaning on the right front fender, grinning from ear to ear! My brother, Dave, and Uncle Gilbert are standing on the driver's side. The black-and-white photo does not convey the true beauty of this Aztec Copper treasure.

Forty years have since passed and I'm currently between Corvettes. In 1978, I bought a '74 coupe with 5,092 miles on it. I bought my first new Corvette in 1985 and in 1989 I bought a '78 coupe with 10,370 miles. This year I hope to own my first Corvette roadster; I have my eyes on a '91 Steel Blue beauty.

Thank you for allowing me to share my 40-year love affair with the "True American Sports Car."

H. Rodger Cottrell
Monroeville, PA

Memories of a '63

My Corvette story began in 1961, when a cousin gave me a ride in a '59 (I think) Corvette. The story swung into high gear in October 1962, when the brand new Sting Ray hit the streets and one cruised by my high school. Someone yelled "Sting Ray" and all heads in the classroom quickly turned to look at the then futuristic looking car.

It wasn't until 35 years later, in 1997 at age 50, that I finally bought my '63 Corvette convertible. It is a restored 327cid, 340-hp, with a hard-top and a customized extra deck lid thrown in. It is even more fun to drive than I imagined, but the side pipes are loud!

Douglas M. Dawson
Ellicott City, MD

Three Brothers Chasing the Dream

I [Guy] can remember my Uncle Herb had a promo-type model of an unusual looking car. He explained that it was an XK 140 C sports car. We were intrigued by the words "sports car" and the then-unknown (to us) world of cars.

Uncle Herb had purchased a '56 Chevrolet sedan in 1958 after graduation from high school. It was powered by a 265 V-8 engine. The valve covers were curious. They were aluminum with the name Corvette cast between rows of fins.

What was otherwise a stock two barrel V-8 gave our uncle great pleasure. He explained to us that a Corvette was a special two-seated Chevrolet sports car built in limited numbers. He also told us about the fiberglass body, fuel injection and four-speed transmissions.

In one memorable ride in this car Uncle Herb was explaining that the standard engine in a Chevy had six cylinders. He pretended to be driving a Corvette by using the horn ring for the steering wheel. He would push harder into the accelerator, demonstrating the power of the optional V-8 he called his Corvette engine.

Well, I don't know if it was the excitement of my uncle's snappy driving or the mystique of the name Corvette, but I was hooked! Horn ring in hand, Herb drove even faster knowing he had our full attention.

That fall, Chevrolet sealed our fate when they introduced the Sting Ray. Life was definitely never going to be the same! Throughout junior and senior high school, Chevrolets and Corvette were constant subjects. I tried to be the first in line to check out each new issue of *Corvette News* from the school library.

In the summer of '64, my younger brother Curly and I were taking a bike ride when we spotted a Corvette Sting Ray in front of the local medical clinic. Upon closer inspection we saw that it was a '64 roadster that

When Did It Start for You?

was silver blue with a dark blue top. Our hearts really started pumping when we spotted the fuel injection emblems!

We decided to hang around to hear the fuel-injected engine run and to see what type of person drove such a magnificent car. A nice looking man came out of the clinic, and to our dismay, put two more hours in the meter. We went to get permission from our parents to return, if possible, to the Corvette.

Upon returning, our wait was over. This time, an attractive woman accompanied the man. I wish we had been braver and asked them about their Corvette. It would have been great if he would have taken the time to talk to us. With the engine fired, we held our own around the block and watched our dreams disappear into the distance.

In November 1967, my older brother, Jack, and I were in Janesville

visiting our Uncle Herb and ran across an ad for a '59 Corvette for $1,200. Minutes later, we were looking at an unmolested black Corvette with silver coves. To our surprise, the mother of the owner said that we could test drive the car. The first thing that we noticed was that the car had 4.11:1 gears and accelerated with ease. We kept the car as long as we thought that we could get away with it! After putting in a couple of bucks worth of gas, smiling, we returned the car.

In 1970, Curly and I purchased our first Corvette. It was a '69 350-hp coupe. The car had 17,000 on the clock and was in excellent shape. We finally had stopped chasing a dream and were living it. In the fall of 1971 we sold the '69 and ordered a '72 ZR-1 off-road performance package Corvette coupe, which we still own. Later we bought a '67 427 coupe, which we also still have.

A few years later, a Honduras Maroon '62 base engine 4-speed with two tops took care of our Route 66 fantasy, but we regrettably sold it. After many years and a family, a base engine 4-speed coupe was purchased so we could again enjoy a Corvette on the road more often. Jack has two '76 base engine 4-speed Corvettes. Corvettes have been a passion over the years, but more importantly, a source of pride.

The Carpenter Brothers:
Jack (2/12/48), Guy (10/7/49), Curly (11/19/51)
Marshfield, WI

Three Dog Night

This picture was taken in the very early '70s. The Vette is a '67 convertible that belonged to my uncle who lived in Boonville, Missouri. I was about 6 at the time and my older brother about 10. In the summer, he would give us rides across the bridge to New Franklin or out on Hwy 87 with the top down, listening to Three Dog Night. I still remember watching the tach and listening to the sound of those side exhausts as he clicked through the 4-speed.

The car had a small block and was originally Sunfire Yellow with black interior. Later it was mildly customized in metallic bronze with flared fenders, Cragar SS wheels and a big-block hood. The hardtop was always stored away properly, right off the foot of this bed propped up against the wall! The car has survived the years and, amazingly enough, I managed to keep track of it.

I guess the affection for Corvettes has stayed in the family. I later owned a '76, my father-in-law has an '87 convertible and my uncle now owns a '73 convertible. When I read that Mid America was putting this together, I couldn't pass up the chance to write in. Those kids in the ad look like us back then. I'm an avid motor sports fan and every year I go to shows like Bloomington Gold just to hear those side exhausts again! Thanks, Ed!

Dale Stuart
Columbia, MO

The Sunflower Christmas Corvette

It was 1972 when I was first bitten by the Corvette bug. My uncle, who lived in Denver, came home at Christmas in his five-month-old Sunflower Yellow convertible, which I thought was the coolest thing on the planet. I was only seven at the time and could barely see over the dash, but I can still remember the feeling as he shifted through the gears and the sound of the engine as we raced down the back streets by my grandparents' house.

I saw the car again a few years later on a short visit as he moved to his new home in Florida. Even sitting on a U-Haul trailer packed to the roof with whatever they could load in it, the car still looked great. I found it much more interesting to look at than my parents' 4-door Ford Maverick.

Over the years, whenever we visited Uncle John, my brother and I would use every imaginable excuse to try to get him to take us out for a ride in "the machine," and on occasion the begging and pleading paid off. We were rewarded with an accelerating trip around Orlando, much to our (and I think his) utmost enjoyment.

Then in August 1991, it happened. My wife and I were visiting my uncle and just as in the past, persistent begging worked and he agreed to take the car out the next morning. We got up fairly early and drove to a small town near his house where he suggested that I could drive the car back! As I slid behind the steering wheel of a Corvette for the first time in my life, I could not believe how nervous I was! My uncle was probably equally terrified! I paused for a few moments to take in my surroundings. I never realized how low you sat, or how high the front fenders rose creating a valley for the hood bulge that proudly declared LT-1 on its sides. This was incredible! The 15-minute trip back seemed to pass in seconds but its effect was lasting. I was hooked! However, because my wife was five months pregnant with our first child, a Corvette was not in our immediate or foreseeable budget.

The call came in June of 1995. My uncle wanted to know if I would be interested in purchasing the yellow machine that I had worshipped for so long. Soon a deal was struck, and in September I was on a flight to Orlando to pick up MY Corvette! I hit the road the next morning to begin the trip back to central Illinois. Twenty-two hours later I arrived at my

       When Did It Start for You?

house tired, but grinning like an idiot! Since then, we have taken the car to a few Corvette shows, met some wonderful people and have had a lot of fun. But our proudest moment thus far was receiving a Judges' Choice Award at Mid America Designs' Corvette Funfest '97! I never thought that a Corvette would be such an exciting part of my life. Now I can't ever imagine being without one!

Scott & Susan Faulkner
Peoria, IL

When Did It Start for You?

First Love

Chapter 3

Prom Corvette

I was 11 years old and my older brother took me along to visit one of his friends. That was the first time I saw a Corvette. It was a '62 with gold exterior, red interior and a white soft top. Sitting there it looked like the fastest thing on earth. I did not know it then, but this beauty was to play a major part later in my life.

In 1977, I picked up an after school job at Miller's British Petroleum gas station. Not until that summer did I see that '62 Vette again. It was sporting a new red exterior to match the interior, rally wheels and black walls. As it happened, the car had been sold a number of times before it came to be owned by my boss, Larry. I could hardly believe it was the same Vette, and the new color looked great.

Eleven months later, in the spring of my senior year in high school, I decided to attend my first and only prom. Almost 18 years old and thinking I knew everything, I asked to borrow that car for the special occasion. Larry said he'd think about it and let me know, which usually meant no, but at least he hadn't said it. Others who had worked at the garage, and had known Larry a lot longer than I, said he'd never give it up.

Weeks went by without a word from my boss. I didn't dare ask him for fear of him saying no, so I ordered my tux and got my car ready for prom day. I drove into the garage at 12:30 and got out of my car. As I was walking toward the garage, Larry backed out the Vette. I can still remember how the sunlight shined on the paint.

He started to fill it up with premium and called out to me. I figured he was going on an errand and wanted to tell me what to work on. As I got closer, he threw something to me which I caught. Before I had a chance to look in my hand Larry said, "Take the rest of the day off, have a good time and bring it back when you're finished with it." He walked back to the garage without saying another word. I opened my hand and there were the keys to the Vette.

That's how it started for me, the first Vette I saw became the first Vette I drove to my only school prom.

Rick Willier, Halifax, PA

When Did It Start for You?

Corvette Angela

I met my husband, Richard, in 1975 through my niece, who had gone to college with him. He had a white '73 Corvette convertible. They were talking one day and she mentioned that her aunt had a '71 Corvette LT-1 coupe. He wanted to meet me, so my niece gave him my phone number. He called me and told me to call him if I ever needed work done on my Corvette. About a week later, my timing chain went and he fixed it. We went out to dinner that night and have been together ever since. That was March 1975. We were engaged in December 1975 and married May 15, 1976. We all had Corvettes at our wedding! His sister had one, our best man had one and my nephew did, too.

In 1978, though we owned both a '73 and a '71 Corvette, we bought a new '78 Indy Pace Car. By then we had had two sons. We put both boys in one bucket seat for a couple of years, but soon they outgrew the Vette. In 1983, against our wishes, we sold my husband's '73 Vette for a new Mercury Marquis wagon. It was like a death in the family or selling one of the boys!

We gave our oldest son the '78 Pace Car for high school graduation and want to give the '71 to my other son, but he does not want that "old stick shift car." I guess I'll keep it for myself, since the license plate reads, "MOMS 71." We all are members of Orange County Corvettes and my oldest son belongs to the National Corvette Restoration Society.

Please note that my '71 Vette was actually my third one. I had a '60 convertible and a '65 coupe. I've had a Corvette since I was 19 years old and my husband since he was 17 years old. Corvettes have always been a part of our lives.

Angela Zarski
Trabuco Canyon, CA

Kentucky Corvettes

As a young teenager I remember my older sister's '72 T-top Corvette. It had a 350 with all of the options, a very nice car. She ordered it and waited three months to get it just the way she wanted it. I guess you could say this was my dream car!

At 17 I went to work in Lexington, Kentucky. My boss found a classic '60 black with red interior roadster. He bought it for $2,500 from an elderly lady whose son was lost in Vietnam. The car needed engine rubber. It smoked, but ran and drove great! The body was perfect, as was the interior. He asked me to help rebuild the engine with him. I couldn't wait!

It was a 283, 2-bbl 4-speed with headers into factory exhaust through the bumpers. We went through the engine with help from a guy at a local machine shop, and two weeks later it was finished. My boss wanted me to have the car, knowing how much I loved it, and sold it to me for $2,500. He said that since I had done most of the engine work that was his gift and the car was mine. Six months later, I was hit and the car was a total loss!

Last year, at 39 years old and with the support of my lovely wife, I started my quest for my dream car once again. I checked with Newton's Corvette Parts and Brokerage and they found me a '72 roadster for $12,000, red on red with optional hard top! The previous owner had restored the car almost completely. After spending $3,000 more and a lot of hours hunting parts and labor, I once again have my dream!

If you're ever in Kentucky on a sunny Sunday and see a pretty red '72 Vette with a pretty blonde lady and a white-haired, 40-year-old driver, it will be Vickie and Paul Kidder. We'll just be out for a ride looking for a '60 Corvette like the one I had when I was 17. Just goes to show you that you really don't know what you have until you lose it!

PS: Thanks to my wife for letting me relive the legend!

Paul Kidder
Louisville, KY

A Memory of the World's Fair

The year was 1964 and the place was the New York World's Fair. I was 9 years old. I remember the General Motor's pavilion and the dazzling display of the new

'64 models, and there it was, a red '64 Corvette Sting Ray. I just had to sit in it and, of course, my parents just had to take my picture!

That was it for a while until the neighbor across the street came home with a Corvette convertible. It was beautiful! I was so jealous because our family car at that time was a '62 Chrysler. Not much of a comparison!

I didn't think much about cars until high school in New Jersey. I had a good friend across the street, Walter Riley, who was into motorcycles. Since he was into them, so was I. Walter bought a '68 Corvette L88 (yes, it was an L88) right after high school in 1973. I moved to Florida to go to college and never even went for a ride in it, but I remember how loud it was when he raced past our house that summer.

Time went on, I married my high school sweetheart, graduated from college, started my career, then we bought our first house and had our first child. Cars, other than ones that run, just weren't a priority. In 1982, I bought an '82 black Pontiac Trans Am. I thought it was awesome, until two years later when the neighbor across the street came home with (you guessed it) a brand new '84 Corvette. All of a sudden my Trans Am became just transportation!

I kept the Trans Am until 1988. My wife was pregnant with our third child and I felt a bigger car was necessary. We also had a station wagon, so it really wasn't needed, but every day on the way to work I passed the local Ford dealer. I must admit I was attracted to the new Thunderbirds, particularly the new turbo coupes. I traded the Trans Am in on a loaded '88 Thunderbird turbo coupe.

I hated it, even though I never had any problems with it. It just seemed like I was now driving my father's car. It was too big! I kept it for one year and took a beating on it when I traded it.

Early in 1989, I noticed that the local Lincoln dealer was advertising an '87 Corvette. It was black with all the toys on it at what seemed to be a good price. I went to look and fell in love! It only had 6,000 miles and was traded by some old guy from Wisconsin in a Lincoln Town Car. His loss was my gain! I traded in the T-bird and still have it today.

That Corvette was driven daily for about six years. During that time, I drove it to New Jersey, all over Florida and even to Texas where my father and I went to experience a hurricane. That was kind of dumb, but it did give us some good stories to tell. Today, the Corvette has 76,000 miles on it and sits under a cover in the garage, only driven on weekends. I'd be lying to say that it was a good car, because I have had a lot of problems. But even though I don't drive it daily anymore, I can't bear to part with it. However, the new C5s sure look good!

Gene D. Heil
Fairhope, AL

Trading in the Honda Aspencade

It all started for me in 1965 when I was about 16 years old, which was when I got my driver's license. I would go up to the local Chevrolet dealer and dream of owning a new Corvette. But it was only that, a dream. I had noticed that it seemed like only "old guys" owned Corvettes.

As the years went by, the thought of owning a Corvette was always tucked away in the back of my mind. After getting married, I told my wife, "Someday, I will own a Corvette! I may be 90 years old, but I will have one before I die." The years went by and purchasing a home and raising two children were more of a priority than a car.

After various cars, I bought a Honda Gold Wing Aspencade, complete with all the goodies and a trailer to tow behind it for long-distance touring. But the birth of my daughter meant the end of my motorcycle, because every time I wanted to go somewhere on it, at least two people had to stay home. After going through a phase of pickup trucks, my wife still knew I wanted that Corvette. Finally one day she came to her senses and said, "You are not getting any younger, so you might as well get yourself a Corvette now if you still want one."

After getting my heart restarted, I informed her that my search would begin as soon as possible. It took me a couple of months of shopping to find a Corvette that I knew had been well cared for, and was one that I would be happy with. In October, 1994 I purchased my first Corvette.

My '91 is an automatic and powered by a 350cid/300-hp engine. I have added the Greenwood Motorsports ground effects kit to it and have so far left the rest of it stock. My daughter thinks she is going to be driving this car to high school in a few years, but I have got some news for that young lady!

Purchasing my Corvette was a very long-term goal for me, and that goal was finally accomplished! Now every time I drive it, I believe that I enjoy it more and more each time. I have also learned another thing: Old guys are not the only people who own Corvettes!

Make the most of your driving experience! Buy a Corvette!

Darrell Singleton

Homecoming Princess or '69 Corvette... You Choose!

In the summer of 1969, infatuation struck hard twice. Once was when I saw a senior homecoming princess, and the other was the first time my eyes took aim at a '69 Corvette. The undeniable lust for those lines and curves, on the latter of course, negated all logic and rationality that a 17-year-old punk could possess at that fragile, delicate and easily impressionable time in life.

As time passed, lust, passion and desire combined into total, absolute and complete love for the Corvette. Roadsters, coupes, dragsters, show cars, even models, all fed my restless yearning and aching fervor. Although all Corvettes caused me to snap my neck and swerve into oncoming traffic for a longer glimpse, it was that '68-'72 generation of sharks that caused me to blush, swoon and stutter.

With my 40th birthday bearing down on me like a locomotive emerging from a dark tunnel, I could no longer bottle up my thirst and emotional denial. I had to admit my destiny.

After six months of searching, I met my fate. She was a '72 350cid, 4-speed coupe, Rally Red with saddle interior, air conditioning, power steering, power brakes, Posi-traction and matching numbers. It was all the desirable qualities any man would crave. Some minor cosmetics, a tuck here, a lift there and some rubbing in all the right places soon returned her pride, dignity and self-respect.

Everyone comments on how great we look together on those summer afternoons when the covers come off and we exit the garage. The anticipation of driving boils over into an explosion of pride and joy at the turn of a key. The rumbling of her V-8 underneath my seat as we enter warp speed is worth the wait of owning a Corvette! As the G-forces erase reality, it is too late to resist the awesome desire of one last thrust of the accelerator to achieve total contentment.

I'm proud that I had goals and waited for the perfect Corvette to come into my life. As time speeds by and life becomes more demanding and unpredictable, it is a comfort to know I can jump in my Corvette and stop or even reverse time for a short while!

Mike Evett, Livermore, CA

When Did It Start for You?

Big Red and The Robertsons

In 1989 my husband purchased a '74 Corvette that was in need of repairs. We spent a year fixing the car and soon realized how much fun it was to own a Vette. Since it was purchased as an investment and I was driving it all the time, my husband decided it was time to sell and we quickly found a buyer. The day we sold the car, we realized we had made a terrible mistake and immediately began looking for another Corvette. In 1990, while driving through Atlanta, we stopped at Tom Jumper Chevrolet and found a beautiful bright red '90 Corvette.

We went home and discussed the purchase, since it was more than we had planned to spend. But then my husband said, "I want it!" As every good wife should do in this kind of situation, I said, "Yes, dear,

When Did It Start for You?

whatever you say." I quickly got him the phone number before he changed his mind!

The next weekend we went to pick it up. You cannot imagine how excited I was when my husband surprised me and put "Big Red" in my name! But a five-hour trip up and a two-hour delay at the dealer made me tired before we began our trip back. Only half way home, while I was driving our other car and my husband was in the Vette, I had to pull over because I was hungry, tired and had a bad headache. My husband said if I could just last another 30 minutes there was a fast food place down the road. Since I still didn't look very happy, he gave me the keys to the Vette. With keys in hand, I quickly got into the Corvette and took off. The faster I drove the less tired I felt. Soon, I wasn't even hungry and my headache was completely gone! (Yes ladies, a Vette can really cure a headache!) When it was time to stop, all I wanted to do was keep driving.

Since "Big Red #2" we have owned a 40th Anniversary, a '96 Silver Collector and, hopefully very soon, a Pewter '99!

The Corvette is part of the family. It has taken us all across the nation to various shows and we are convinced that the nicest people are Corvette owners. I feel very fortunate not only to own the most beautiful car in the world but to be able to drive it daily. It is amazing how much the Corvette has changed our lives. I cannot ever imagine being "Vette-less" and I plan to drive Corvettes forever!

Charley & Jim Robertson
Marianna, FL

Corvette Radar

From the time I was old enough to know what it was, I have always wanted a Corvette. My dad used to tell me that I had radar: I could spot one coming down the road a mile away. I even dated guys who drove Corvettes just so I could be in one. But the car, not the guy, would always steal my heart and I would move on!

As I got older the dream was in the back of my mind, and life went on. I got married, had a son, bought a house, a minivan and faced the reality that I would never own a Corvette, or at least maybe not until I was 50 years old.

Then in 1997, a friend told my husband and me that he had gotten a Corvette from the Carolinas that had been a little abused. We went to take a look and what we saw would have broken the heart of any Corvette lover. The paint was chipped and cracked from years of sitting in the Carolina sun. The interior was faded and broken and just all-around neglected. But it was reasonably priced and my husband said, "Your birthday is next month. If you want it, it's yours."

The next day, I raced to the phone to talk to my insurance agent and as I bubbled to the guy about how great this car was going to be, he stopped me mid-sentence and said, "Judy, are you sure you're getting this car? After all, it is April Fool's Day." I thought, no, this can't happen! I paced and panicked all day until my husband came home and I could look him in the eye and ask if the car was really mine. He said, "Yes, I have the money right here in my pocket."

We went and picked up the car that night, and I felt like a little kid. Over the next months, we replaced door panels, the dash, the molding, stripped the paint down to the fiberglass, replaced emblems, rebuilt the engine and everything that you can imagine. The result is the sharpest '79 Ice Blue Corvette you have ever seen! Now people can spot *me* coming down the road a mile away.

And my husband, well, he is my hero. I still have to be the responsible mom, drive the minivan to ball practice and such, but whenever I need to make sure my heart is still beating, I jump in that car and remind myself that I got the greatest husband and car.

P.S. When my son is older, I'll warn him how to spot the girl who only loves the car.

Judy Simpson
Newton Falls, OH

Speedy, Little Brother & Acer

"Once upon a time" in the land of Oklahoma, a new Air Force 2nd Lieutenant, having sold a Chevrolet Corvair (his practice Corvette) and having bought a Ford Galaxie, needed a second car for his wife. She was a teacher and needed transportation.

Together they decided to buy a Triumph Spitfire. This was a great little car that had no power and twin side-draft carburetors that were hell to keep synchronized. Another 2nd Lieutenant friend went down to a used car lot and came home with a really neat '63 Corvette and showed it off to all who would stand still, including me. As fate would have it, several weeks later the Triumph Spitfire was forced off the road, rolled over and suffered serious damage. Fortunately no one was hurt, but I had to look for a replacement car. Guess what? In a used car lot there was a '62 Dark Red Corvette convertible that just begged for a new home. Now, I too, had one of the cars from which dreams are made!

Towing this wonderful car behind our Ford Galaxie to my next duty station, my wife and I planned on living "happily ever after." This was not to be! This car also became a statistic when it ran over a manhole that

When Did It Start for You?

was being installed on a new road where we lived.

This might have ended the saga except for the fact that in 1971, while looking for a '55 Thunderbird, my wife, Mary Ann, spotted an advertisement for a '68 blue Corvette convertible. It found a new home very quickly. It has stayed in our family since that day and is what our daughter considers a true sports car.

After "Speedy" in 1982 there was "Little Brother," followed by "Acer," Mary Ann's red convertible in 1996. On my birthday I bought a blue '98 convertible, "Speedy 2." It was delivered right after New Year's Day in 1998.

Corvette ownership has affected everyone in our family. Our daughter, Kim, introduced us to Brad, her future husband, by saying, "You'll like him. He has a Corvette." The fact that it soon went into major repair was only a temporary setback. Soon, Kim and Brad bought a yellow 1974 T-top.

That brings this Corvette saga to the present day. It covers 34 years, from 1964 to 1998. Brad and Kim have two daughters, Victoria, four years old, and Elizabeth, three months old. The elder daughter, Victoria, also known as Tori, now asks her grandmother, "When can I drive 'Acer,' Na-na?" The tale continues!

Michael and Mary Ann Decker
Evansville, IN

Margo

I used to think it was funny how people had names for their cars. This affection seemed to go way beyond a nice paint job. It appeared to be a connection between human and machine, based on a very unusual friendship. I used to wonder how a hunk of metal and four rubber shoes could garner such importance in a person's life. When I met "Margo," it all became clear!

I currently reside in Petaluma, California. You may not have heard of Petaluma, but chances are you have seen it because it is a popular location for Hollywood production companies. A locale like this is perfect for early American nostalgia collectors (fanatics) like myself. I think my fascination with collecting old stuff has become an obsession. It's hard to explain the satisfaction felt in owning a piece of history, to reflect on its previous owners, to appreciate the craftsmanship, to marvel at the ingenuity of the creator and to be transported back to a

simpler time. My ultimate dream has always been to own a classic car, specifically a Corvette.

When the first Corvette rolled off the assembly line in 1953, an American cultural icon was born. In the early 50s American automakers were feeling the pressure from foreign competition and needed to create a symbol of performance that truly represented America. The Corvette was the answer and became the standard thereafter. I have always loved the early years, the first generation. My personal favorite has always been the '59. My dream would only be complete by actually owning this automobile.

Finding a specific vintage Corvette is not as easy as it may appear. Forget the local papers, the selections are too few and far between, wrong color, wrong year, no engine, two engines and no seats. Some of the larger automobile magazine classified sections offered some promise, but it's hard to separate fact from fiction. Just when I thought I had looked in every barn in Northern California, I finally found Margo, a black '59 Corvette. This was the car, there was no doubt. We have been together two years and my life hasn't been the same.

Why the name Margo? Well, I have always been a big fan of "The Shadow" from those classic radio shows. Lamont Cranston (The Shadow) always relied on his companion, Margo Lane, for help, and they shared many adventures together. The first day I had the car, I turned on the Wonderbar radio looking for my favorite old-time AM radio station, and Margo's was the first voice I heard. It just kind of stuck. It is hard to explain the satisfaction of driving a classic Corvette. The car suddenly takes on a life of its own. It's almost as if the car takes control and you are only along for the ride.

Like a piece of moving art, the Corvette touches people's emotions. It is that moment when I start to realize how generic our society has become. Margo reminds the world that newer isn't always better. She represents not only an era of auto making, but an era of history, when values were different and when American quality was not questioned. I always get a kick when a very expensive new car drives by. Very often people seem to go out of their way not to acknowledge it, as if the car seemed to represent the arrogance of the driver. But a classic Corvette is a part of everyone, all Americans. I have yet to experience "road rage" in this car!

Some advertisers have tried to convince us that simple and practical is better; obviously they are not Corvette owners. What fun is it to be practical? Life's true enjoyment comes from feelings, like behind the wheel of a Corvette. A recent discovery seems to support this point. While repairing the seats, I came across an old speeding ticket from 1966. I can only imagine the wonderful drive the old owner was enjoying before it was unfortunately cut short!

I continue to enjoy my time with this car. I have been given the opportunity to be involved in numerous parades, car shows and even a calendar. I have learned it is experiences like these, shared between human and machine, that cause a person to name a car. As I said earlier, Margo made it all clear. Owning a Corvette is more than owning a car; it is much more. Cars only provide transportation. Corvettes inspire passion. It's this enthusiasm that sets the Corvette owner apart from the average car owner. Some people arrange their whole lifestyles around their Corvettes such as clubs, clothes, etc. Who can blame us? How many people have the opportunity to spend some time with a legend?

Joe Noriel
Petaluma, CA

Converted Trans Am Owner

My husband and I have been involved with Corvettes since before 1986. We currently have three Corvettes: a '78, '73 and '84, all coupes. Since 1986, we have belonged to the Lancaster County Corvette Club in Lancaster, Pennsylvania.

My husband always had large luxury cars. One day he came home and said, "I'm buying a Corvette!" I don't know how or why. We went to see this beautiful blue-green '73 Corvette; the rest is history. He tried repeatedly to get me to trade in my '85 Pontiac Trans Am Firebird. I said, "No way!" After constantly bugging me, I said okay. I drove my first Corvette and I wasn't impressed. But after driving about three different ones, I drove my Trans-Am to the dealer's lot, left it and never looked back. To me there is no other car! None!

My husband is currently first in autocross for the East Region. I'm very proud of him. He eats and sleeps Corvettes. Our den looks like an extension of a garage! My dream is to someday own an '86 yellow Pace Car convertible.

I never thought a car could over take your life, but Corvette did it. There's nothing to compare to the thrill of driving one!

Janis & Joseph Yacobenas, Lancaster, PA

A Fateful Corvette Test Drive

I always liked having a neat car, and when I married my husband, Shayne, cars became a big part of my life. We always worked on cars, had a '55 or '57 Chevy and belonged to a car club. As we grew older, our cars became more practical: a Grand Prix, Cutlass or Toronado. Our family vehicle was often a station wagon, suitable for getting groceries and hauling around our daughter and her friends.

As my 40th birthday approached, someone offered us a good price for my Malibu station wagon and I quickly accepted. When my husband asked what I would like to drive next, I declared, "No more old-lady station wagons! I want something a little sporty!"

One day we pulled into a dealership to see a Blazer, one of a half dozen we had looked at. All of them had been disappointing. It had been a long, discouraging afternoon and now it started to drizzle. "There's the Blazer," Shayne said. It was red, which is a color I dislike.

"I'd rather look at that," I pointed to the far corner where there was a brilliant yellow '81 Corvette. Yellow is my favorite color!

The sales manger knew Shayne and offered us a test drive in the Corvette. We had no intention of buying it and told him so. The price was several thousand dollars more than I wanted to spend and the whole idea was totally impractical. Although I'd ridden in a couple of Corvettes, I had no idea how to handle one, yet pulling out from the shoulder, I felt like the car was made for me. I had found the perfect car!

We told the salesman how much I wanted to spend and he said they could never let the yellow Vette go for that price, so we thanked him for the test drive and left. We never did drive the red Blazer, and all I could think was how wonderful the Vette looked and felt. I dreamed about it that night.

On Tuesday, the salesman phoned Shayne and offered to drop $1,000 off their price. "If they drop another $3,000, we'll buy it," I joked. By Thursday, they had done just that, so we decided to take another look.

We knew nothing about Corvettes at the time, so we made a committee decision. Shayne went to look the Vette over thoroughly and took

When Did It Start for You?

two friends along. One was a body shop foreman who had painted several of our show cars and one was an expert on parts who had owned several Corvettes. I waited at our house and late that evening they brought my car home!

Friends and neighbors already thought of us as eccentric and now they were convinced that we were crazy! It really amazed everyone that the Corvette was mine and not Shayne's. But he always impressed upon everyone that the car was in my name and I drove it every day. It was a combination 40th birthday present and inheritance from Grandma, and I knew she would love what I had done.

A month after we bought the car, I had breast cancer surgery. Shocked and frightened, I faced a six-month session of chemotherapy and a deep insecurity about my prognosis. The Corvette became a talisman. If I had an uncertain future, at least I would have had the experience of owning this wonderful car.

Following surgery we took a couple of weekend trips, cruised around visiting acquaintances and gathering friends around us whenever we could. Anxious to spend time with our only child, Cyndi, I taught her to drive the Corvette. We spent hours each day practicing, and while we practiced we talked about my health and the future.

I celebrated my seventh cancer-free anniversary this year, as well as

A Fateful Corvette Test Drive, Cont'd

my 47th birthday June 30th, which is apparently also the birthday of the first Corvette. Since we bought my car, our lives have been more fulfilling, and "Corvetting" has become a big part of our leisure time. We moved to a larger city and Shayne bought a Corvette of his own, a red '86 roadster. We joined the local Corvette Club and have had unbelievably good times with the members, forging some solid friendships along the way.

Having cancer taught me and those around me the value of life and its pleasures. For me, a major pleasure is owning my yellow Corvette and remembering all the happy moments of Corvetting. I know my grandmother looks down and smiles each time I back out of the garage, and I still consider the car a factor in giving me the courage to fight off cancer. Mystical reasons aside, I just plain love my car!

Lee Parent
Regina SK Canada

When Did It Start for You?

Cut Right at the Corvette

The fall of 1966 was like any other fall, except it was the year it started for me. The neighborhood kids organized the almost daily ritual of choosing teams for football games in the street. Play was only interrupted by the occasional shout of "Car!" This normally elicited groans and epithets as only 10 and 11 year olds can give. This day, however, the shout was "Vette!" It sweetly pulled up the block and every rumble and twitch of it brought oohs and aahs from this young but easily impressed group. I can still see it. It was brand new, Nassau Blue, with side pipes and blue vinyl interior. As beautiful as any '66 coupe could be, it stopped to pick up one of the opposing team's sisters. The game was called while we all inspected the car and quizzed the owner. Many a game was canceled in reverence to that automobile!

The summer of 1978 was like any other. I was working to put myself through college and on the way to work I saw her, a brand new '78 Corvette. She was a light blue T-top with dark blue leather interior, the most gorgeous thing I had seen since that '66 coupe.

One day in 1995, a co-worker said her husband was selling his Corvette. I asked the usual questions until I realized she was describing the very same light blue T-top Corvette with blue leather interior! She was still all-original, still beautiful and still running strong! My wife gave me her blessings on the purchase and a week later my 17-year fantasy had come true! Yes, it's only a '78, but it's my '78. I can tell by the looks on the kid' faces when I interrupt their football games in the street that maybe, just maybe, my Corvette may start "it" for them, too!

Mike Hale
Erie, PA

Bob's '66

It was early in the summer of 1966. I was 12 years old and would turn 13 in a month. I had just completed seventh grade and was facing the eighth grade, the last year of junior high. It would be three years before I would receive a driver's license and five years before I would receive a lottery number for the selective service draft.

The Vietnam War was still going strong. The limited understanding I had of the war came from the short glimpses on the evening news of U.S. soldiers patrolling through the various types of terrain of Vietnam, the jungles and open areas, carrying their weapons, radios and sometimes their wounded comrades.

My sister, who is eight years older than me, dated a guy named Bob in high school. Before they graduated, they had decided they were just friends and he remained a friend of my whole family. Once, when I was 9, Bob even went on a long trip with us in the middle of winter. The weather became so bad that the road signs were impossible to read because they were covered with snow. My mother pulled the big white station wagon onto the shoulder of the major highway we were driving so that Bob could throw snowballs to knock snow from a road sign that we desperately needed to read.

A few years later, Bob became a soldier and went to Vietnam. My family no longer lived in Ohio where he and my sister went to high school together, but had moved to southern Indiana. Shortly after his tour of duty, he looked up my family and pleasantly surprised us with a visit.

Just seeing Bob again and knowing that he survived Vietnam was what was important to us. But he had with him some things that were very impressive to me, as I was only 12 years old at the time. He had a very large knife and a 35mm camera, something to show for his sacrifices. Items like these were made very affordable for soldiers overseas. But these were just accessories for what really made an impression on me, a new '66 silver Corvette Sting Ray convertible with factory side pipes. After showing us how to drop the convertible top and stow it in the compartment behind the seats, he took my brother and me for a ride. I've never forgotten those times and those moments. I didn't fully realize it then, but that's when I decided that was the kind of car I

When Did It Start for You?

wanted.

I didn't understand it at the time, but now I know how much that car must have meant to Bob. He had experienced war and with it some of the worst of what the world has to offer. I believe Bob had earned the right to experience some of the best the world has to offer. We are fortunate to live in a country that gives us the opportunity to enjoy freedom and some of the finer things in life. Today, the Corvette is still a symbol of many kinds of freedom.

I wanted a Corvette not as a status symbol, there are much more expensive cars for that, but as a symbol of another kind. I wanted a symbol of the feeling and mood of good times like that summer day in 1966, times when all was well and things were good and right.

Nick Redden
Lafayette, Indiana

When Did It Start for You?

Hangin' With the Guys

Chapter 4

The Poster at Mission Chevrolet

When did it start? It happened to me in 1953. My friends and I ran to Mission Chevrolet in San Gabriel, California, to look at the all new '53 Chevrolet Bel-Air hard top. While checking it out, I saw some pictures

and good-size posters of a white sports car. It was called a Corvette. Fast forward to 1959, married, kids, out of the Army. One day my friend Al came over to visit, driving a new '59 black with silver coves 4-speed roadster. Al said, "Ray, let's go." We did, and I was hooked! I found my dream Vette in October, 1990. It was a single-owner, '61 black with silver coves roadster Vette with power windows.

I am now a proud owner of two roadsters, my '61 and a Gun Metal Blue '91 L-98. I could go on and on, but I have to stop. Oh, how I remember when. Dreams do come true. Only in the good 'ol U.S.A.

Ray & Imelda Flores
Huntington Beach, CA

Born With a Toy Car in Hand

My exact age when it all started is hard to say. I think I was born with a toy car in my hand. I even remember my first childhood pedal car. However, it was my first ride in a Vette that bit me hard. In high school I was taken for a ride in my friend's '69 black 4-speed, small-block Vette. It was best with the T-tops off, leaning out the window to hear the sound of the side pipes. The fact that my friend enjoyed shortening the life of his rear tires every chance he had didn't hurt either! I had a nice Camaro, but it wasn't the same after that ride.

College and dental school put a Vette on hold for a while, but I finally bought a '72 Vette, painted it black and put on those side pipes. I still own the car after 13 years. I've also added a '58 290-hp fuelie and an '85 to my collection. Although I maintain the cars to show quality, I drive them often and have the same enthusiasm as I had on that first ride!

Bill Stolfi, Hopewell Junction, NY

The Trip to the Corvette Nationals

Ever since I was 12 years old, I have been fascinated with America's favorite sports car, the Corvette.

Every time a Corvette passed me on the road, I would stare in awe and wonder when my time to own one would come. I told everyone I knew that someday I would own a Corvette of my own. My dream finally came true in 1996.

It was Saturday, May 4, 1996, and my friend Greg Dixon and I had gone to the Corvette Nationals here in Indianapolis. The day was cloudy with rain threatening the show all day long. That didn't stop us from walking around and looking at all these beautiful cars.

We stumbled upon a stunning white '76 Sting Ray with red leather interior. I had always loved the Sting Ray because it reminded me of my high school days. I stopped and spoke to the gentleman who stood beside his prized possession. He told me in a sad voice that he had to sell it because he needed some extra cash for his son's college education. I told him that I was interested, we negotiated a price and I became the proud owner of an American legend!

On the way home, I called my parents' house to give them the wonderful news. My mother answered the phone and couldn't believe that I had actually bought a Corvette! She knew that my lifelong dream had come true.

Maria Tabares, Indianapolis, IN

When Did It Start for You?

Straightening Out the Curves in Las Vegas

My Corvette dreams started in high school. A friend of mine picked me up in a heavily modified '68 drop top. It had been set up as a slalom racer and could really handle the curves. What a thrill! I ran into him about five years out of school. He had totaled the Vette and was working in a Subaru dealership.

A few years back, I was stationed overseas with the Navy in Japan. I was not able to bring my family, which made for a rather difficult tour. I bolstered myself up by making it my goal to save enough money over the two years to buy a used Corvette when I returned. I read every piece of Corvette literature I could find at the Stars and Stripes bookstore. I saved quite a bit of money, but when I returned I found there were no cars in my price range. I was dismayed!

About a year later I ran into a former co-worker who owned an '81 Corvette. I asked if he still had it. When he said he did, I asked if he would give it to me! He laughed and said, no way, but he would sell it to me. His price was reasonable and within a week it was mine!

My '81 Corvette isn't in concourse condition. It needs paint and interior work, but the engine is strong and it is a thrill to drive. The wife and I even took it to Las Vegas and had a wonderful time. The old girl took the mountains like they had been rolled flat. It was the best driving experience I have ever had. In a couple of years when I have more time, I will make my baby a real showpiece. But for now, I still get a thrill every morning when I walk out my front door and realize that I get to drive a Corvette to work!

Walter Hefty
San Diego, CA

The "Cool" Guys' Cars

In 1955 I saw my first Corvette. It was being driven by one of the local "cool" guys named Jerry Godkins. It was a white '54 Vette with a red interior. The sound of that Blue Flame six was about the neatest thing I'd ever heard. I was only 10 years old, but I was into cars in a big way. You could ask and I could name and spec just about anything and even at that age, I knew something was amiss when I saw the Powerglide. For a car to be really cool it had to have a stick shift, but Chevrolet was on the right track and I knew I wanted one.

Five years later a local doctor's son bought a black '61 fuelie and my love affair stirred again. I actually begged a ride in it and it was worth the groveling. I was gone. With the top down, going through the gears, pressed back against the seat, it was a sensation unlike any other. This is what dreams of a 16-year-old are made of. And someday one would be mine.

In 1964 I was pumping gas at Jerry Godkins' Union station, when a guy I'd never seen before rolled in with a Frost Blue '60. I was surprised. Where had this car been? I knew every car in Juneau, Alaska, and had missed a Vette! I stuttered and just about died when he told me that he was selling it because it just wasn't big enough for him and his wife. "Gee," I thought, "Women ruin everything." But I had enough brains to ask, "How much?"

"Oh," he said, "$1,500 would about do." I forgot my pity for the guy and realized I had a chance at a dream. Now, you have to realize that I was working for, $3.00 an hour, and $1,500 in cash was a long way away. I didn't have the money, so I did what any enterprising young man would do; I asked Dad. He hemmed and hawed a bit and said, "For $1,500, you're sure not getting much." But he loaned me the money anyway. I could sell my '57 Bel-Air hardtop and pay some of it back, and the rest he would except as payments. A while later I decided that the 283 was tired and I needed just a little more power, so I dropped a 327cid/365-hp with the help of my friend, Jeff. Did we have fun! My dad's garage was the center of the cruise on a Saturday night and we were the stars. We rolled up the sleeves on our greasy white T-shirts, just like Jimmy Dean. It was neat.

Later the newness wore off and I got my hands on a '65 Sting Ray with a 327cid/365-hp engine. But it just wasn't the same. To me, it wasn't a Corvette. It was something refined. You could hear yourself think at speed and it didn't leak. I missed that little round back end.

Aviation school and a family won out and Corvettes were off the list! However, I loved that '60 and vowed that someday I would have another. Last year, I turned 50. My daughter is on her own, so I bought myself a birthday present. Yep. It was another Turtleback, a '59. No cherry, but one I can work on and drive without feeling that I desecrated a museum piece. And there is peace in the valley again as I tool down the coast on Highway 101 listening to the Beach Boys and enjoying the sound of a '67 327cid/350-hp engine with the top down. Now that's the way to have a second childhood! And yes, a woman made it possible! Aren't they great?

Ed Fleek
Cannon Beach, OR

Car Craft Magazine

My love affair with the "American Dream" started back in 1977 when I was in junior high school. I was sitting in study hall looking through *Car Craft* magazine and spotted a '73 Corvette. Wow, what a car!

From that day forward, I dreamed of owning my own Corvette. As a teenager, I cut out and pasted every picture of a Corvette I could find. What fun this was to do! As the years went by, it became evident that I would probably never be able to purchase a Corvette. In 1982, I got married to my childhood sweetheart and shortly thereafter had two young children.

In 1992, after working day and night at the same job for 10 years, things finally started paying off for us. I got promoted to general manager and the possibility of owning a Corvette was, for the first time, within reach. In January 1996, I told my wife that I was going to start looking for a late-model used Corvette. She thought I was joking.

The next week, I was in Davenport, Iowa, at a meeting. After the meeting was over, I started back home and had to stop to get gas in my truck. While at the station, I picked up a *Car Trader* newspaper and there it was, a '92 white Corvette coupe with almost every factory option. It was in immaculate condition.

My wife and I went to Peoria, Illinois, to look at it that same weekend. Once we laid eyes on it, our dream came true. It was a two-owner car with all the documentation. Every ounce of fuel ever put in the car had been recorded, along with all maintenance items, tire changes, etc. What a magnificent machine it was! To our surprise, the car had been personally autographed by Mr. Dave McLellan and dated September 25, 1992. That date was our tenth wedding anniversary. Was this fate, or God saying, "Rodney, you've made it! This car is meant to be yours!" To this day, I still sometimes have a tear run down my cheek as I drive my Vette. It took me 18 years to make my dream come true.

P.S. Anyone who has a dream of any kind, please don't give up, regardless of how bad things may seem. Time heals all, and hard work still pays off in America. A special thanks to my wife, children and my parents, who gave me the will to achieve. I love you all!

Rodney E. Bailey, Taylorville, IL

Serving Time in a '52 Chevy Pickup

We call ourselves enthusiasts. We subscribe to all the car magazines, attend automobile races and shows. We lovingly polish our machines during every spare moment. Probably even called in sick to work a few times in pursuit of the great American road trip.

But now it's time for a reality check, fellow Corvette lovers. If you want to experience the full range of the automobile experience, I challenge you to abandon your pavement-ripping sports car and your cushy climate-controlled Cadillac for a step back to the way it used to be. Try driving the next 50,000 miles behind the wheel of an early '50s pickup truck. It was from this perspective that my Corvette experience took flight.

For all the love and discipline my parents gave, they just never made a splash financially. They struggled at times from one meal to the next while raising three children, one of whom was a budding auto enthusiast whose first job was as a $3.35-an-hour pizza cook. Needless to say, Corvettes and Ferraris were never parked on our driveway, but they did make several flights of fancy in my mind.

The reward for these exotic car fantasies came in 1982. I had just turned 18 when manna from heaven fell into my lap in the form of the most decrepit '52 Chevy pickup you ever saw. No, it wasn't a Porsche, but the Chevy did become a welcome friend at a time when I was desperate for wheels. It was old, slow, drafty, noisy, leaky, smelly and rusted, but soon earned my admiration for its dependability and classic styling.

Then one rainy day in 1983, while continuing to rationalize away the inconveniences of my only ride, I gazed through the cracked glass at the most amazing automobile on the planet. The reason for that particular outing escapes memory, but the sight of the two-tone, silver-and-gray car and the place she was parked in the corner of a movie theater parking lot is still vivid. That first glimpse of the exotic new C4 was hampered by my truck's partially inoperative vacuum wipers. Not satisfied with the view, I removed the folded newspaper "wedgies" used to keep the channel-less side glass from rattling, grabbed the makeshift vise-grip window crank, lowered the window and stuck my head out for a closer look.

What a contrast it was! I was looking at the most stunning, technically advanced automobile in the world from behind the wheel of a vehicle that hadn't seen a fresh coat of paint in over 30 years! The truck reeked of gasoline, grime and rotten upholstery fibers, all mixed together. But you could almost smell the "new"on that Vette as it perched cat-like across the street! It had a high-tech mix of electronics that would give you info on any engine or trip mileage function you could imagine. If the looks or the powerful engine or the handling of that car didn't get your blood flowing, then maybe those cool flip-over headlights would. My truck wasn't totally void of some of those things, though. It had a dip-stick-style gas gauge I had fashioned when the dash unit quit working. It even had headlights that worked. Whoopee!

At that point in life, imagining myself in a Corvette was as realistic as Roger Penske recruiting drivers at the state motor vehicle office. Finally in 1994 those years of study, minimum-wage jobs and the associated headaches from trying to make ends meet on a minimal budget were nearing an end. Graduate school was over and for the first time in my 30 years I began to see a comfortable financial future. Additionally, I had the support of my wife, Barbara, who always had a keen eye for sharp cars. We made a pact that we would get a sports car when I got a decent job after graduation.

The job came in March and by mid-summer I was chomping at the bit for a Corvette. Prudence dictated that we should wait just a few more months before that purchase in order to get all of our other financial details ironed out. Then the phone in my office rang one afternoon. Seems Barb had checked the mail that day and we had received a promo mailer from the local credit union offering obscenely low finance rates on new car loans. That was just the impetus we needed to act!

We first went to the dealer on a Wednesday evening where the validity of the sweet deal was confirmed. Unfortunately, I had a workshop to attend all the next week and was anxious to see a deal go through before leaving. A day or two was spent while the dealer checked the availability of the vehicle we wanted and by Saturday afternoon, my dealer had been able to locate just the car. He assured us it would be there the following Friday when I returned from the business trip.

Man, what a week of anticipation that was! The car was black on black with a 6-speed tranny. None of that automatic stuff for me! I intended to enjoy this car to the fullest and that included slamming a few gears.

The night before the four-hour return drive from the workshop, I barely slept a wink. But the waiting was almost over. It had been raining all the way back from Atlanta and continued even now as we drove onto the dealer's Nashville lot. The dealer told me that I had a choice of two. Both were black, but one had red leather interior, which was a little too bold for my taste. After that cursory glance, I stepped over to get a serious look at the car that had been the object of my lust for nearly two weeks. Or had it really been 11 years? Whatever the case, this was a moment to be savored!

I slowly circled the car in the same manner as I had examined used cars many times before. There wasn't a scratch to be found, not a single rip in the seats or any oil stains on the engine or floor underneath. The reality of this situation was still sinking in. This was a brand new Corvette! And in a few moments, it would be mine!

When the salesperson handed me the keys, my anticipation was mixed with euphoria. I lifted my leg over the high doorsill and nestled into the soft leather seat. I depressed the clutch with my left foot and slid the key into the ignition as if by instinct. The turn of the key was quickly followed by a smooth rumble. The beast was alive! The digital dash was awake in an orange glow and my eyes fell on the odometer. Eleven miles! Only 11 miles! As Barb stepped to her car to make the trip home, my lungs filled with the sweet smell of virgin leather and new carpet. The rain was lightly falling, so I turned on the wipers, then those flip-over headlights. It was way cool.

As we drove off the dealer's lot I had an ear-to-ear grin, and for a moment my mind popped back to another rainy day 11 years earlier when I had gotten my first glimpse at the new C4. Briefly, I struggled to hold back tears of joy for finally having achieved the dream. But the emotions were no match for the physical sensations I felt when I lowered my right foot, keeping the car just short of wheel spin. She accelerated like a missile, pushing my upper torso back into the seat as no other car had ever done. The engine revved so fast under hard acceleration, I almost thought the tachometer needle had spun off the gauge!

She begged to be driven hard. The shifter seemed much easier to use when shifting hard and fast and if done carefully, my novice hands had no trouble finding the right gear. With each shift it felt as if I had been rear-ended by a tractor-trailer rig! A few quick gear changes and I was doing 100 miles an hour!

The 40-minute drive ended all too soon, yet I was happy to have the car home for a more detailed inspection. There was a welcome space in the garage right beside the old '52 Chevy, whose windows had once framed the face of an optimistic teenager who saw magic in the Corvette.

The old Chevy was much better now, too. It had proven a dependable daily driver for many miles and had earned the right to rest from regular duties in these later years after becoming the benefactor of my first auto-motive restoration. Will the Chevy ever be for sale? No way! She holds sentimental value and is a great reminder of the struggle to finally reach Corvette status. As for the Vette, she's the vehicle of choice for just about any outing.

When we're not on the road, that garage is now the perfect place for a leisurely wax job, an oil change, or just relaxing. I can close my eyes, reflect on the memories and sometimes, when the mood is right, I just listen to the heartbeat.

Scott G. Sensing
Murfreesboro, TN

Keeping Peace

I was 12 years old in 1978, a student at the only middle school in the tiny, rural farming town of Wautoma, Wisconsin. My family was extremely poor, living on welfare checks and cherishing the monthly allotment of government cheese and consumables. I remember my class was at recess when a brand new '78 Corvette Pace Car slowly crept onto the very field where we were all at play.

Maybe it was the way that car rippled with automotive muscle and wore its two-tone paint and decals in such a brazen manner. The smooth lines of that fiberglass body, well adorned in ground effects, almost made me forget all about the poster of Farrah Fawcett so lovingly pinned to my bedroom wall. All the students outside that day slowly approached the Vette, eyes wide in disbelief, mouths open in awe. I recall the owner of the car was wise enough to not let this horde of sticky-fingered children inside his new baby. We sure smeared his windows, chrome and deep black paint, though!

It was unreal, with its silver leather seats, CB radio, power everything and "Official Pace Car" tattooed on the doors. I was jolted back

When Did It Start for You?

from dreamland when the bell rang. As I headed toward the school door, I glanced back for one last look and thought to myself that one day, I would break away from the poverty that surrounded me and get myself that very car.

Nearly 20 years later and now living in Denver, I flew up to Spokane, Washington, to help a cousin drive back a 4x4 and a gorgeous '72 Corvette Sting Ray he was buying from his father. When I got behind the wheel of that '72, the childhood memories of that Pace Car came rushing back and I was stricken with full-fledged and incurable Corvette fever. That same cousin, Bret, was with me the day I found my pristine '78. It sat in a heated garage for eight years. This car with only 18,000 miles on it had cobwebs in the storage area and suspension and was still sporting the original tires (full of flat spots from sitting). The original battery was removed, but available, as was the window sticker.

I bought that car not just because it was a great deal, but because I had made a promise to a 12-year-old boy.

David Schmidt
Highland Ranch, CO

Making the Move on a '62 Corvette

"Did you buy it new?" "How long have you owned the car?" "Why did you decide on a '62?" At any given car show, the frequency of these questions never ceases to amaze me. The first two questions are easy to answer. "No, I didn't buy the car new. I bought the car in February, 1989." The last question is one that takes too long to answer. I usually respond by saying something like, "I have always liked the straight axles and this car became available, so I decided to buy it." But this is only a fraction of the story.

In 1962, my junior year in high school, the conversation in the locker room and in the parking lot revolved around the new models of the year. The discussion at times focused on the Anniversary Gold 327 Super Sport Impala, as well as the 409. The major topic of discussion centered on the "new" Corvette with the 327hp engine.

All of the "gear heads" talked about how fast it was and how it would clean up at CDR (Continental Divide Raceways, Castle Rock, CO) in the coming summer months. Every red-blooded male enrolled at the school wanted one. I was no exception. As a stock boy at Burt's Shoe Store, I knew I would be lucky if I got to stand near one. To make matters worse, my best friend's grandmother presented him with the keys to a brand new '62 Anniversary Gold Super Sport 4-speed Impala. We cruised around in that and couldn't wait for the drag race season ahead.

The summer drag race plans were not pipe dreams. We arrived at the strip as race prepared as 17 year olds could be. I will never forget the first time I saw that white '62 Vette driven by Judy Lilly roar down the strip. I had read practically all that was written about the wonders of the '62, but it was another thing to personally see it. All summer we watched Judy Lilly and her white '62 clean up everything in her path. It was this summer that I vowed I was going to own a '62 327 Corvette. My friends laughed. No one believed me, but I knew. So what if it took me 27 years? I am laughing the hardest now because I own a '62!

John Marsico
Broomfield, CO

Fuelish Dreams

It was a great time to be a teenager in America in the early '60s, especially if you had a driver's license and you were into cars and cruising. We would sit at a soda fountain and drink chocolate cokes, cherry phosphates and check out the latest car magazines.

In those days, most of the cars featured were way-out customs with chopped tops, fender skirts and 3-bar spinner hubcaps. We all liked American V-8 power and knew of no other kind. Fuel injection was by Enderle and reserved for 'slingshot' dragsters, so when we laid our eyes on an article featuring a '61 Corvette with fuel injection, we wondered in amazement at this new kind of street induction.

Then came the big news from Detroit, specifically Chevrolet. It hit the automotive scene like a lightening bolt. Sting Ray! What was this hot new American car on the scene? Every year in the fall, the new cars were introduced and we would get to the car dealerships however we could. Sneaking around, we would try to spot the new models arriving on the transports. In those days the dealers made a big thing of introducing new styles. They would put big covers on the cars on the transports and paper over the windows of the dealership right up until the day of introduction! If any Corvettes came in, they would go out right away and we would be looking at Impalas most of the time.

In the spring of 1963 and on the verge of high school graduation, we would gather at the home of one of our group. This was usually the guy who had the most car magazines to look at, the most records to play and the latest AMT customizing kit to look at. Here is where I saw the picture that would capture my imagination. It was the May 1963 issue of *Motor Trend* magazine and featured an Ermine White, split window coupe. I stared at the cover for a long time and my buddies had to shake me out of my trance.

The summer of 1963 passed without once seeing a Sting Ray on the street. This could most likely be attributed to the fact that the town I was living in at the time, Rockford, Illinois, was a working-class town, and a high-priced car like a Corvette was relatively rare. The streets of Rockford resonated to the thunder of big-inch machinery, such as 409 Impalas, 390 and 406 Ford Galaxies and 383 and 426 Dodges and Plymouths. It seemed like every corner gas station had one of these machines parked there belonging either to the owner or one of his employees.

The next year for me was taken up by college work, and it wasn't until the summer of '64 that I would have an experience that I remember even now like it was yesterday. By then, a lot of the "new" cars we saw on the street were showing up on used car lots as trade-ins for '64 models. We had a grapevine of information on the whereabouts of some of these cars, and we often cruised around town looking for a car lot that had a car we wanted to sit in and touch. The '62 Olds Starfires were a favorite, and we saw an example of most all the others previously mentioned. However, the one I wanted to look at, the '63 split window coupe, never showed up on a lot. That is, until one day in late summer.

We were parked in one of our parents' cars at the local eatery where we parked in a row so the local hot shots could cruise through a gauntlet to show off their cars. We wanted to see this new car from Chevrolet, the "Chevelle" and the hot one from Pontiac, the "GTO," and to see which one of our former classmates was lucky enough to be able to have one. One member of our group rolled up and told us he saw a Sting Ray on a car lot across town! Man! I got goose bumps and could hardly wait for the weekend when I could ask my dad to take me there. At the time, my dad was on the road in sales most of the week so the only time we had to spend together was on the weekend. We would play a game with car dealers, going around looking at cars, pretending to be interested in buying and getting them to let us test drive them. We only did this to confirm previously held opinions we had about various makes and models, but it was all in fun. Except I was dead serious about getting to that Corvette.

We drove into the lot, and sure enough, my information was right on the money. It was an Ermine White, split window coupe. The salesman threw open the hood and I beheld the engine of my dreams. It was the 340-hp engine complete with ribbed valve covers and the holes in the air cleaner. When the salesman handed the keys to us, I looked at Dad and he said, "Let's take it for a spin!" I got in and my dad took the passenger seat, and it hit me that I had never driven a 4-speed car before in my life! I pushed in the clutch and turned the key at the same time, pushing the accelerator pedal halfway down like I was an old hand at it! That 327 fired to life and I quickly found neutral across the "H" like my buddies had taught me in our hangout sessions. I snickered the T-bar shifter into first, let the clutch out and into the street we went!

This was no time to foul up, I told myself. What kind of fool would get rid of a car such as this, I thought! My eyes fell to the spun aluminum dials on the dash, those bent red needles rising and falling to the revolutions of the engine. I looked out the rear window through the rearview mirror. I had no earthly idea who Zora Duntov was or why he didn't like that split window! I loved it and had no thought about vision obstruction. That Sting Ray spine from the front of the roof to the rear of the deck was about the most glorious automotive styling theme I had ever seen!

We found ourselves at the intersection of a street where we were facing a steep incline. This was no time for one of my friends to come along and see me stall in the middle of the street. I gave the Vette the gas and squealed out onto the main drag. By this time I was really confident of myself and decided to get into this car. I ran through the gears, hoping now that one of my friends would see me driving this fantastic car. I then learned what one of my friends meant when he said, "There's nothing like a solid lifter Chevy. Man, those lifters were talkin' my language!"

The mechanical cacophony of the engine and the exhaust rumbling beneath me were more than I could stand and the reality soon hit home. I could no more buy this car than fly! It had to go back to the lot, where I reluctantly shut the engine off. The salesman walked up and said, "Well, what do you think of this baby?" I said, "Wow! What a car, but I don't think it's for me. I would probably just wrap it around a tree!" We left the salesman with a puzzled look on his face. Little did he know I had a knot in my gut at having to leave that car there. I wanted it so badly!

Over the years, I saw the Corvette ebb and flow yearly but never gave up on getting one someday. Job, family and house payments took precedence, but in 1986 GM decided to have a big clearance sale after years of high interest rates, and my wife and I decided it was now or never. We brought home a brand new '86 coupe, which we still own.

That's my Corvette story, but what about the future? The new C5 guarantees that the Corvette will be around well into the next century, it is that good. What will our children and grandchildren think of the Corvette? For its survival, it is essential that they become interested in the car and that they see a C6 Corvette.

The answer to the question may lie in what happened on a recent visit by our two-year-old grandson. On his first visit to Grandpa's house he decided to check out the garage. Enclosed is a photo snapped by his mother who wisely followed him around with camera ready. As you can see, he is lifting up the cover on our Corvette. He has discovered Grandpa's Corvette! Is this where it starts for him? Only time will tell, but our daughter-in-law reported that upon finding that shiny aluminum wheel, he looked up at her and exclaimed, "Oh, gosh!"

And the beat goes on!

Steve & Sandra Palmer, Richmond, TX

Never Too Old for a Corvette

I just turned 69 years old this year. We bought our first Corvette in the spring of 1997, exactly 40 years from my first ride in a Corvette. My friend, Roger Swiney, invited me to ride with him on a Poker Run in his red and white '57 Vette. When I got home, I told my wife that someday I would own one.

Three kids and five grandchildren later, we bought a beautiful '82 Corvette with 50,000 miles on it from our friend Jerry Frisgy, who still owns an '81, an '82 Collector's Edition and an '89. In fact, he took the picture I'm sending with this letter in Roslyn, Washington, in 1997.

Angie & Janice Butrick
Renton, WA

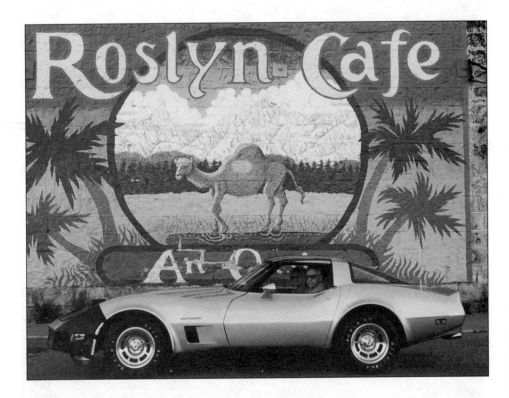

When Did It Start for You?

The Long Walk Home

The first Corvette was a '66 coupe, silver with black interior. The time was fall of 1968. I was in the eighth grade. Walking to and from school every day, I saw this car sitting in a nearby front yard. I would stop and stare at this Vette until I'd be late for class. Years later, after high school, I was working at a service station part time. The owner of the station was the brother-in-law of the owner of the '66. This guy was about 15 years older than I was, but we became close friends. Together we worked on this car, keeping it going. I told my friend if he ever wanted to sell the Corvette, just to let me know.

In 1982, he was in the process of getting a divorce and needed money. Needless to say, I jumped to the checkbook and wrote him a check. The '66 sat in my driveway until I started to return it to street-driving shape. Someday I plan to do a frame-up restoration. Until then, it's my daily driver.

Jim Cahill
Muskogee, OK

Corvette Spotters

Small Oklahoma towns are not necessarily hot beds of automobile activity. But in the early 50s the art of customizing the family sedan and hot-rodding were in, and people were making their way eastward from California via the "Mother Road," Route 66. These were the days of '50 green Oldsmobile Rocket 88 coupes, "Fordillacs," Hudson Hornets and Pan American Lincoln racers. Chevrolet was not a "runner." But the Ford/Chevrolet debate raged among those of us already polarized by our fathers. Unfortunately, Ford had not only the image, but the V-8.

Weekends were spent sitting on the corner of the main drag, which happened to be a U.S. highway and the only paved thoroughfare in town. We spent our time identifying the model year (a lot easier then than now), type of engine and making real and imaginary assessments of top speed. A leaded-in '50 Ford in primer, lowered and sporting twin turned-down spotlights was high excitement. Anything with just two doors that was not a pickup was cool.

While updating the automobile census in town during a warm summer day in 1954, a small white car the likes of which had not been even imagined came speeding down the street. It was driven by an Oklahoma Highway Patrolman with the local Chevrolet dealer riding shotgun. "It's headed for the Chevy dealership, yelled someone, and four young teenagers broke all local track records for the three-block distance between the hangout corner and the dealership.

We arrived before the two passengers could exit this machine. It was the first Corvette. It was resplendent in white with red interior. Time, heartbeats and breathing stood still. A vow of future ownership was sworn on the spot that we knew would be fulfilled. A passion in life had been kindled that will never be extinguished.

That first sighting is still as vivid and as nourishing to the senses now as it was then. I have no doubt it always will be. Growing older is not a process to relish. But it's been glorious to watch the beloved Corvette grow up with me, from its adolescent years to tough kid on the block, from man-about-town to world-class bon vivant!

Paul & Barbara Mariano
Goleta, CA

When Did It Start for You?

Neighborly Advice

Chapter 5

Gary's Car Wash

On December 27, 1958, my family and I moved three miles north to a new neighborhood. To an 11-year-old kid, three miles from all my friends may as well have been 3,000 miles. Across the street from my new house lived a man who would soon introduce me to the world of cars. Gary owned, but rarely drove, a '58 Corvette. My most vivid memory is one of Gary washing the Corvette and then slowly driving it down the short dead-end street on which we lived. If I close my eyes, I can still see the chrome spinner hubcaps sparkling in the sun and hear the low rumble of the engine.

Gary added about 1,500 miles per year to the odometer and most of them were with me in the passenger seat. I learned how to care for a car from Gary. The Vette never saw rain, never parked next to another vehicle, and every time I climbed in I was reminded not to put my shoe on the chrome doorsill.

Most of our rides were with the top down and the radio off. The fuel-injected 283, 4-speed, with 3.70:1 Posi-traction rear was music to our ears. In the late '50s, nothing on the road could match us, except another Corvette. Even though it was a rare occurrence, the sight of another Corvette brought huge smiles and energetic waves.

I've now added 40 years to the 11 and I've envied every driver of every Corvette I've ever seen. About five years ago, I bought my first Corvette, a '76 red Sting Ray. About a year ago, I added a '64 300-hp 4-speed convertible Sting Ray to my collection. It's fast, it's fun, and sometimes when I'm shifting through the gears and the wind is blowing what little hair I have left, it's 1958 again.

Richard Johnson
Rose Hill, KS

A Lasting Impression

My "Love At First Sight" Corvette story began in the early '80s. I was a teenager influenced like many other youths by the sight, sound and thrill of new adventure and fast cars. The neighborhood I lived in was void of hot rods until that oh-so-fateful day. It caught my eye in an instant. I was like a hawk that with sharp, keen eyesight focusing all attention on it. I was unaware of what it was. I knew, though, that this one machine would fulfill every teenage dream of sight, sound and the thrill of adventure. My emotions wound out of control like an explosion sparked by this one car. I had to have it! Later I found out it was a Corvette.

Although that car has been long gone for many years, I know now it was an early '60s Sting Ray. In '89 I had the opportunity to finally own the American dream, the Corvette. It was a '67 model with a drivetrain and in need of extensive bodywork. Sight unseen and in as rough condition as I heard it was, I jumped at the chance to buy.

Unfortunately, the owner backed out. I smiled and waved good-bye to this Sting Ray I never had the pleasure of seeing, knowing that soon my day would come. Although that day has not yet arrived, I hold to my faith that tells me that my Corvette is out there. One day, when the time is right and opportunity comes my way, we will cross paths, my Corvette and I. What a glorious day that will be!

Edward Prado
Corpus Christi, TX

The Sound and the Power

I was 15 at the time and the neighbor who lived behind our house had just brought home a new '64 coupe with a 327cid/365-hp engine. It was a red 4-speed. I remember running out to the alley behind our house just to listen to that car run when he would start it up. When I turned 17, with help from my dad, I bought a red '59 Vette 283cid 4-speed. Some friends of the family had a red '57, so mine just had to be red.

In '69 I was drafted into the Army, so I sold the '59 to my brother for $1,100. He still owns it today and I've tried to buy back the car many times. It's not going to happen!

After a tour in Vietnam, I returned home, bought a house, got married and in 1975 bought a '72 T-top 327cid, 4-speed. It's a nice driver that we still own today. Later in '85 we bought an '85 coupe and kept that car for eight years, sold it and bought a '65 convertible red 327cid/300-hp 4-speed that I am currently redoing. We just put the body back on the chassis in February. My brother also owns a red '89 coupe. We both have liked these cars since we were kids. The C5 sure looks fine, doesn't it?

John E. Hucik
Edmonds, WA

Corvette Rocket Ship

It was the late '50s when friends of my parents came over to our house. Normally, this was not all that exciting, but this time was different. My parents' friends, Gerald and Lois, had just bought a new car. It was a Corvette. Gerald asked me if I wanted a ride. This was to be my first ride in a Corvette. I do not remember the year. It was white with colored coves. The interior was impressive. The bucket seats made you feel like you were in a rocket ship. There wasn't even a glove box where the glove box normally was. One of the most memorable items was the speedometer. It went to 160 mph. My dad's Buick only went to 120 mph. This car must be something special. Although the ride was short, it got me hooked.

Since that day, I have always wanted a Corvette. When I was 16, in 1969, my barber had a '63 red coupe for sale for $2,000. I kept trying to come up with a way of buying it. Looking back, it was probably better that I did not get a Corvette at that time. By the way, that barber still has the '63 coupe. The last time I saw him, around three years ago, he said it was now part of his retirement plan.

In late 1995, my wife finally agreed that I should buy a Corvette. At this time, both of our daughters were out of the house and just about done with school. I did a lot of looking, reading and calculating. In November 1995 I found a bright yellow '77 Corvette, the last year of the straight-back window. Although all Corvettes are beautiful, this one really got to me. One of my dreams came true.

By the way, both of my daughters are back home again, so my timing was perfect.

Eric A. Gordon
Roselle, IL

Want to Go for a Ride?

In 1962, my next-door neighbor, who was just out of the Navy, drove up in a new convertible red Corvette. My friend and I were doing what 13-year-olds do in July, which was nothing! Our jaws dropped when we saw that car. My neighbor quickly sensed our wonder and to our astonishment asked, "Want to go for a ride?"

The three of us went for many rides and every time it was more exciting. We sure did get a lot of looks and thought we looked so cool! One evening I half-jokingly asked if I could drive the auto into the garage. After stalling it several times I managed to drive the car all of 30 yards. That's when it all started for me and America's sports car. I made a promise to myself that one day I would own a Corvette.

I finally bought the Vette of my dreams. Check it out! And Bill and Jimmy, if you're reading this, I hope you're both still cool!

Ed L. Grieco
Denver, CO

Dad's Friend's '74

My story started in 1974 when I was four years old. My dad's friend let us use his orange '73 Vette for about a week. I remember how awesome it was to sit in it and go for a ride. Everyone had an interest in that car wherever we went. I knew then that Corvettes had to be something special.

Then in 1987 another family friend brought over a recently purchased '66 Vette, with a 427/425-hp engine. After going for a very fast ride, I was hooked! I even got to take it to school that next spring. What a riot! Everyone thought it was totally awesome.

I now own a restored Riverside Red '64 coupe with a 327cid/300-hp 4-speed. I also have recently acquired an all-original '76 silver/red leather L82-M21 beauty with rare no air and no power steering, one of 173. It's a great feeling cruising in either one, or just standing in the garage looking at them. Whatever it takes, Corvettes are a dream come true!

Kelly Johnson
Elkhart Lake, WI

The '36 Chevy That Couldn't Compete

It all started for me in 1953 or 1954. I was walking home from grade school and I saw a lady in a '53 or '54 Corvette. I remember it had grilles over the headlights, and it was either powder blue or white. I fell in love with Corvettes right then! My parents were driving a '36 Chevy at that time, so the Corvette really looked like a genuine sports car to me.

In 1958 I was 18 years old and had just started my first full-time job working in a grocery store. I went to the local Chevy dealership, where a friend of my sister was a salesman, and he also raced a '58 Corvette called the "Purple People Eater." I talked to my mother and dad and they agreed to let me trade in the '55 family Oldsmobile for a new '59 Corvette. I had never ridden in a Corvette or even sat in one, but I had to have one!

I ordered a '59 Inca Silver Corvette with both tops, red interior, 290-hp, fuel-injected engine with 4-speed and 4.11 rear end. About six weeks later my car came in. My dad rode with me to pick it up. While we were in the showroom signing all the papers, I could hear this whistling noise coming from the service area. It was my Corvette! Dad then told me that the car had cost more than our house! The car cost $4,300 and my parents paid $4,000 for our house in 1929.

I started drag racing my Corvette and did pretty well. It turned a best of 14.08 seconds at 98.9 mph. I also drove it to work every day. I then traded it in for a '63 split window, also silver with black interior and 4-speed, 360-hp, fuel-injected engine with 4.11:1 Posi. I paid less than $6,000 for that one. I also drag raced it and drove it to work daily. I think it ran a best of 13.8 seconds at 101 mph.

My next Corvette was a '65 convertible with both tops. It was Glen Green with black interior, a wood steering wheel, 396 engine, 425-hp with 4.56:1 gears and 4-speed transmission. That car really ran! It turned a best of 11.19 seconds at 119 mph.

I sold it in 1969 and bought a '69 Burgundy T-top Corvette. This was a big block with air conditioning and automatic transmission. I didn't race this one! All this time I was still just a grocery clerk. My yearly salary was always about the same as the price of a new Corvette.

In 1980 I bought a used '71 Corvette with both tops for $4,500. It had a replacement 396-cid block that I had rebuilt and blueprinted. I drove to Chicago to Gary Dyer's shop to pick up a 6-71 street blower with two 750 Carter carbs. This is the blown street Corvette I had always wanted! It is painted Competition Orange with black interior and it really turns heads. I don't race it or show it, I just really enjoy driving it around town. It does sit in the garage more than I like, but when I drive it I feel like a teenager again!

The only reason I don't drive a new Corvette is that I am still a grocery clerk and my salary hasn't kept up with the price of cars.

PS: I still wave at every Corvette I see on the road, but I find a lot of the newer Corvette owners don't. To me, they don't deserve to drive the legend. They probably don't know a spark plug from a freeze plug.

PSS: If I ever hit the lottery, I will be driving a new Corvette, and yes, I will be waving at all Corvettes!

Fred Hofer
St. Louis, MO

Corvettes Can Be a Drug

Like most people, I caught the Corvette fever at a young age. I was eight years old, which was old enough to know what a Corvette was. My mother worked with a pharmacist who owned a '70 Sting Ray in Daytona Yellow. From that day on, I was fascinated with the look of the Sting Ray.

In 1989 I joined the Air Force and bought a vehicle for the daily grind, thinking I would never own a Corvette until I was 40 years old. Was I wrong! Five years later, things were about to develop. As soon as my truck was almost paid off, I thought about getting a Corvette. I was getting tired of receiving a Corvette magazine subscription in the mail and not even owning one myself. I wanted a Sting Ray just like the pharmacist's. That day, my mother told me about a Corvette that was for sale down the road from where she lived. I traveled to my parents to visit and decided to check out the car.

To my surprise, it was an '84 model. I was never really fond enough of the C4 generation to own one, but something about this car reached out to me. It was the color. It looked sharp painted in light blue metallic, reflecting the sunlight as it sat upon the pedestal. After talking to the salesman and checking the car out, I had to come back to reality. Although I wasn't able to buy the car, I had to take it out for a test drive, just so I could find out what I would be missing. I went back to the car lot and told the guy about the situation, and he was nice enough to let me take the car out for a drive.

Never having driven a Corvette before, I didn't know what to expect. Sitting in the driver's seat and looking out the windshield over the wide hood was intimidating, but felt great. I think the handling and the overabundance of creature features was the selling point of the car. But what were the odds in finding another light blue '84? From that day on, I was hooked on a C4 Corvette! How ironic!

For the next year I did my homework on what I should know about '84-'86 Vettes. Thinking that I had every *Car Trader*, I saw one on the bookshelf that I didn't have. I flipped through it and came across a dream too good to be true, a well-looked-after '85. A quote from the ad said, "You can't find a better looking Corvette. You be the judge." If that wasn't enough, it was from an area that wasn't too far from my parents. After meeting the owner and looking at the car, I knew it came from a good home. This car was immaculate! To make this long story short and sweet, this was the end of my year-long search for an '84-'86 Corvette. Not only did I get a late-model Vette, but one with tuned-port injection. And best of all, it was two-tone blue.

This was one weekend I would never forget! It was the greatest feeling and sense of accomplishment in my life to be driving away in a Corvette. As much as I couldn't believe that I finally owned one, it felt so natural to climb in and drive it. It was like I was meant to own a Corvette.

Last but not least, it's great to finally be able to get the satisfaction when waving to another Corvette owner driving by. After 17 years of dreaming and waiting to finally own a Corvette, I don't know what could possibly be better! Except maybe a second Corvette.

Dave MacDonald
Kingston, Nova Scotia, Canada

Never Lose the Corvette Dream

I must have been about 6 or 7 years old when I fell in love with a car for the first time. I remember seeing my first Corvette in about 1956 or 1957. It was a white '55 sitting in the carport on the west end of Main Street in Mitchell, Indiana. Those headlight screens and that perfect white body always caught my eye as my dad drove us past in the old family sedan.

Later in life when I was about 13 or 14 years old, I fell in love again! Three guys who had just graduated from our local high school had all somehow managed to buy '62 Corvettes. Although they were all young men, they still had that boyish streak. They would park their Corvettes in the church parking lot facing the street and trade imaginary driving time for the use of some bicycles. My friends and I were always willing to give up our bikes for an hour or so to sit in the church parking lot and cruise out our dreams. I guess we each had our favorite car. There was a red one, a black one and a fawn beige one. The fawn beige was my favorite. Those hours of imaginary cruising with my imaginary girl by my side or the imaginary race of three Corvettes down the extra-wide dragstrip had to be some of the best used dreams of my life. Once, I even got to take a real ride in the fawn beige '62. I fell in love for real!

As time went on, I never lost the Corvette dream. I always knew, someday, I would own a Corvette. In real life, dreams get put on hold. Marriage, family, education, and a job to support dreams had postponed the Corvette fantasy. I had two wonderful sons, one married and on his own and one who was in high school. I had two careers going at the same time. I was a supervisor for General Motors and a helicopter pilot for the Army National Guard. As for marriage, I was twice divorced. My car dreams had come close a few times. I bought an '84 Pontiac Indy Fiero and an '85 Camaro Z28. I even had a '64 MG. Still, reality takes its toll on dreams.

Some time after my second divorce, the Corvette dream came back. I decided it was time to do something for me. I had been seriously dating a beautiful lady and we were talking marriage. I found and bought a two-tone silver '84 Corvette. I was cruising on cloud nine when I drove up to her apartment. I jumped out, ran up the steps and started pounding on her door. When she finally came to the door, I was standing there beaming. "Come see what I bought." She stepped out on the front step, looked at the Corvette and sat down right there and started to cry. It is a joke now, but then it was serious. Through the tears, I heard, "We'll never get married now. You can't afford me and the Corvette both." Well, we've been married for five wonderful years. We still have the '84 and last summer we bought a maroon '65 coupe. Dreams do come true!

Robert Barnett
Bedford, IN

When Did It Start for You?

The Dream Machine

Chapter 6

Parking Lot Love

It first started for me November of 1975 in Teaneck, New Jersey, during my junior year in high school. I took a job washing dishes after classes in the kitchen of the local hospital. On my first night of work, I fell in love in the parking lot. Way off in the corner of the lot, under a light, was a white '67 roadster with "427" boldly displayed on the hood, side pipes and knock-off wheels.

For nearly two years, I admired that beautiful Vette. Having no car of my own, I walked to work and made a point of always crossing through that part of the parking lot on my way in. It was owned by another employee, no doubt a doctor, so I was able to actually touch it, admire it and dream of someday owning one of my own.

In September of 1977, I went to college for four years, never again to see that roadster. My civil engineering degree took me to Las Vegas, Nevada, where I always needed a 4x4 for work. The daydream of owning a Corvette never faded, though. A few years ago, I met the girl of my dreams and convinced her that she should sell her Mustang GT, park herself in a new Vette and then marry me.

She accepted, and the big day was set in her hometown in Colorado. Due to complications with getting a marriage license out of state (aren't all marriage license bureaus open 24 hours a day?), we had to get married

here in Las Vegas first. So we removed the top on our '95 Polo Green LT-1 coupe and headed for the world's only drive-up wedding chapel. We tied the knot June 16, 1996, drove the famous 'Strip' and headed off into the sunset. Occasionally I think of that '67 roadster, but now I live the dream in the Corvette my bride, Shara, and I were married in.

Thanks for allowing me to relive that great memory.

Brian and Shara Walsh, Henderson, NV

A Corvette's Best Friend

I am enclosing a picture of myself with my master, Rory Alexander, in his shiny Torch Red Corvette. My name is Sabby and I am an English Setter. My pal, Rory, bought his first Corvette in 1992, but it had black cloth seats. I never got to ride in that car, since I shed white hair on anything I touch.

In 1994 my master pulled into the driveway in a '94 Vette with leather seats. Fur wouldn't stick to that! Rory waited a day or two until the floor mats had some dust on them and then said, "Hey, Sabby, let's go cruisin'!"

I thought I had died and gone to heaven! I leaped into the car without any hesitation and sat up in the seat as proud as I could be. He backed out of the driveway and put it in gear. My ears flew back and even my lips were flapping from the wind and acceleration! What a thrill!

I ride around with Rory every chance I get. We are great friends. I wanted you to know that this is where my love for Corvettes started!

Rory Alexander
Page, AZ

When Did It Start for You?

Ruining a Perfectly Good 16-Year-Old

Hello, my name is Bryan Ratliff. It all started when I was 16 years old. I went to look at an '84 Vette. I could not buy it, but I wanted to look anyway. The guy let me drive the car and the minute I sat in it, I fell in love. I took the car out for a drive and had not driven a mile before I was dreaming of owning one.

From that day on, I told myself I would stop at nothing to get a Corvette. Two and a half years later I had worked about 60 hours a week and given up a lot of things in my teenage years in order to buy a Corvette. In April of 1996 I bought an '88 Corvette and got to drive my dream and love to the prom. I still own it today! The fever has only gotten worse since then. I am now 20 years old and hope to become a Corvette engineer someday.

Bryan Ratliff, Hayes, VA

It's America

I wanted you to know the very first time I took a second look at a car. It was a blue '63 Sting Ray coupe. I knew I would own one someday. The problem was that I was only 11 years old! I got my first Corvette when I was 25 years old. It was a '77 white coupe. I bought my second one in 1996, also a white coupe. In May 1998, I customized it to a Callaway Supernatural 450-white coupe. Now I'm looking for my favorite, the C2 series, only this time it will be a convertible! Corvette is the only car there is. It's America!

Joan Spoerndle
Milford, CT

On a Mission

I feel that the Corvette is the truest sports car there is. I was first enthralled when I was a little kid as we drove by a Corvette show. I saw an '85 Corvette that was fully decked out with the ground effects and chrome wheels. I knew even at that young age that I had to have one! As soon as I was old enough to drive, I made it a mission to own a Vette. I was 19 years old when I said to myself, "I am going to buy my dream car."

I went shopping for the Vette, but was out of luck as nobody had one for a reasonable price. Later that year, I found an '84 Vette and was hooked. I paid $9,000 for the car and ever since then my motto has been, "Vettes for life!"

I enjoy going to Corvette rallies and seeing people wave hello as I pass by. I feel bad when I break down on the side of the highway and the only people who stop are either fellow Corvette owners or the police. All I can say is that having a Corvette is cool and driving one is an experience of a lifetime. My story may seem very vague, but describing how much I love my Vette is difficult. I hope you guys can help me out by confirming that Corvettes are number one!

David Mitchell
Radcliff, KY

Brother's Basket Case

My first love started more than 36 years ago at the young age of 13. I was the third son out of five children. My father had a policeman friend, a single man who owned a '58 Vette. My heart beat a little faster whenever I saw the car!

One day, I overheard the car would be for sale. I begged my father to purchase it for a family car, kind of unrealistic for a working man with a wife and 5 children. Several years later my oldest brother went out on a limb and bought a "basket case" '60 Vette. I was ecstatic! We finally had a Corvette in the family. I was the envy of all my friends. As teenagers do, we all vowed to own one of these cars right after graduation from high school. Some of us kept that vow.

My dream stuck with me and soon my wife also shared it. Eventually we started a family and had the various responsibilities that go with it. About a week after our last daughter was married, my wife and I looked at each other and asked, "Now what?" We talked about the past, the future and our dreams. It was then that my wife, Linda, strongly encouraged me to pursue my childhood dream and almost immediately the hunt began.

In January, with below-zero temperatures in Green Bay, Wisconsin, my dream car showed up on the market. After a short test drive, we owned the Vette on the spot. It was an '80 L82 T-top in nearly mint condition. Spring up north seemed like years away, but when the first 70-degree day arrived, the T-tops came off and my honey and I felt like teenagers again. Our daughters and sons-in-law think it s the only way to go through a mid-life crisis!

Mike Grall, Green Bay, WI

Go Cart Corvette

I was nine years old the first time I drove. My aunt and uncle put me to work driving their Farmall Cub tractor. I did well enough that a neighbor hired me to drive his John Deere.

The next time I drove I was age 11, and I drove my dad's '50 one-ton Chevy truck. In 1957, when I was 14, my parents made me the chauffeur for my younger sister, and I used the family's '57 Plymouth. That same summer, an older friend had a '55 Bel-Air red-and-white convertible. Long before it was fashionable, I was his designated driver on Friday and Saturday nights. What a thrill for a 14 year old!

The next summer, I worked at a local grocery store. Sometimes I was allowed to drive to work in the family Plymouth, although I still did not have a driver's license. My route took me past the Chevy dealer. That summer he had a Vette parked in the showroom. It was identical to the one in the photo I have enclosed. There is not much I would not have traded for that car. I vowed that someday I would own a Vette.

That fall my parents decided to buy a new car, a '59 Chevrolet Bel-Air hardtop. In the showroom the dealer had a Vette on display and was giving it away. I registered and vowed to win it. A few weeks later, I got a call that I had won! I hurried down to pick up my new car.

I have to admit that it was simply a go-cart with a Vette body, but it was my very first Vette. The "transmission" was simply a V-belt with an idler pulley. The gas pedal worked the carburetor and transmission simultaneously. The more gas you gave it, the tighter the V-belt got, and the faster you went. The brakes consisted of a 5/16-inch bar, which rubbed across the tread of the rear tires when you pushed on the brake pedal. That combination provided two speeds, fast and stop.

The local cops didn't seem concerned that it didn't have plates or registration, or that I didn't have a driver's license. My sister (see enclosed photo) and all of the neighborhood kids drove it hard all fall and winter. In fact, we drove it so hard that the body mounts (which consisted of a 2-inch angle iron in the front and rear on which the body simply rested) caused the body to break! I wrote a letter to the manufacturer and within a couple of weeks, I had a new body.

The next summer we moved and I decided to leave it with my older sister, who had a three-year-old son. She later had another son, and they eventually grew into the car. They and the neighborhood kids drove it until it was taken in pieces to the local dump.

With marriage and all the other things in life, I was not able to buy my own Vette until I was much older. Although I now own two: a '62 red/red and a '79 red/red coupe, I often dream of how I could restore my first Vette if it were not rusting away in the city dump!

Dickie D. Lewis, Clifton, CO

"Goldie"

It was the summer of 1956, Elvis was singing Jailhouse Rock, and something was about to happen that would change my life forever. I was 9 years old, riding my bike through the neighborhood, when I first spotted it; a really cool car with only two seats and no roof! It was Cascade Blue with beige coves and wide white walls. The name on the hood emblem spelled Corvette.

I had never seen such a beautiful car before. The following year, we moved a few blocks away, but I was always drawn back to the old neighborhood to catch a glimpse of that Corvette. The seed had been planted!

I don't remember seeing another Corvette until I was a senior in high school. A junior drove a really cool-looking silver '65 Sting Ray coupe to school; his daddy and mommy had money. I vowed to own a Vette of my own when I grew up.

While studying aerospace engineering at Penn State, I'd see a Corvette every once in a while and it kept my dream alive. Then, in the fall of '67, I saw a new '68 parked outside a fraternity house, and I was in love. It was the most beautiful machine I had ever seen! I marveled at its bold flowing lines, just oozing with character.

Then came the summer of 1968, which was my last before graduation. My best buddy, Keith, and I went out to the Chevy place in State College to see if they had any Vettes. Fortunately, there was one in the showroom; I was awestruck! I opened the door and slid in behind the wheel, while Keith got in on the right. As soon as we shut the doors, I looked at him and said, "Man, I've got to have one of these." This is my kind of car and I'm gonna order one as soon as I get a job!

I flew out to Los Angeles for my first job, but nobody would give me enough credit to buy a Corvette. Begrudgingly, I bought a pale green '62 VW Beetle with 92,000 miles on it. I promised myself this situation would be short-lived!

After two months on the first job I was ready to move back east. I called an aerospace company in Connecticut and they gave me an offer I couldn't refuse. As soon as I got home to Harrisburg, I went to three Chevy dealers and got quotes. Then on December 14, 1968, I placed an order for the car of my dreams.

Three agonizingly long months later, and after many phone calls to Tom Yesconis, the salesman, my "baby" finally arrived. A couple of days later, March 21, 1969, my dad rode with me to the dealership in the trusty VW, where I gladly exchanged cars. It was one of those special events that happen only once in a lifetime.

Going from a Beetle to a sleek, 300-hp Riverside Gold Sting Ray with saddle leather interior was almost overwhelming. My childhood dream had come true! I was 21 and on top of the world. I owned the best car in the world, a Corvette Sting Ray.

Goldie became the focal point of my life. She faithfully took me on many adventures from learning to fly and going to grad school, to dating and building my own business. She was the one constant in my fast-paced life. She was the one thing I could count on.

By the fall of 1988 though, I had added about 6,000 more miles to Goldie's clock. Unfortunately, I ran into some personal and business challenges, and reluctantly put her up for sale. The guy who bought her lived only 50 miles away, and I asked him to please call me if he ever wanted to sell her. I had Lou's phone number and a secure feeling that I could call him at any time. Deep down inside, I knew I

eventually would!

Then in February, 1996, after yet another discussion of how much I wanted Goldie back, Marjie asked, "Why not give Lou a call and ask if he might consider selling her?"

A week went by and I called Lou. Much to my relief and boyish delight, he still had her! I started getting excited. I asked if he might be interested in selling her, and he said he had been thinking about it. He told me he'd think about it some more and call me in a week to let me know.

That was the longest week of my life and I just couldn't sleep! I tossed and turned every night just thinking about how great it would be to have Goldie back. Seven days went by and no call, but I kept my cool. Then on the tenth day, Lou called and said he had just had her inspected and was ready to sell.

I hardly slept a wink for the next three days. Finally I called Lou and asked if Thursday, March 21, would be okay. He said yes, and I got goose bumps. It was exactly 28 years to the day that I originally bought Goldie, March 21, 1996! At last, Goldie was mine once again, this time forever. I would make good on my promise by finishing her restoration and showing her.

Our target completion date of March 21, 1997, was missed, but she was ready just in time for my 50th birthday, May 23. What an awesome present!

I told Marjie that it was better than getting a new C5! It was such an incredible experience to restore Goldie to better-than-new condition.

No matter what year Corvette you may prefer, focus on your dream and go for it! The results will blow your mind. Everything you need to do to make it come true will pay you more dividends than you could ever imagine. Enjoy the trip and don't spare any expense. You just can't put a price tag on the emotional value you'll get from your own plastic fantastic.

You deserve the Corvette you really want. Haven't you already waited long enough?

Mike Markowski, Hummelstown, PA

Frozen Out of the Bidding

When did it start for me? My obsession for Corvettes started early. When I was 9 or 10 years old, I saw the new '78 body style and the two-tone Indy Pace Car paint job and fell in love. I started reading about Corvettes, learning about the history and its evolution. I announced to my parents that someday I was going to own a Corvette. I started saving my pennies, literally. After a few months I decided to save every coin I got. This went on for years, through high school and college. When I turned 16 years old, I even bought a Corvette key chain and kept it in a box until I could put the keys to "my" Corvette on it.

In my senior year at college, I started going to car auctions hoping to get lucky. I found a bank repo auction that was going to sell 23 Corvettes. It was the middle of January and the weather was terrible. Out of the 23 Corvettes, 18 were brought in for bidding. I was not able to afford any of the ones in good condition. The auction then went outside and only two of the remaining five Corvettes were going to be sold.

The first one was not in very good shape and did not run (you just want to find the previous owners and slap them). The second one was a '72 or '73, 454 big block, canary yellow with T-tops. The door locks were frozen shut, so it could not be brought inside for the auction. I spoke briefly with a guy who worked at the auction house and he indicated that the car was in great shape. This was it, the big opportunity finally came.

Very few people stayed to go out in the cold and no one knew what condition the car was in. I put in an opening bid and soon had no one else bidding against me. The auctioneer wanted more for the car, so they tried to open it again. My bad luck, the car opened and they started it right away. After revving the engine a few times, the bidding went higher. I had the car with a bid of $500 more than I could afford (hoping someone would loan me the money). The auctioneer then asked the assistant to open the hood. After breaking it free from the ice, the hood went up and so did the bidding. I had to walk away when the bidding was $4,000 more than I could afford. I never did find out what the final cost was.

After college, I got a good job and saved my money. I got married and my wife and I moved into a starter home. After a few years, I accumulated enough credit and savings and started shopping for Corvettes again. I found a red '82 with mirrored T-tops in great condition at a used car dealer. Winter was coming, so I was able to work a good deal that would trade in my car. The deal was to be made that Saturday when my wife could see the car. I went to the bank and cashed in my coins, which at the time amounted to over $1,500. On Friday I left work bragging about the Vette I would be driving to work on Monday.

That night, my wife announced that she was pregnant with our first child. After celebrating the great news, we took the money and traded in her car for a minivan. The following Monday was a long day. All day I answered questions like, "So where is the new sports car? A minivan, does it have wood panels and a luggage rack? Should we line up our cars and see who wins?" (I drove a Hyundai.) I still haven't lived that down!

At that point, the dream of owning a Corvette was fading. Don't get me wrong, I wouldn't trade or change anything (except maybe that auctioneer). I just couldn't see myself getting a Corvette until I was old, bald and fat!

In October 1997, one month after our second child was born, I stumbled across a '79 Vette in good condition and for a great price. The money would be tight for a while, but I thought I could pull it off. After a quick call to my wife, she laughed and said that if I thought we could afford it, I should go for it. Her best comment was, "This is your dream;

if you say we can do it, then do it. You just have to love her!" The next day I drove home in my snow-white '79 Vette with T-tops.

I don't know if I will be able to afford to keep it after this spring, but when the weather turns warm, you can be assured that I will be driving it every sunny day. My dream has been fulfilled, even if it will only be for a short time!

When did it start for me? Twenty years ago!

David B. Wilson
Worthington, OH

Anniversary Promise

In September of 1997 my husband and I went to Pigeon Forge, Tennessee, for our eighteenth wedding anniversary. There we saw several Corvettes and even took some pictures of them. Before we left, we decided that a Corvette would be our next car. That is when it started for us.

We are now the owners of an '81 white Corvette with 48,900 miles that is in very good shape. We have replaced a few small things, bought from Mid America and enjoy your catalogs very much.

Jim & Debbie Watson, Irvine, KY

When Did It Start for You?

On Tour With Their '72

I've always been interested in cars. I've owned a '37 Chevrolet and a '65 Pontiac Catalina, plus other performance cars. The Corvette experience started when my wife, Lori, said, "Lets buy a Corvette." We started looking and found a '72 L-48 coupe with automatic transmission and air-conditioning. Everything is original except the tires and paint, which is '85 GM Light Green (my wife wanted red). After working on the brakes and air-conditioning, we have a daily driver if so needed.

We have been to Bloomington Gold, Funfest (which is great) and a tour of the Corvette factory in Bowling Green, Kentucky. While touring the plant, Lori helped assemble a door panel. Our kids are Vette fans. We would like to own either a C4 or C5 someday.

Charles & Lori Leeper
Niantic, IL

Triple Black

I always wanted a triple black Corvette. To me, that is the most prestigious ride on the planet! One day I was tending bar and these two gentlemen walked in and ordered a round. The one guy, Carl, was wearing a Corvette hat. I asked him if he owned a Corvette. He said that he owned 14 Corvettes! He had one triple black, but that was his wife's. I told him that I always wanted a Vette, but it had to be a triple black convertible. He said to stop by his car lot and test drive one. He had enough nerve to say, "You might not like it."

When you work nights, it's hard to get up in the morning. I never made it to Carl's place to check out the Vettes. About two weeks later, Carl came into the bar and was upset. He informed me that he bought his wife a new Corvette and she didn't like it! She said that people stopped her all the time to praise it, and she was also afraid to park it anywhere. I told him to bring it to the bar and I'd check it out. The next night, Carl pulled in with a '95 Pace Car. I had mixed reactions at first. It was overwhelming. I thought it was kind of loud. By the time Carl parked it under the lights - it was mine!

Buying a Corvette was a big decision. It's a big chunk of change. I live in Ohio and that's basically a six-month state for cruising. I personally would not drive a Corvette on our salt-covered streets. I still live at home and even though I am an adult, I still had to ask my dad for help. We both went over to Carl's house to take the car for a test drive. Once Dad and I got out of the driveway and went down the street, my dad just lit up with excitement. We were always best friends, but the car just brought us closer together.

Needless to say, we bought the car. Even with our hectic schedules, we always found time on sunny days to sneak away in our '95 Pace Car and go for an ice cream. Dad wouldn't even let me polish it! For some reason, the car would always be out of gas and I would hear him say, "I better go gas her up!"

In 1997, my father passed away from a massive heart attack with no warning. I lost my dad and my best friend. I will never forget the memories we had together in that Corvette. There is emptiness now, but when I hop into that driver's seat, put my seat belt on and go 90 mph down the street, I can still hear my dad say, "Slow down!"

When Did It Start for You?

David A. Rogers
Brook Park, OH

Stu Murray's Split Window

At the age of 11, I was standing outside of my father's office in this historic town of Hyde Park, New York. Each day after school I would go to his office and stay with him until it was time to go home, as there was no one home to watch me. As I watched the cars go by and stop at the nearby traffic signal, I would drool over some of the nice cars. But this day one in particular caught my attention, a brand-new '63 Corvette split window coupe! The car was dark blue with a bright red interior and a rumble of power emitting from the dual exhaust. It was awesome!

I have three older brothers, so I just couldn't wait to get home that night, as I had a story to tell! When we all gathered around the dinner table that night and I told my story, my brothers turned to me and said, "You know whose car that is? That's Stu Murray's car." Stu had gone to school with my oldest brother and they knew him very well. I never got a ride in it, but I did get to see Stu pass my dad's office every night on his way home from work and he'd wave to me. It was the highlight of my day.

Years went by and I kept dreaming. I would wait with great anticipation every fall to see what the next model year would bring. I got married to my girlfriend, Joann, and had two sons, Jay and Kevin. Well, you know the typical American life of a '50s baby boomer. Family values, but still no Corvette in the garage, only a Malibu station wagon!

In 1991 I purchased a '73 Z28 Camaro in mint condition with only 28,000 miles. I thought this was the closest thing I would ever have to a Corvette! Behold the 40th Anniversary Corvette introduced in the fall of '92. I began reminiscing about my childhood all over again. I just couldn't get over the absolutely beautiful exterior color with the matching Ruby interior and convertible top. Again, I thought it would be just a dream.

After many years of buying Chevrolets from Audia Motors in Millbrook, New York, I called to talk to the salesman. I said, "Pete, what's the chance of finding a 40th Anniversary Corvette roadster with a 6-speed?" Peter responded by saying that the plant was preparing for the '94 model year and that one could not be ordered, but he would search through the GM dealership locator system. Low and behold, a week later he called me and told me he had found not just one, but six. Unfortunately, either the cars had options that I didn't want, pushing the cost too high, or the dealers just would not part with them. He continued to search and was finally able to talk to the sixth dealer, who graciously agreed to give up the car!

Audia Motors made arrangements to pick up the car from Hawthorne Chevrolet in Hawthorne, New Jersey. Bob Audia, the owner, took my '73 Z28 Camaro in on trade for the '93 Corvette 40th Anniversary roadster 6-speed. Wow! The car that I had been dreaming of since age 11 would finally be a reality!

I took delivery on Saturday, September 11, 1993. Presently the car has 2,708 miles on it. I've entered many car shows, taking four First Place and three Second Place trophies. The car is extremely well documented. Audia Motors gave me all the original paperwork (they kept the copies), including the dealer's copy of the '93 Chevrolet Corvette Product Guide. I have photo documentation from day of delivery to present, and the car is registered in the National 40th Anniversary Corvette Registry. I have also collected many 40th Anniversary promotional items. I've had a custom 6-foot, waist-high glass display case made in Ruby Red to display these items.

I've learned two important things in my life: First, dreams do come true, and second, there will always be a little kid in all of us. Thanks for letting me share my story.

Mr. & Mrs. Paul Rinschler
Hyde Park, NY

When Did It Start for You?

Chance Encounters

Chapter 7

Hit By a Frisbee

It's been more than 20 years, but it seems like yesterday.

I was 14 years old growing up in the central Texas town of Fredericksburg in the mid-'70s. It was spring and the countryside was once again awakening from winter's chill. Golden Earring's Radar Love was heating up the airwaves, and I was just beginning to take notice of cars. Not just cars in general, but more specifically, hot rods, race cars and the like really caught my eye. Things like duals, 4-barrels and metal flake were the rage.

I was being chauffeured home one afternoon by my mom and aunt, when pulling up to the stop sign in front of us was this car that left me totally awestruck. Its color was bright orange, and I'd never seen anything like it before in my life. The radically flowing body lines, small cockpit, flat back window and stance made it look like it was flying standing still. The license plate read FRISBE, which only added to the fantasy that it must fly. The rumble of those exhausts as it took off and the Corvette nameplate disappearing in the distance had me excited well into the next day.

The years rolled on and as I grew up, so did my love affair with cars. I have many fond memories of fixing up and hot rodding three early Camaros and even a (gasp!) Mustang Mach I. But in the back of my mind, I still longed for a Corvette. I read all the print I could find on Corvettes and even did a research paper in my junior year on the history of the Corvette. Later on, an early morning drive in a '76, with the T-tops off and the sun coming up over the horizon, firmly cemented my ongoing love affair with this awesome sports car.

To date, I have owned two Vettes, a '75 and a War Bonnet Yellow '72 with a base 350-hp and automatic.

No, my GLASIC (my license plate) is not the fastest or rarest Corvette, or even a "Top Flight" car. It is, however, driven with much pride on sunny days, starry nights and to an occasional car show/cruise. The Corvette lifestyle is even better than I had imagined as a kid.

Dan W. Heimann
Austin, TX

Keeping the Promise

I was interested in Corvettes at an early age, back when birthdays were still measured in single digits. Living in a small midwestern village, a Corvette was an interesting sight that captivated my attention until it was gone from view. But even then, there was still that sound.

My parents went to the local Chevrolet dealership one evening, and in the showroom was a mid-year convertible painted midnight blue. I can remember reading it on the window sticker. I now know that this was not a factory color for mid-year Corvettes, this was a custom-painted car. I looked this car over as intently as any prospective buyer. But I was too young, and like the GM magazine ad says, "When you were a kid you made yourself a promise (to someday own one)."

The next chapter in my Corvette life was when I worked as a mechanic at a local Honda motorcycle dealership. The other mechanic owned a '65 big block with side exhaust and aluminum wheels. This car was awesome. It shook the ground at idle while the tach bounced at 1,100 rpm.

We would drive this machine along county highways at night about 100 mph, listening to Jethro Tull over the wind noise.

One day I got to drive that car, and I got to feel a real teak wheel, a 4-speed Muncie and handle 425-hp. As I completed a left-hand turn, I stabbed the throttle. The car fishtailed wildly until I let up on the gas. I was hooked for life!

My first Corvette purchase was not until years later. It was a '77 that I proudly kept for ten years. But this was not the car of my dreams. I began the hunt for a mid-year roadster with an L-76. But what I settled for was a '63 split-window coupe with an L-75. This Corvette has been my mistress for almost five years, and I hope will be a friend for many more.

Kingston Wulff
Reno, NV

Such a Flirt

It all started out while I was driving a conversion van with my son, looking for a used car for him.

We were across town, when all of a sudden the most beautiful, shiny, charcoal metallic '81 Corvette with wire wheels appeared right in front of the office of that used car lot! It took your breath away as it sat "flirting" with the public.

We pulled in, got out of the van and it was love at first sight! Needless to say, we both got so caught up in the excitement of it all, looking for my son's used car became secondary. I signed the deal, the van was history, and I bought a used Cadillac (which turned out to be a disaster) and the Corvette. I kept the Caddy and the Vette for about a year, traded both in on a brand new Chevy conversion van and thought, "I'll probably never be able to own a Vette again." I was sick! It was gone.

Not so! When you have Corvette fever in your blood, it doesn't ever go away. A few years later my heart still ached to fill that void in my life. Then the best thing that could ever happen to me did: There sitting and waiting just for me was my love, my joy and my present-day baby, an '82 Collector's Edition!

Now we have the van and the Vette! And as the story ends, "They Lived Happily Ever After."

John R. Underwood
Galloway, OH

When Did It Start for You?

Corvette Custom

It started for me in the late '70s, when the custom van craze was in. I had a show van that won many trophies and was even in a couple of magazines.

At one show in Ohio, there was a '60 Corvette with beautiful blue metalflake paint, Cragar SS mags and lots of chrome. I was in love! I had to have a Vette! I spoke to the owner of that car and he said he just happened to have a '59 for sale and it was on a car trailer outside. For $2,600, I owned my first Vette! Yes, a real dud, but it was mine!

That was over 20 years ago. For the last 15 years, I have been restoring them. I have owned over 60 Corvettes, dating from 1972 and earlier. I have five right now: a '56, a '62, a '63 coupe, a '66 and a '67 (the last two are big blocks). Is it an addiction or a love affair? Maybe both. I love redoing them and watching them slowly come back to life. No matter what year, they all have their own style and personality. And if they could talk, I'll bet there would be some good stories to hear. I'll stop here, because it sounds like I'm talking about a person! I'm going to get wrapped up and taken away!

Ron Spontak
Burgettstown, PA

Can We Get That One, Mom?

My willpower to resist contacting you regarding my first Corvette experience has finally collapsed! I was 10 years old in 1960. With my grandfather and my brother living with us, there were five in our household. When we went on our biannual car-shopping excursion, we made our way into the local Chevrolet dealer. To my immediate right as I walked in the door was a gorgeous silver Corvette with white coves. Knowing full well who handled the purse strings, I immediately went over to my mother and said, "Can we get that one, Mom?" She could rarely handle telling me no, but posed the question, "Where would we put you, dear?"

My parents then went on to close a deal with a salesman on another car while I loitered around that beautiful Vette, trying to figure out how this dream machine could accommodate five people. After finally coming to the inevitable conclusion that I just didn't have the heart to squeeze my brother and grandfather in the trunk, I opted to accept my mother's invitation for input on a silver Impala sport coupe. I also asked her if we could get dual-rear antennas set at 45-degree angles, which we did. Though this was the best compromise I could come up with at the time, I promised myself, "Someday." I am now on my second Vette, a black '84 coupe!

Thanks for listening.

David J. Fife
Elmira, NY

On the Road to the Indy 500

I was sleeping in the back seat of my dad's car when my "Love at First Sight" with the Corvette happened to me. I was 13 years old at the time and I will never forget that magic moment in my life. My dad and older brother and I were driving from our home in Liberty Center, Ohio, to the Indy 500 time trials and it was very late at night. I was catching a few winks in the back seat when we drove into a small Indiana town and pulled up to a stoplight. That's when I woke up and heard the Corvette engine roaring opposite us at the stoplight. I'll never forget the powerful sound of the engine as the driver was revving it up. It was the most awesome car I had ever seen (a '63 silver coupe) and at that moment, I decided that was the car for me.

I have owned four Corvettes since that time, and I am currently in the market for another. I am now 46 years young and , yes, I am still "in love!"

Tom A. Kern
Liberty Center, OH

From Cows to Corvettes

As a child I grew up on a dairy farm in Vancouver, Washington. My parents had a herd of about 70 Jersey cows, 20 of which we took to several shows in Washington and Oregon.

When I was 12 years old, in 1969, we went to the Clark County Fair in Vancouver. It was there that I noticed a '64 Corvette convertible parked on a lawn next to the entrance to the fairgrounds. This thing really caught my eye. "Wow, what a cool-looking car! I bet that thing can really move," I thought to myself as we drove by with a load of cows to take to the fair. Later that week, I told some of my friends about it and they told me that the guy who owned the car was Dennis Larson. He had some cows just around the corner in another barn, so I walked in the direction of where he was supposed to be and there it was.

I could not believe it, this thing was so incredible! Wow, the paint was shiny, the top was down and man, you should have seen the tires - they were huge! My friends told me the wide tires are to keep good traction at high speeds. That was it. I knew that someday I was going to have a Vette just like Dennis Larson's. I wanted so badly to talk to him about his car, but I could never get up the nerve to approach him. He was 18 or 19, and I was 12 years old.

When Did It Start for You?

Later that week, he saw me several times looking at the car. He watched it like a hawk. No matter where he parked the car, I would find it. He must have told someone about me, because some guy came out of the barn one day and said to me "Hey kid, why don't you take a picture of it, maybe it would last longer." I really felt stupid because I didn't think it was that obvious. I still kept an eye on the car, but not quite so close.

Ever since that time in my life, I have been a Corvette buff. I am 40 years old now, and I've finally gotten my car, a '72 coupe. It is so much fun. What a beauty! Part of the fun is watching my 12-year-old son, who also has "the fever!"

I saw Dennis Larson at a cruise that the Mustangs Unlimited Club had last year in Vancouver. I had not seen him since the fair days. He looked like he was having fun visiting with friends so I didn't bother talking to him. Maybe in 30 years I will see him again in a nursing home or something like that, and I can thank him with a glass of prune juice instead of a glass of beer!

P.S. To my lovely wife of 23 years, Debbie, "What do you think of a second Corvette, dear?"

Brian Curtin
Washougal, WA

Cruisin' In the Mercedes

Strange actually that I had never had any interest in cars, until that day. I don't know the exact date anymore, but it was a lovely Sunday summer afternoon in 1992. I was 18 years old and I was finally enjoying the freedom of driving my parents' Mercedes around the countryside with my girlfriend. Sometimes we drove more than 100 miles on one day.

That particular day on one of those abandoned back roads we passed an old garage with a large show window and there it was, a large blurry item with some chrome-like bumpers in front. We both looked at each other and we knew we had seen something very special, but we didn't pay any further attention to it. One week later, it was still in my mind, and we decided to go back and take a closer look at it.

Upon our arrival, I immediately fell in love with that car. Even though it was covered with inches of dust on top, the dark brown paint was faded, the

When Did It Start for You?

chrome bumpers were rusted and the windshield was broken, it was the largest, meanest, most styled car I had ever seen! Like most Corvette people, you can say this car toggled a switch in my mind. The old showroom looked a bit like a small museum. There were old motorcycles, army parts, tools and that one car with that small script on the finger, 'Sting' and something else. You can believe it or not, but I had no clue which car this was, or where it came from. I never had seen it before in my life.

Through some research, I finally found out what it was; a Chevrolet Corvette Sting Ray! These words sounded like magic and I knew I had to have a car like that! This was when my Corvette mania started. I guess my discovery had a positive and a negative aspect. When you're young, you just don't have the financial capabilities to own, restore or drive a Corvette in Europe (base price for a soft-nosed Vette in bad condition is over $11,000, plus another $3,200 for road tax and insurance every year). To compensate the negative side, you have the opportunity to start with Corvette collectibles. My scale model collection of Corvettes now includes more than 200 items in all the different sizes, types and forms.

In 1994, I finally had the necessary finances to start looking for my very first Sting Ray. I went back to that particular garage, but it was completely gone! I hope I will someday find the time to investigate where this car went.

You probably know the rest of the story. I bought one too quickly for a too-high price compared to the condition it was in. It's a '74 coupe with worn-out suspension and interior, a bad engine and two layers of different paint on it that chipped away when the car was washed. We just don't want to learn!

Now, four years later in 1998, I have the car in running condition with the most worn components replaced, but it hasn't received a new coat of paint yet. It's too bad that the Corvette is the only love in my life anymore, and that the other one is gone!

Thanks to GM for building the greatest car of all time, the Chevy Corvette. Greetings to all the Corvette heads, especially to my American friend Joe Vopal in Sheboygan, Wisconsin, with his super '67 rat. Any correspondence is welcome! This is dedicated to Soraya; you still owe me a '67 in wrapping with a large ribbon around it.

Dominick Joos
Lokeren 9160 Belgium

When Did It Start for You?

Odd Jobs

Chapter 8

Keeping in Tune with Corvette

As long as I can remember, I have been an avid Chevrolet fan. It seems only fitting that in 1961 I started my working career as an inspector at a GM plant in Indianapolis. In the spring of 1966, I spotted a white '61 Corvette at a local Ford dealer. I owned a new '66 Impala SS 396 at the time, but I had to have this Corvette. My wife and I were in the market for a second car at the time and I convinced her this was it.

With very little negotiating, I bought the car for $1,500 and drove it daily for three enjoyable years. In the summer of 1969, I sold the '61 for $1,550. The reason for the sale was a '67 Elkhart Blue small-block coupe which I purchased for $3,600. I drove the '67 for two years and traded it for a new Mulsanne Blue '71 coupe. Due to an accident, I only had this car for a short two months.

I replaced the '71 Coupe with a War Bonnett Yellow '71 convertible, which I drove for about two years. I sold it to a friend in 1974 and went without a Corvette until the summer of 1976, when I purchased a very nice black '62 for $5,000. I drove this car for six years and was forced to sell in 1983 due to a divorce.

In May of 1985 my new wife and I found a beautiful '78 Anniversary Model with only 12,000 miles. We bought the car on the spot for $10,500. We logged over 100,000 miles on this car in nine years until it met with an accident in Key Largo, Florida, in the summer of 1994. The other party was at fault and we received $11,585 from their insurance company to replace the car, which was declared a total loss. With this, we bought an '84 Medium Blue coupe for $10,000. It has performed flawlessly to date.

I am now retired from GM and my wife and I and the '84 coupe live happily in sunny Florida.

Ted & Linda Von Tress
Bradenton, FL

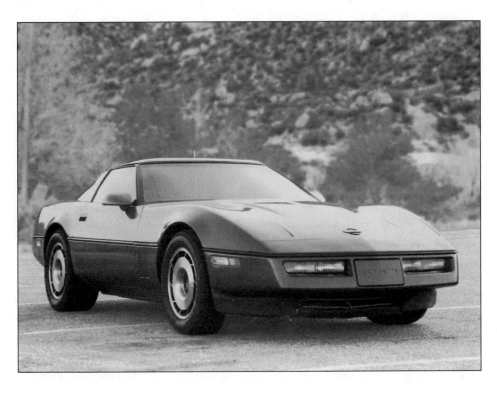

Repo Man

Let me tell you about the time I knew that, without a doubt, I would one day own a Corvette. I was in a small bank in the town of Havre, Montana, waiting to see if my college education would come to an end for lack of funds. I sat in the waiting room thinking my senior year might not happen when my loan officer called me in.

"Well," he said, "we feel you're a good risk." I thought, thank heavens, and I signed the papers. As I was about to leave, I noticed he was pacing the floor and rubbing his chin, as if there was something wrong. I was almost to the door when I heard these words, "I need a Corvette repossessed. Can you do it?"

I stopped dead in my tracks and said, "You bet!" In my small farm town, Corvettes were not commonplace. Winters were below zero, a four-wheel drive pick-up was a necessity and it seemed the only place fiberglass was used was on the chemical spray tanks. To a 23-year-old whose pride and joy was a '73 Plymouth Satellite, the question of taking my first drive in a Corvette was a no-brainer!

The loan officer explained the plan. I was to go to the guy's house, get the car and bring it back to a warehouse behind the bank. He gave me keys for the car door, the ignition and the warehouse.

Leaving the bank, I wondered whether I would actually pull off the stunt. I talked with one of my buddies and convinced him to drop me off at the house where the Vette was located. It was a warm spring afternoon. I walked up to the house and rang the doorbell. There was no answer. So far, so good! Out of the corner of my eye, I turned to see my buddy drive away, leaving me on my own.

My choices were to snag the Vette or walk home. There was a side door into the garage, and through the window I could just make out a '76 silver Corvette. I was really nervous. I walked through the gate that led me to the side door. The door was open. I couldn't believe it, because I didn't have that key to the side door. I hurriedly rolled the overhead door open, ran to the Vette and found the car door was unlocked. As I jumped into the cockpit, I was so nervous I don't think I could have told you the color of the interior. I turned the ignition key and the L-48 fired to life. Putting the car into reverse, I backed out enough to close the overhead door. Taking it real easy, I drove away. It was just me and this poor guy's

Vette!

The farther I drove from the repo scene, the more relaxed I felt, so I just drove and drove. I began to notice the color of the leather seats and enjoyed the most beautiful view the fenders and hood had to offer. I ripped through the gears, hung a few corners and felt the splendor of 4-wheel disc brakes. This was truly a gorgeous spring day! After I parked the Vette, I locked the warehouse door behind me and was unhappy that the fun was over.

I never found out who the guy was that lost his Vette. But from my driving experience that day, I felt sorry for him. After finishing college, landing a job, getting married, buying a house and becoming a father, I managed to become the proud owner of a '96 Corvette. Let me say this, I'll make the payments in full and on time!

Ken Holme
Renton, WA

Beauty Shop Blue Vette

It all started for me in the summer of 1965. I was 13 years old with little outlet for a growing fascination for those great muscle cars of the '60s.

I washed my father's Galaxie 500 and the neighbor's Impala with regularity. Noting my fervor, my mother offered my services to her hairdresser, a young woman who owned a new Nassau Blue Corvette convertible. I also washed that car with regularity and passion. It was an experience that bordered on spiritual. That summer I made an unspoken promise to myself.

Timing is everything. As luck, or lack of luck, would have it, I graduated from college just in time for the gas crisis. During those dark days of the '70s and early '80s, you had to look long and hard to find any remnant of those V-8 powered '60s. Through those days, however, the Corvette hung on.

Fast forward to 1993, when my wife and I were both working. The family was growing. Auto performance was back, but $30,000 price tags were abundant. While walking through a car show corral, I saw a '77 Corvette. It was red, and I'm a sucker for red cars! The paint was good. The black leather interior was very good. The price was fair. Within a week, the car was mine and the dream was fulfilled.

Little did I realize that I had bought more than a car, I had bought a hobby and a project seemingly without end. Over the last four years, I've read and studied as much as I could. I've spent money as well as many pleasurable hours working on this car. I regret neither. There have been times of frustration, but there have also been many more moments spent at car shows and cruise nights that were rewarding.

While not the mid-year Sting Ray I first dreamed of, I've found the 350 V-8 'shark' satisfying enough for me after the 4-cylinders I've driven. But the truth is that for the money, no car gets more second looks than this red Vette. The fun continues!

Scott Gay
Cortland, NY

When Did It Start for You?

Insurance Adjustments

I first became fascinated with the Corvette in the early '70s. I was working as a body man in a Chevrolet dealership at the time. Most of my friends in the early '70s were fixing up old Chevy pickups and so was I. One day an insurance adjuster came by and said he had just totaled a car that had a drivetrain and bucket seats. It happened to be a '62 Vette. I loaded up the wife and kids after dinner and drove out to see the wreck. It was love at

first sight! The first thing I did the next morning was call my adjuster friend and tell him that I wanted that car. The salvage price was $500 and I was a happy man. Needless to say, my pickup project was history!

I had not previously worked with fiberglass, but I quickly learned and took plenty of advice from my dealership buddies. I glued every piece of that car back together during Saturdays and evenings. It took me several months, but finally I finished. I drove that car to work during the week and raced it on the weekends. That car was the first in my over 25-year long love affair with the Corvette. I have bought, sold and rebuilt more than two dozen Corvettes, but that red '62 will always have a special place in my heart.

My current driver is a '94 Admiral Blue convertible. I still work on Vettes

and now share this love with my 27-year-old son, Joey. He works a different day job, but is over on the weekends working on car projects.

Mickey Wheeler
Arlington, TX

Dad and the Legend of General Motors

In 1992 I retired from the GM Powertrain Division, Engineering. My last work assignment had been as the development engineer on the LT5 engine. I was assigned to the Proving Grounds to assist the Lotus on-site personnel. The LT5 was the all-aluminum, dual overhead cam 4-valve engine basically developed by Lotus engineering. This engine was specifically designed and built for the ZR-1 Corvette by Mercury Marine in Stillwater, OK.

In 1997, I went to the Proving Grounds as retirees do for the Christmas luncheon, and went around to see some of my friends. Dave Wikeman and Jack Gillis were there and Dave said, "Hey, I've been thinking about you and I've got something for you." It turned out to be the Sept/Oct 1997 issue of the *ZR 1 Legend.* That's a periodical put out by the ZR-1 Registry and he'd saved it for me because I was named in an article written by Graham Behem. I'd not seen a copy of it before. Appreciating Dave's thoughtfulness, I took it home and went through it from cover to cover.

I noticed an ad in the very back put out by Mid America Designs, Inc. I thought it was a very cute ad, because it pictured two kids in an old barn and the kid in the foreground is slowly lifting the cover off what appears to be an early Corvette. The kid in the back is playing with a tennis racket or something he found in the barn. It's captioned, "When Did It Start For You?"

My dad started life as an Iowa farm boy back in 1903, pre-flight and at the dawn of the automotive industry. It was one of the most exciting periods in modern history. His first job was working in a railroad back shop in Lincoln, Nebraska. Married in 1925, he wanted to work for GM for a long time. After my parents were married they decided to move to Detroit, but things were pretty slim at that time there. He ended up working in the salt mines that were under the city, but he kept his eye on the want ads and eventually was hired by Cadillac Motor Division as a motor repairman. This was about 1927 and this was his entry to General Motors Corporation.

In about 1932 or 1933 he became the Cadillac representative on the team to help Clark Equipment Company develop an auto-train. Its purpose was as a people-mover using existing railroad tracks. When he was in the engine lab, he met Ed Cole. Cole later became the president of General Motors, and he and Cole were lifelong friends from about 1932 on.

My dad was one of six people involved in the early development and production of the first fully automatic transmission in the world, the Hydra-match. During World War II, Dad got very heavily involved in tank development, and it was at this time that he and Ed Gray designed the torque converter that went in the front of the Hydra-match.

When did it start for me? It partially started with my dad's Buick because that is the car I remember spending a lot of time backing in and out of the garage. When Dad sold the car, the guy across the street had to have it so bad he could taste it.

In 1950, Chevrolet came out with the Powerglide, which at that point was a non-shifting unit. Ed Cole was drafted to head up Chevrolet's activity, and he asked my dad to come over and convert Chevrolet's non-shifting Powerglide into a shifting Powerglide.

And then, in 1953, there was the Corvette. At that point in time, my folks had a '53 Bel-Air. Shortly after the announcement of the '53 Corvette, Dad was going to bring the car they'd been working on home for the weekend. Friday came and it wasn't ready, so the arrangement was made that the boys would bring it out to meet him near our house. He and I went down to the corner to meet them. I remember being all excited about this thing and wondering how we would know it in the distance. My dad told me it would be lower and wider than anything on the road. I sat there with my eyes glued down the road and all of a sudden here came this very low, very wide convertible with the top down. That was an awfully exciting time for a 14-year-old boy!

In 1954, the proposed 265cid engine was put in a '55 Corvette for evaluation and Dad brought it home. My folks were going to go to a party that night and Dad wanted to drive that car there. Mom didn't want to come home in it, because she never liked the breeze. The idea was that they would drive it to the party, but I would then take the family sedan to the party then drive the Corvette right back home.

When I got to the party, I knew that if I fired that thing up, Dad would hear it, give me sufficient time to get home and then call. So, my friend, Charlie Randall, and I decided to push the car down the road a ways and fire it up where the noise wouldn't be quite so obvious and Dad wouldn't know we'd left! There we were, two kids pushing this experimental Corvette down the road after dark, and our local police came by! I knew him fairly well and we waved and he went on about his business and we ducked into the car. We had one wild ride that night!

Dad was interested in superchargers and possibly using them on production cars at Chevrolet. Dad and Art Latham (of Latham supercharger fame) borrowed a new '57 Bel-Air hardtop from the local dealer and installed a multi-stage supercharger. Art knew of an abandoned airstrip and we went out there to compare a fuel injected '57 to the supercharged '57 Art 'warmed up' for us. I got to drive the fuelie as we drag raced the cars. Dad rode with Art in the supercharged '57 Bel-Air. It was quite an experience for an 18-year-old kid and gave me a lot of respect for super-charging an engine as the 'blown' '57 walked away from the fuelie. I was amazed.

Eventually I needed my own car, so Dad and I went out to look for one. Considering our budget, the earlier Chevrolet with the torque drive wouldn't do the trick, and it couldn't be a Ford, so it ended up being a Kyser. Some of you may remember the Kyser. It was ahead of its time in terms of styling, but behind the times in terms of power. With Dad's help, it was pretty easy to accommodate a V-8 engine. The car was made to accept a 283cid, 4-barrel, dual exhaust Corvette mufflers and a 4-speed.

That was my car for several years, and needless to say, I had many great experiences in that car. With the 4-barrel it was a good runner, but a year or two later we decided more power was the way to go and we re-built the engine incorporating fuel injection and aluminum big valves heads, Duntov camshaft and solid lifters with a 3.90:1 Posi-traction rear end. That was a car that would get by almost anything on the road. It would actually beat the 270hp Corvette. In essence, this was the same configuration as the 315hp Corvette, but the Kaiser was a bit heavier. The exhaust was cut off and came out in front of the rear wheels, but I left the rest of the tailpipes out the back so that it would look stock. We had a lot of fun and many drag races with this Kaiser. (And we won most of them too.)

In the summer of 1957 I took a job as a test driver for the GM Proving Grounds. What an opportunity! This put me right in the middle of things that were of great interest to me. I would spend my time looking through the garage and sizing up what was going on. At that time I met Bob Clift, the Corvette Development Engineer at the Proving Grounds. He was a real Corvette fan in his own right and raced them at Waterford. He and I became friends.

I remember working with him in 1958. I don't know what he was trying to accomplish, but he was using a 1958 Impala to run some kind of top speed test. It had a 348cid engine and 3 x 2bbl carburetor with open exhaust, a 3.08 axle and high speed tires. He needed someone to go along and read the fifth week instrumentation so he asked me. I thought this was neat. I remember going North on the North-South straightaway at 150mph in that car actual speed!

I also remember going for many rides in Corvettes with Bob on the handling course. Wow, what a wild man he was! It took a lot to scare me, but I'll tell you he got me there many times including spinning out on one occasion. I really didn't care to ride with him much after that.

In 1965, I moved to the downtown offices of Chevrolet's Central Office Service department. This was also the year my father retired after 38 years from the position of Executive Engineer for Chevrolet…Corvairs, automatic transmission and ultimately ZR-1 engine development.

The past 59 years of Corvettes and cars is hard to cover in this letter. I hope that this is interesting for Mid America and those who read it.

Gary Rosenberger
Brighton, MI

The Test Vehicle

I purchased my first Corvette during the summer of 1990. It was a Bright Blue '87 coupe with the Z-52 handling package (license plate CAWVETT). I drove the car until 1994. At that time, one of my associates had invented a new type of spark plug in need of testing, so from

that point on, the vehicle was used specifically for testing purposes.

I then purchased a low-mileage '91 Torch Red convertible to use for work, and in May of 1995, I purchased a new Dark Grey Green Impala SS (license plate BIG VETT), which I still drive today for work and pleasure. In 1997, I was caught in a torrential downpour and my '91 convertible was flooded. My beautiful convertible was now a low-mileage Jacuzzi! Again, no Vette to drive. The insurance company handled the paperwork and authorized the flood repairs, but by this point I wanted a new Vette. The '97s were hot and in great demand, fetching about $10,000 over sticker. The prices eventually started to come down by mid-year and I asked my saleslady, Mo, at Bachrodt Chevy in Coconut Creek, Florida, to find me a '97 Sebring Silver

coupe with no body side moldings.

Since there weren't any new Vettes available that had the options I wanted, in 1998 I decided to custom order my '98 Sebring Silver couple (license plate CO VETT, short for company Vette).

On May 3, 1998, I received delivery of the car at the National Corvette Museum in Bowling Green, Kentucky, an awesome experience for Vette enthusiasts. I have described this as "King-for-a-Day." With new options available such as the dual zone air and Yaw control, the '98 was worth the wait. My '87 coupe is now undergoing a body-on restoration and was completed in Christmas 1998.

I expect to hold onto my first Vette for many years to come. I remember my close friend once telling me, "It's gorgeous. Keep it forever. It will never go out of style." I couldn't agree more.

Robert Montemarano
Clearwater, FL

When Did It Start for You?

Movies, Music and Magazines

The Beach Boys

I remember a warm summer day coming back from a family reunion with my parents in my father's '49 Dodge 4-door sedan in the summer of 1955. We were on the back roads of Ohio when this fantastic all-white sports car with a red interior went flying by, my father hollering  at them for driving fast and crazy. The two occupants looked like they were having the time of their lives. I asked my father what kind of car it was. He said it was one of those new Corvettes that Chevy was selling. He went on to say how rough they rode and that they could only carry two passengers. I didn't hear the last part. I was hooked for life!

I started seeking out information about Vettes and started dreaming about owning one at the young age of seven. One of our neighbors' sons owned a black '58 fuelie and drove it past us kids on the way to work everyday while we waited for the school bus. I can still remember the sound of that fuel-injected Vette as he roared off and caught a little second gear rubber, to the delight of us all.

If you remember the "Shut Down" album by the Beach Boys, there were two Sting Rays on the album cover. I was in high school during the mid-60's, driving my cherry '57 Chevy and still dreaming of owning my own Corvette. One of the young men I worked with had an older brother who was shipped off to Vietnam. He had left behind his '64 split window coupe covered up in the family barn. I begged my friend to show it to me.

One night after work we went to the barn to sneak a peek. He pulled off the cover and there to my delight was the most gorgeous-looking Cherry Red Corvette I'd ever seen. It had a white interior. My friend opened the door and allowed me to sit in it. This was my first experience of sitting in a

Corvette! I can still remember the thrill of looking at the dash with all the cool gauges, and that 160-mph speedometer. Gripping the wheel with one hand and holding the shifter in the other, I knew this was it!

During college I took a job at a medical center where I was the lot attendant. There wasn't much going on after five, so it gave me a great place to study and get paid for it. The reason I am telling you this was there was an older doctor who drove a new silver '67 435-hp three-deuce, four-speed coupe. It had factory side exhaust and knock-off wheels. When he would leave the garage you could hear him catch rubber in all four gears. I told myself that when I got old, I wanted to be doing that!

My cousin had purchased a '68 427 roadster and invited me to go along with him and the Dayton Corvette Club to the Indy 500 in '69. That was the last year for the all-Corvette parade lap at the beginning of time trials. They filled the infield with Corvettes from '53s to brand new Vettes, including customs and race prepared vehicles. I was in Corvette overload! Being able to drive around Indy with thousands of Corvettes was awesome.

It was only one year later, after college, that my dream came true. My graduation present from me to myself was a brand-new '70 Donnybrook Blue big-block coupe. I was looking for an LT-1, but when I saw that beautiful 454 big-block coupe, I knew it had my name on it. I never will forget the look on the salesman's face when I told him I didn't want a factory stereo because I wanted to put my own in it. He didn't know that my stereo was a set of custom chrome side exhaust headers. After that, you couldn't hear the radio anyway. I was going racing with the local Dayton Corvette Club as soon as I had her broken in. I have fond memories of driving hours after work on the twisty back roads around where I lived. That car and I became one!

I took her out to KillKare dragstrip for the first time and took first in my class with a 13.45-second e.t., this with street tires and a 3.08:1 rear end! I still have the trophy today. I met and married my wife, Carla, one year after buying the Vette. I taught her how to drive a stick in that car. Carla loved to race also. When we were still engaged, I let Carla drive my Vette to school while I drove my beater to work. Someone told me about some girl in a big-block Vette that was blowing the doors off the locals in our small town of Troy, Ohio. After they described the car and driver, I knew it was Carla. The only thing I ever said to her was, "Don't ever get beat." Now that was true love!

After 10 years, two custom paint jobs and over 98,000 miles, we sold the Corvette. I wasn't interested in the latest smog-motored Corvettes. I just couldn't bring myself to buy a car that was a Corvette in name only, with no performance.

Then in '84 the next generation Vette came out. Wow! The juices started flowing again. I had heard about the new tuned-port fuelie due out in 1985, so I waited. I took one look at that tuned-port tunnel system and I was hooked! Except for the looks of the '65 fuelie motor, I think that the tuned port system on the '85 is the neatest-looking engine Chevy ever put in a Corvette. We kept the last Vette for almost another 10 years. It had all the toys on it, and we logged nearly 90,000 miles and still got over half of our investment back.

I thought that at the age of 48 I had finally gotten the Corvette bug out of my system. Wrong! Have you seen the next generation Vettes yet? I am waiting for the first spring day to take a test drive in the all-new Corvette. I guess when I'm 99, if I am still around, I'll be cruising around in my Corvette. I am just a true Corvette fanatic.

P.S. The two pictures show the '70 in her last paint scheme and the '85 the day before I sold it. Looking forward to my next Vette!

Gary Webb
Troy, OH

Autoweek

It was 1974, my freshman year at college, and I was an art major, a racing fan and a dreamer. I was flipping through an *AutoWeek/Competition Press* on IMSA-Road Atlanta.

John Greenwood shocked the racing world with his plastic-fantastic, slab-sided Can-am style wide body Corvette, the most ground-pounding monster ever built! It was the last of the real race cars not born in a tubing factory but on an assembly line, with factory-stock frame and components modified to the extreme.

I was in the salvage yards within the week, but $800 wrecks were out of reach with college expenses. Eleven years later, in 1985, I bought my first Corvette, a '66 small-block roadster.

In 1997, my search ended in Munich, Germany. I found and purchased the '74-'75 Greenwood Team Car. It was the exact car that did it for me! I have restored it to its most famous Sebring '75 paint scheme, the one in which it won Daytona and set (and still holds) the all-time trap speed record there of 236 mph.

So now the love affair has started. This most exotic piece of Corvette racing history is out of hiding and back in fire-breathing form, making Corvette and non-Corvette people smile again.

Come see it, hear it, feel it, smell it, sit in it and dream the way I have for the last 24 years!

Lance Smith
Villanova, PA

Hot Rod Magazine

Actually, as I think about it, I have been a Chevy man for as long as I can remember. In 1960, my dad bought a turquoise-and-white '56 Chevy 4-door Bel-Air. The old six-banger was dependable and it ran well. I guess my dad's love for that old car rubbed off on me. I was always rooting for any little 283 Chevy to wax any 390 Ford at the local street drags.

In my hometown of Cabool there was this fellow named Murr who drove a '61 Corvette. It was a beautiful car. The Vette magic had a hold on me and I began to read car magazines like *Hot Rod*. The Corvette was always the street machine to have, but owning one in those days seemed like an impossibility.

About five years ago, I began to think that it just might be possible to buy a Corvette. There was a guy at 3M, where I work, that had a red '75 Corvette coupe. I began to ask him about his car. I had heard that Gary went to the Bloomington Gold Corvette Show every year. He advised me to learn all that I could about Corvettes before I bought one and gave me his brochure on the Bloomington seminars. One of the classes offered was called, "How To Buy a Corvette." It was just what I needed to know!

That night I showed my better half, Rosemary, the brochure and we began to talk about the possibility of taking a short vacation to Bloomington. I could hardly believe my eyes when I got my confirmation back for the Corvette seminar. I really enjoyed the class.

I have been going to Bloomington Gold ever since. I subscribe to *Corvette Fever* and *Vette* magazines. I like them both. Gary Pauley and I have looked at virtually every car for sale at Bloomington Gold since 1991. I enjoy talking to Vette owners about their cars because you can learn a lot.

I learned at the seminar to read about Vettes and to drive cars that you may be interested in to find out what you like and what you don't like. Rosemary and I agreed early on that we really liked the style of the mid-year '63 to '67 Corvettes. The only problem was that they were pricey! Over the next four years I drove a lot of cars and also joined a local Corvette club. It's a good way to learn about cars for sale and to learn from car owners the strong or weak points about particular years and models. Plus you make some good friends!

In January of this year, I told Rosemary there was no way that I was going to be able to make it through another summer without a Corvette! So I began to seriously plan how I could pull together enough money to buy one. By March I was ready and began to make phone calls, but couldn't find the right car.

About the middle of April, Rosemary and I took a Friday off and went to St. Louis to drive some LT1 6-speeds. We decided to go to the north side of St. Louis to a dealer that had advertised several late-model Corvettes for sale, including a '66 427 coupe. Every time I mentioned looking at a 427 car, she said, "You don't need that, you'll just kill yourself with that kind of power."

We pulled into the dealer and there in front was the '66 and a whole row of late-model Vettes! I couldn't take my eyes off of the '66, but Rosemary chose to ignore it and walked over to look at the late-model cars. Next thing she heard was the 427 roaring to life. That was Friday, and by Saturday, my new strategy was to search for all the Corvettes I could find with 427 motors.

Sunday evening arrived and I had a handful of possibilities. I began to make calls. On Monday, I called about a red '67 427 convertible and spoke to the owner, Larry, who told me that it didn't have the original motor, but had a real good 427 in it. The car had been wrecked and stored for a number of years, but the bonus was that it had side pipes. It was a two-top car with original interior, but the mileage was unknown.

Here's the kicker. I heard a loud noise on the other end of the phone during the conversation with Larry. After asking what it was he told me that he was sitting in the car in the garage. I said start it up again and let it idle this time. Man, it sounded good! I made an offer immediately on the phone and to my surprise, he came down on his price.

During this time Rosemary had run to town on errands. When she returned, I informed her that we had bought a Corvette. By noon Tuesday I had the down-payment wired to Larry's account, and I was making travel arrangements to the Twin Cities that Friday.

Just before leaving for Minnesota to pick up the car, I received a call from Larry, indicating that he had lost the title and that there might be problems. We decided to make the trip up and at least take a look at the car. Happily, after intervention by his lawyer and a quick bout of DMV paper shuffling, we were able to obtain a clear title necessary for the sale.

We were at Larry's house by 9:30am and the car was sitting in the garage looking great. My nerves were just beginning to recover from the prior week of worry and waiting. We fired her up, and she sounded great. Larry took me over to his mechanic's shop to check out the car. We put it up on the rack and checked the frame and numbers. Everything looked good and mechanically solid underneath. On the way back to Larry's it was my turn to drive and I was hooked. After a trip into downtown St. Paul for paperwork, we signed our check over to Larry, and are now the owners of our own '67 red Corvette.

You see, when I first started looking for a Corvette and anyone asked what my favorite was I almost always replied, "A '67 Corvette. And one time before I die, I would love to own a 427." This is one time that I didn't have to compromise. God blessed me with my dream Corvette!

Terry Geisler
Columbia, MO

When Did It Start for You?

Road & Track

I can remember an image in my mind of a '67 Corvette driving toward us as my father pointed his '70 RS Camaro down the two lane toward Connecticut. It was the odd shape that caught my eye, and due to my father's fascination with imported cars, particularly Alfa Romeos, it was odder still that I would have even noticed it. Dad had played with Alfas and MGTFs in the early '60s, and handling was his hot button. "Pirelli tires and handling, that's where it's at." Yet, I can well remember one blast to 90mph as a kid with Dad at the wheel of the Alfa. But that was not the norm, the little red convertible rarely pressed its few ponies to the limit.

But I was a speed freak. I loved reading all my dad's *Road & Track* magazines, especially the road test charts that gave the performance figures. I'm certain I was able to pass high school chemistry based solely on my ability to read those *R & T* test tables. I loved Lamborghini Muiras and AC Cobras. But Corvettes? I was intrigued by the performance numbers, but come on, fiberglass? Give me aluminum!

It wasn't until 1980 that the Corvette bug really bit. It was on the heels of finishing the modifications to a '69 Camaro Z/28 for *Hot Rod* magazine where I was the associate editor. The Camaro was decked out with the dual four barrel-crossram carb option, and a recent engine rebuild and new Marina Blue paint made for an amazingly quick and fun car to drive. I took the "Z" up to Willow Springs Raceway and had a blast but got my hat handed to me by the Cobras and Shelbys in attendance. Time for more power. Time for a Corvette.

My first Corvette was a knee jerk reaction to the "pocket full of money" syndrome fresh off the sale of the Camaro. A quick read of the *Los Angeles Times* on a Tuesday night resulted in a jump in my '70 340 Duster and the peeling off of $5665 for a '66 Corvette coupe (I went with Bruce Caldwell from *Hot Rod* magazine; the ultimate wheeler and dealer of all time who cut an unusual final price for the car). The Daytona Yellow couple featured the original 427cid/425hp "IP" code block: very important stuff for us magazine types. After all, if you write it for a living, you certainly ought to live it, too, right?

I went through the '66 from top to bottom, stripping off the layers of

When Did It Start for You?

paint with aircraft stripper (a bad idea, by the way), reapplying original Sunfire Yellow and completing a full drivetrain and interior redo chronicled in the pages of various Petersen Publishing Magazines during the '80s. It was a great car and aside from the loss of a front right knock-off on the way home from the *Popular Hot Rodding* magazine offices on Wilshire Blvd. and calling Dick Guldstrand from the hospital (it just happened to be the nearest pay phone) for a ride back to his shop, the car performed well.

Since that time, I've owned two more Corvettes: a real honest to truth "IT" code '68 silver-on-silver convertible 427 L88 I bought from Al Maynard in Michigan and a '67 427cid/435hp Marlboro Maroon convertible that I purchased in wrecked condition in Ventura, California. Both cars were wonderful, and never babied. The L88 was restored to original specs when I purchased the car. It made one pass through the L.A. County Raceway traps at 13.08, 111 mph on the Polyglass tires with the top down. The '67, after eight years of restoration effort, made its way down the same track at 13.42 seconds at 114 mph (the 427 had been warmed up a bit as the mph numbers attest).

Through car magazine adventures and the graces of GM, I've had the opportunity to drive many high performance Corvettes. I was present on the '84 Corvette introduction in Santa Barbara and the ZR-1 debut in the south of France in '89; certainly two high points in my career.

Corvettes and magazine work has satiated the speed freak in me.

Cam Benty
Stevenson Ranch, CA

Corvette Summer

As a teenager, I remember seeing my first Corvette on television in a movie called *Corvette Summer*. That might not be a big deal for an American, but just try buying a Corvette in Australia! Movies are about the only way you get to see these hot-looking cars.

Three years ago I got married, moved to America and now live with my wife in Nevada. As you can imagine, I was eager to get my hands on a Corvette. But after the expense of a wedding and a move to a new country, little money was left to buy a dream car. I began begging my wife in a joking way, "Honey, if I find a Corvette for less than $5,000, can I have one?" "Of course you can," she said with a firm belief that it would never happen.

One day, completely by accident, I stumbled upon a beat-up '78 Sting Ray with a blown engine. After some thought I decided this project was a little out of my league, but it got me thinking that I could probably get a better car for less money.

One weekend with a fistfull of $50's I flew down to Los Angeles to go car shopping. With the help of my Corvette black book and a buyer's guide, I knew exactly what I wanted, a C3 Vette '80-'82. Color and condition didn't matter, only that it ran and would make the 400-mile trip back to Nevada! I was looking for an inexpensive project car to clean up and repaint. Few were in my price range. Then, when I least expected it, there it was! I could tell from 20 feet away that this '80 Corvette was good but needed a lot of work. This yellow beauty, unregistered but still carrying the license plate MISS USA, was the perfect project car for me!

The 400-mile trip back home was a blast! In my mind, I practically rebuilt the entire car. It's a good thing I did, because that's exactly what I

When Did It Start for You?

had decided to do. Any car can be good, but a Corvette should be great and that's what it was going to be. Many people have asked me when the project turned into an obsession. I say, what obsession? Just wait until you see my next one! The hardest thing about rebuilding my Corvette is the desire to drive it again. This owner is patiently waiting, the project is still under construction.

Tony & Cheryl Arends
Vallejo, CA

Red Alert

You've heard of love at first sight in the supermarket, soul mates swept off their feet amid kiwi and kumquats. Well, I lost my heart in the magazine section early in 1983. There on the glossy cover against a black background was the stunning new white '84 Corvette. It was like being struck by lightning!

I took that magazine home and everywhere else I went for literally weeks. Infatuated, obsessed, I had to have one. The only problem was, not even wildly creative accounting could stretch the bank account that far. The object of my affections was just out of reach. I bought a Trans Am on the rebound, but every time I passed a Vette, I died of envy.

In 1989, another magazine rekindled Corvette fever. Joking, I told my husband that if he could buy me a Corvette, I wouldn't care what color it was. (That was a small fib, I swoon for silver.) Another magazine featured an '88 demo model, loaded, 4,500 miles with full warranty and it was red, the color Dave wanted! But, a deal is a deal. When we got it home that night, he just stood there and said, "All that red takes my breath away!" It did mine, too, and still does.

"Red Alert" was joined by "Raptor" in 1994. Remember the storms that ravaged the gulf coastal states that summer? We drove nine and a half hours in two red Vettes from Florida, where it was delivered in tornado winds and rain with trees and power lines coming down around us. We got out just before the flood. Sort of squelched the joy you would normally feel while breaking in your first made-to-order fiberglass baby!

A third addition to the family garage arrived via the National Corvette Museum delivery program in 1996. I finally got my silver car, a Collector's (Dave still had to have some red, so he picked the interior). "Kwik Silver" took its break-in trip to Bloomington Gold and the weather was perfect.

Our Corvette family is now complete. We play with our "kids" nearly every weekend along with the North Mississippi Corvette Club. We take them to shows, races, parades and events of all kinds. If it's true that the family that plays together stays together, then this family fun should last forever!

When Did It Start for You?

Patti C. Harris, Oxford, MS

Route 66

My love affair with the Corvette began in 1953 when I was 11 years old and I read about the new fiberglass American sports car. I followed the car's yearly progression from then on and eagerly awaited the release of each year's model. In the early '60s I couldn't wait for each week's episode of Route 66 to drool at Martin Milner's roadster, the show's plot being secondary to the car.

In 1968 the release of the third generation "Mako Shark" Vette confirmed that at some time in my life I had to own a Corvette. I remember going to the March 1969 Melbourne Motor Show to see a Metalflake Orange 'Shark' roadster and considered it the most beautiful and exciting car I had ever seen. Over the years the '68-'73 and '80-'82 Vettes have been my favorites.

Four months ago, my lifelong ambition was realized when I acquired a magnificent 24,000-mile original '81 Corvette. It is completely stock, with the exception of a $7,000 Glasurit two-pack paint job in Maranello Red (a GM Australia color). The car has medium-red leather seats and the usual standard L81 motor, 350cid auto, air, electric windows and locks. Options include FE7 Gymkana suspension, alloy wheels, 255/60 radials, power drive seat (now the passenger seat), cruise control, rear window defogger and power antenna.

I note from the Black Book that only 7,803 cars were sold with the FE7 setup out of 41,000 or so made in '81. From the VIN it appears the car was number 5,377, produced at the end of 1980 at the St. Louis plant. It was purchased for Bob Stall, The Chevy Capital, in La Mesa, California. I am at least the car's third owner in Australia and it has been professionally converted to right-hand drive. Despite the FE7 suspension and Australia's less-than-perfect highways, the car is virtually free of the creaks and groans reported in a lot of U.S. road tests.

In the short time I have owned it, I have fitted a new heavy-duty radiator and low-temperature switch to the auxiliary electric fan to help cope with our hot summers, fitted a 180-degree thermostat and replaced an inlet manifold gasket to cure oil leaks. The only thing I don't like about the car is the lock-up feature of the auto transmission; it is fine when gunning the car, but annoying at low speeds.

When Did It Start for You?

I live in a small town of about 2,000 people and there are five Corvettes here. Considering there are only about 3,000 Corvettes in Australia, we are quite unique.

The Corvette is revered here in Australia as the epitome of American style and performance, and we owners are passionate about our cars.

Barry Volk
Tatura Victoria, Australia

It's Never Too Late To Start!

Do you have a "When Did It Start for You"
story that you'd like to share?
Send it in! Simply submit your *story (500 words or less),
along with a transparency, slide or print (past, present or both),
and a copy of the photo release form, at right, to:

Mid America Designs
ATTN: Start Book
PO Box 1368
Effingham, IL, 62401

OR: E-mail mail@madvet.com

*Stories MUST be typed; photos will not be returned unless a
self-addressed, stamped envelope is included..*

While everyone has his or her own
unique first encounter, one thing is for certain...
once a Corvette enthusiast, always a Corvette enthusiast!

When Did It Start for You?

Release

I consent to the sale, publishing, reproducing and/or use of my story & photograph for Mid America Designs' "When Did It Start for You?" book and any other ancillary programs to accompany this publication. Mid America may edit for reasons including space restrictions, style, grammar, syntax, content, or other purposes deemed appropriate.

I give permission to use these materials for other promotional purposes, including advertising, display, exhibitions, editorial illustration purposes and trade. I do hereby grant Mid America Designs, Inc. permission to copyright said photograph, and all of the above-mentioned uses are granted without restrictions, reservations, or limitations whatsoever.

_____   _____

Signature   Date

_____

(Please Print Name Here)

Share When Did It Start for You With A Friend!

If you're reading this, chances are you've already enjoyed Volume I of <u>When Did It Start for You</u>. And it's likely that you would like to purchase a copy for all of your friends and family, especially if you were among our featured stories! It's a great gift idea for any occasion and the perfect addition to any Corvette enthusiast's library. Give our Sales Team a call at 800-500-VETT.

20000.....When Did It Start for You, Vol I.....$14.95

2 Thumbs Up!

Funfest '97, '98, '99 and the making of the Last C4 vdeos feature exclusive, behind-the-scenes footage, capturing Funfest '97, '98, '99's astounding turnouts and the 1996 Last C4's momentous final assembly. Each video is 25 minutes. **$10.95 ea**

30644....."Last C4"   30648 ..Funfest '98
30643 ..Funfest '97   30654...Funfest '99

Load 'Em Up!

A. Volume III

B. Volume II

C. My Garage

The Vette Lover's Screen Savers cycle through some of the more spectacular Corvette photos ever to come across our desks. My Garage is a collection of shots from our R & D Center. Both require Windows 3.0 or higher, minimum 256 color VGA monitor and 1.5 MB hard disk space. PC version only. **$19.95 ea**

A ...190115 ....Volume III
B ...190113 ....Volume II
H...190114 ....My Garage

The Host With the Most!

Make a date with Mid America Direct, host to 3 annual customer appreciation celebrations, including Corvette Funfest—*the best Corvette party of the year*. Registration, Fun Display Car Show, Saturday evening entertainment & more are all FREE to show registrants. So, what are you waiting for? Mark your calendar or phone 217-347-5591 for more information.

Corvette Funfest

September 16-17, 2000

September 15-16, 2001

Porsche Funfest

July 15-16, 2000

July 21-22, 2001

Beetle Funfest

June 10-11, 2000

June 9-10, 2001